"I have to say, I'm always impressed with what you write." —Craig Robinson, editor of theiowarepublican.com

"Thank you...for your spirited argument, which advances the important argument." —George F. Will

"Brilliant...excellent." Jan Mickelson, host of WHO Radio's *Mickelson in the Morning*

"I think it is very, very good." —Steve Deace, syndicated talk radio host

"Your writing is smart and interesting." —*The Philadelphia Inquirer*

"Your command of the material is impressive." —*Akron Beacon Journal*

THE FREE WILL OF

GOD:

The Joy of the Clay in the Freedom of the Potter

NATHAN W. TUCKER

1689

Reformed Baptist Press

Dedicated to all who come, by God's grace alone, to love the absolutely sovereign free will of God.

The author wishes to express his heartfelt gratitude to all those who have taken of their valuable time to edit this material and offer suggestions to make this book better. All errors and mistakes in this book are my own. The author would be indebted to any reader who, so desiring, wishes to send corrections to him at reformedbaptistpress@gmail.com.

TABLE OF CONTENTS

	Preface	i
1	The Free Will of God	1
2	The Purpose of the Free Will of God	19
3	The Free Will of God in Creating	43
4	The Free Will of God Over Sin	69
5	God's Free Will in Definite Atonement	103
6	God's Free Will in Effectuating Salvation	135
7	Gods Free Will in Reigning	181
8	Conclusion—The Good News of God's Free Will	207

APPENDIXES:

A	Who is the World?	217
B	Who is "All"?	231
C	Does God Desire All to Be Saved?	241
D	But Can't You Lose Your Salvation?	251

PREFACE

*I*n concluding the penultimate chapter of my book *Are My Babies in Heaven?: A Grieving Pastor Finds Hope in the God of Scripture*, I wrote, "O!—that we serve a God so free, sovereign, and independent in all that He does, for only such a God is worth worshipping!" That line, in due time, gave birth to this book—a book rejoicing in the free will of God.

For I wanted to write a book demonstrating how only such an absolutely sovereign God is worthy of worship. I desired to show the splendor and majesty of the absolute freedom of God's will. I longed to display the Potter's freedom as glorious, as humbling, as comforting, as our sole hope for life and eternity. I hoped to make the God of the Bible—of the doctrines of grace, of Reformed theology—irresistibly beautiful.

For this is the greatest need in the Church today—a return to the God of Scripture, of Augustine, of Luther, Calvin, and the other Reformers, of the Puritans, of Edwards, Whitefield, and the First Great Awakening, of Hodge, Warfield, Spurgeon, J. Gresham Machen, and Martyn Lloyd-Jones, and of countless others.

The Church today is shallow in its theology. Man-centered in its worship. Compromised in its lust for political power. Trendy in its mimicry of the world. And we have created a weak god. A pitiful god. A god who serves us by giving us our best life now. A god who births lukewarm Christians in Name Only (CINOs) who profess God with their lips but they hearts are far from Him (Matt.15:8). God—the true God of the Bible—would be ashamed to be called our God (Heb. 11:16).

Arminian free-willism is the cancer, but the free will of God is the cure. We desperately need today a revival of Reformed theology. Not merely of Calvinism (or TULIP), for Reformed theology—biblical theology—is far more than the doctrines of grace. Rather, it is nothing less than the full counsel of God. It is the Gospel in full bloom. It is the entirety of Scripture applied to the entirety of life. It is the soul permeated with a Big-God-centered mindset and heartset. It is Scripture full-orbed; a God-besotted vision for living. TULIP is but a subset of Reformed thought; an essential outgrowth but not the whole of the Redwood tree of biblical theology.

This book, therefore, was written to demonstrate that biblical theology—or, more accurately, the God of biblical theology—is gloriously beautiful, worthy of all praise, and the only God worth worshipping.

Nathan W. Tucker
Omaha Indian Reservation
March 13, 2025

From my childhood up, my mind had been full of objections against the doctrine of God's sovereignty, in choosing whom he would to eternal life, and rejecting whom he pleased; leaving them eternally to perish, and be everlastingly tormented in hell. It used to appear like a horrible doctrine to me.

But I remember the time very well, when I seemed to be convinced, and fully satisfied, as to this sovereignty of God, and his justice in thus eternally disposing of men, according to his sovereign pleasure. But never could give an account, how, or by what means, I was thus convinced, not in the least imagining at the time, nor a long time after, that there was any extraordinary influence of God's Spirit in it; but only that now I saw further, and my reason apprehended the justice and reasonableness of it. However, my mind rested in it; and it put an end to all those cavils and objections.

And there has been a wonderful alteration in my mind, in respect to the doctrine of God's sovereignty, from that day to this; so that I scarce ever have found so much as the rising of an objection against it, in the most absolute sense, in God's showing mercy to whom he will show mercy, and hardening whom he will. God's absolute sovereignty and justice, with respect to salvation and damnation, is what my mind seems to rest assured of, as much as of any thing that I see with my eyes; at least it is so at times.

(Jonathan Edwards)

1 THE FREE WILL OF GOD

*G*od has free will. The debate over divine election often overlooks the fact that God has free will. That He must have free will. And that it must be absolutely sovereign. When we do think of it, we talk of it in terms of His providence or His sovereignty. But we usually don't think of God as a volitional Being whose will is the universe's command. Unfortunately, the debate over Calvinism and Arminianism often takes place over man's free will rather than over the supremacy of the divine free will.

Any discussion of biblical, Reformed theology must begin and end with the freedom of God's will. It is an essential, innate attribute of being God. To be God, He must have free will. And not just any free will, but it must of necessity be ultimate, unconditional, and unfettered. In other words, God's free will must be ultimately and decisively self-determining. Because God is autonomous, His free will must be as well.

I. God Alone Has Free Will:

In the third chapter of Exodus, God provides us with the most profound and fundamental self-revelation of Himself found anywhere in the Bible. God appears to Moses in the burning bush to anoint him to lead His people out of Egypt, and Moses asks: "'Indeed, when I come to the children of Israel and say to them, "The God of your fathers has sent me to you," and they say to me, "What is His name?" what shall I say to them?'" (vs. 13). God answers Moses:

> [14] … "I AM WHO I AM." And He said, "Thus you shall say to the children of Israel, 'I AM has sent me to you.'" [15] Moreover God said to Moses, "Thus you shall say to the children of Israel: 'The LORD God of your fathers, the God of Abraham, the God of Isaac, and the God of Jacob, has sent me to you. This is My name forever, and this is My memorial to all generations.'

1

(Ex. 3:14-15)

Though God has revealed Himself by many names throughout Scripture, the most common name by which He is referred to in the Old Testament is Yahweh. In Hebrew the name is written with but four letters—YHWH. It occurs a total of 6,828 times in the Old Testament, which is more than three times the number of occurrences for the generic Hebrew word for God (*El* or *Elohim*).

Unfortunately, in nearly all English versions of the Bible Yahweh is not translated as Yahweh but rather LORD in all capital letters.[1] This is unfortunate for two reasons. First, the God of Scripture is not a generic deity but rather a specific Person who is God of all other so-called "gods," Lord of all lords, and King of all kings (Josh. 22:22; Ps. 82:1, 86:8, 95:3, 96:4-5, 97:7, 9, 135:5, 136:1-3; Dan. 2:47, 11:36; 1 Tim. 6:15; Rev. 17:14, 19:16). Yahweh refers to a specific deity, just as do the personal names of the "gods" of false religions—whether Allah, the thousands of individual gods of Hindu, Wakanda[2], Zeus, Jupiter, or any other so-called god.

But, secondly and relatedly, Yahweh is not simply first among equals among the ranks of "gods," but He is the sole and supreme God. This is reflected in His personal name Yahweh, whose meaning comes from this passage in Exodus. Notice the three names God uses in these verses:

- **Verse 14:** I AM WHO I AM
- **Verse 14:** I AM
- **Verse 15:** Yahweh (translated as *the LORD*)

All three are used interchangeably as the name of the God who is sending Moses to Pharaoh, and all three share the same Hebrew root *hayah*, which simply means *to be*. There is no more profound declaration than that—"I AM WHO I AM." The God of

---

[1] Though some translations from the 19th century make the good faith but ultimately inaccurate translation of the name as *Jehovah*.

[2] The name of the god of several Native American tribes.

the Bible, therefore, is the Great I AM—the uncreated, self-sufficient, self-existent, unchangeable, limitless One who has no beginning, no end, no need, and no weakness (Ex. 3:14-15; Num. 23:19; Ps. 33:11, 102:27; Mal. 3:6; Jn. 5:26; Heb. 13:8; Jas. 1:17; Rev. 1:8, 22:13).

No one made God, for He is life in Himself. He is not dependent upon anyone or anything else. His holiness has no end. He exists outside of time. And He cannot be improved upon because He has always been and always will be infinitely perfect. Neither Allah, nor the gods of Hindu, nor Wakanda, nor Zeus, nor Jupiter, nor any other so-called god can make such a claim, but only the Great I Am Yahweh.

In short, God is holy. In Isaiah, chapter 6, we read:

> [1] In the year that King Uzziah died, I saw the Lord sitting on a throne, high and lifted up, and the train of His robe filled the temple. [2] Above it stood seraphim, each one had six wings: with two his covered his face, with two his covered his feet, and with two he flew. [3] And one cried to another and said, "Holy, holy, holy, is the LORD of of Hosts! The whole earth is full of His glory!"
>
> (Isaiah 6:1-3)

In this passage the word *holy* is used three times, which is a Hebrew literary device to emphasis the weightiness and magnitude of the word. Here the seraphim thrice cried out, "Holy, holy, holy" to stress the infinite and unsurpassed holiness of Yahweh of Heaven's Armies. God's holiness is to the superlative degree—His holiness is perfect, unable to be improved upon, and shared by no rival.

Again, in the fourth chapter of Revelation we find the Apostle John describing a vision of Yahweh:

> [1] After these things I looked, and behold, a door standing open in heaven. And the first voice which I heard was like a trumpet speaking with me, saying, "Come up here, and I will show you things which must take place after this."

2 Immediately I was in the Spirit; and behold, a throne set in heaven, and One sat on the throne. 3 And He who sat there was like a jasper and a ruby stone in appearance; and there was a rainbow around the throne, in appearance like an emerald. 4 Around the throne were twenty-four thrones, and on the thrones I saw twenty-four elders sitting, clothed in white robes; and they had crowns of gold on their heads. 5 And from the throne proceeded lightnings, thunderings, and voices. Seven lamps of fire were burning before the throne, which are the seven Spirits of God.

6 Before the throne there was a sea of glass, like crystal. And in the midst of the throne, and around the throne, were four living creatures full of eyes in front and in back. 7 The first living creature was like a lion, the second living creature like a calf, the third living creature had a face like a man, and the fourth living creature was like a flying eagle. 8 The four living creatures, each having six wings, were full of eyes around and within. And they do not rest day or night, saying:

"Holy, holy, holy,
Lord God Almighty,
Who was and is and is to come!"

9 Whenever the living creatures give glory and honor and thanks to Him who sits on the throne, who lives forever and ever, 10 the twenty-four elders fall down before Him who sits on the throne and worship Him who lives forever and ever, and cast their crowns before the throne, saying:

11 "You are worthy, O Lord,
To receive glory and honor and power;
For You created all things,
And by Your will they exist and were created."
(Rev. 4:1-11)

Holiness refers to Yahweh's uniqueness, His utter set-apartness from anything or anyone else. It is the magisterial perfection of all His attributes—His love, mercy, grace, anger, wrath, justice, faithfulness, righteousness, goodness, sovereignty, all-powerfulness, omnipresence, all-knowing, and wisdom, to name but a few.

Holiness is Yahweh's intrinsic value and worth; the essential or innate splendor and beauty of being God.   Necessary to His essence, therefore, is that Yahweh is the most supremely valuable Being imaginable in the magisterial perfection of all His attributes which He exercises in perfect harmony one with the other.   Yahweh is all His attributes all the time in all that He does for all eternity.   And therefore He alone is the source of infinitely perfect joy and delight for His creatures.

By very definition of being God, God alone must have autonomous free will or He is not God.   He must have absolutely sovereign freedom to do as He pleases or He is not God.   If free will is defined as ultimately and decisively self-determining, then God and God alone has free will.   If free will means to act without restraint, conditions, or control, only God and God alone has free will.   If free will means infallibly achieving what one desires, then God and God alone has free will.   If free will means not being under necessity to something outside of oneself, then only God and God alone has free will.

In other words, to be really free, the will must be independent, autonomous, and supreme.   And therefore only God is capable of free will, for there can only be one independent, self-sufficient, and supreme Being who, by very definition, is God.   Creatures, on the hand, by very definition cannot exercise such free will for they are dependent and impotent beings unable to govern themselves, much less things outside of themselves.[3]

----

[3] Every non-Calvinist Evangelical stream of Christianity holds that at some point man will no longer have decisive salfivic free will. Arminians, for instance, believe man loses such free will at death, and those Arminians who hold to eternal security believe he loses it at the moment of salvation.   And neither of these traditions believes that such loss of free will dehumanizes man by defiling the volitional accept of his *Imago Die* (being made in the image of God).   The question, therefore, is only over the timing, rather than the justice, of depriving man of his free will.

II. Man Is a Responsible Moral Agent:

If, however, free will is defined as the ability to freely (i.e., without coercion) make choices based on our preferences, then human beings absolutely have free will. And if free will is defined as choosing to do what we most desire, then we absolutely are morally responsible for the exercise of our free will. The problem is, man is unable to choose God. Unable to do good. Unable to please God. Man is only free to choose sin.

For all mankind is totally depraved from conception. For the Bible tells us that we are not born as an innocent blank slate free to choice whether to be either good or bad. Rather, as a descendent of the First Man Adam, we have had our sin nature from the moment of our conception. For instance, the psalmist declares, "Surely I was sinful at birth, sinful from the time my mother conceived me" (Ps. 51:5 NIV84). Elsewhere we read, "Even from birth the wicked go astray; from the womb they are wayward and speak lies" (Ps. 58:3 NIV84). Therefore, the problem we have is not that we commit sins, but that we are sinful. We are not a sinner because we commit sins, we commit sins because we are a sinner.

Not merely our actions, thoughts, or behaviors, but we ourselves are sin. Our soul is black as night and uglier than hell. We have been as grotesque in our evil as any demon of hell from the moment we were conceived and, therefore, have always been under the rightful sentence of eternal damnation. This is why we sin—because we have been a sinner from conception. This is why we cannot stop sinning—because we have been a sinner from conception. This is why we will die a physical death —because we have been a sinner from conception. This is why we will roast for all eternity in hell—because we are a sinner from conception.

And we not only commit evil acts because we are inherently evil, but because we delight in our evil (Prov. 2:14, 21:10). We have a sin nature of inborn, spiteful rebellion against God that we cannot reform on our own. We cannot tame it. We cannot control it. We are hardwired to sin and cannot stop doing it. We have become it's slave, for Jesus tells us that, "'Most assuredly I say to you, whoever commits sin is a slave of sin'" (Jn. 8:34). The Apostle John writes, "8 He who sins is of the devil, for the devil has sinned from the beginning...6 Whoever sins has neither seen God nor known Him" (1 John 3:8, 6).

The book of Genesis points out the obvious, "...the wickedness of man [i]s great in the earth, and that every intent of the thoughts of his heart [i]s only evil continually" (Gen. 6:5). It isn't for naught that a two-year-old's favorite word is, "No!" We do not have to train our children to be bad, but to be good. And as every parent knows, if we did not discipline our children, they would do whatever was right in their own selfish eyes.

Let's say that on my right hand I had a gourmet meal freshly prepared and laid out on the finest of china, and on my left hand I had pig slop. If I brought a hog into this room, which meal do you think he is going to go to? It is a hog. It doesn't care about the culinary arts or fine dining, it wants slop. He was conceived and born with a desire for filth.

And so were all of us in the First Man Adam. "Can the Ethiopian change his skin or the leopard its spots? Neither can you do good who are accustomed to doing evil" (Prov. 13:23). As God Himself proclaims, "'The heart is deceitful above all things, and desperately wicked; who can know it?'" (Jer. 17:9). The author of the book of Job writes, "What is man that he could become pure?" (Job 15:14; see also Job 25:4), for "who can make something pure out of what is impure? No one." (Job 14:4). Therefore, the Bible concludes that no one, "can say, 'I have made my heart pure; I am clean and without sin'" (Prov. 20:9). "All of us," Isaiah the prophet tells us, "have become like one who is unclean, and all our righteous acts are like menstrual rages" (Is. 64:6 NYLT).

Furthermore, because of our sin nature, we are utterly biased against, and disabled and antagonistic toward, God. For instance, the Apostle Paul tells us:

5 For those who are according to the flesh, *the things of the flesh they do mind*; but those who are according to the Spirit, the things of the Spirit they do mind. 6 For the mind of the flesh is death, but the mind of the Spirit is life and peace. 7 *Because the mind of the flesh is enmity to God—for it does not subject itself to the law of God, neither is it able.* 8 *And those who are in the flesh are not able to please God.*

(Rom. 8:5-8 NYLT; emphasis added)

James, the half-brother of Christ, admonishes us that, "Do you not know that friendship with the world is enmity with God? Whoever therefore wants to be a friend of the world is the enemy of God" (Jas. 4:4). In Galatians, Paul writes that "the flesh lusts against the Spirit, and the Spirit against the flesh; and these are contrary to one another" (Gal. 5:17). And in Philippians he warns that, "18 many live as enemies of the cross of Christ....19 Their minds are set on earthly things" (Phil. 3:18-19). Finally, in Romans 5, the apostle describes the unregenerate as enemies of God (Rom. 5:10).

Without the New Birth, therefore, we are:

- Unable to please God (Rom. 8:8).
- Unable to subject ourselves to the law of God (Rom. 8:7).
- At enmity with God (Jas. 4:4).
- Contrary to God (Gal. 5:17).
- With minds set on sin (Rom. 8:5; Phil. 3:19).
- Enemies of God (Rom. 5:10; Phil. 3:18; Jas. 4:4).

Furthermore, from the moment of conception we are children of lawlessness. For we not only sinned in the first man Adam's sin, but we also commit our own sins every single second of every single day of our entire lives. The Bible tells us that, "'no one is good but One, that is, God'" (Mk. 10:18). The Apostle John warns that, "Whoever commits sin also commits lawlessness, and sin is lawlessness" (1 Jn. 3:4). The Apostle Paul writes:

9 ...For we have previously charged both Jews and Greeks that they are all under sin.

10 As it is written:

"There is none righteous, no, not one;

11 There is none who understands;

There is none who seeks after God.

12 They have all turned aside;

They have together become unprofitable;

There is none who does good, no, not one."...

18 "There is no fear of God before their eyes."...

23 ...all have sinned and fall short of the glory of God,

(Rom. 3:9-12, 18, 23)

From conception each and every single one of us have rejected and ridiculed God's right to govern our lives as we blasphemously declare to Him, "Not Your will be my will be done!" We are in a state of insurrection, of rebellion, in which the Bible tells us that everyone does what is right in his own eyes (Num. 15:39; Deut. 12:8; Judges 17:6, 21:25).

In conclusion, therefore, man absolutely has free will to exercise genuine, real choices—freely and without coercion—to do what we most desire. But what we most desire—nay, what we only desire—by nature is sin. An therefore we absolutely have free will to sin, just as a pig has free will to act like a pig, or a dog as a dog, or a chicken as an chicken. And in so acting, we are responsible moral agents who will one day justly give an account for our sins to God. We freely choose our sin, we will be rightly judged for our sin, and we will be justly punished in hell for our sins.

III. But God Authors Our Choices:

But we must never lose sight of the fact that our choices are scripted for us by God. Underneath our will is God's will as the Author, the Potter, the Director of every detail of every second of all history in the entire universe. For God is either absolutely sovereign, or He is not God. He either controls everything, or

9

everything controls Him. Limits Him. Frustrates Him. Resists Him. Just as fictional characters do not dictate to the novelist, or clay to the potter, or the building to the architect, so creation does not, cannot, dictate to its Creator. It is a divine impossibility.

Which is why we read that, "The king's heart is in the hand of the LORD, like the rivers of water; He turns it wherever He wishes" (Prov. 21:1). Yahweh channels men's hearts! Men freely will what God first wills them to will. In another place Scripture tells us that, "Many are the plans in the mind of a man, but it is the purpose of the LORD that will stand" (Prov. 19:21 ESV). Men freely plan, but only what Yahweh has first decreed them to plan. Or as we read in the thirty-third Psalm:

> 13 The LORD looks from heaven;
> He sees all the sons of men.
> 14 From the place of His dwelling He looks
> On all the inhabitants of the earth;
> 15 He fashions their hearts individually;
> He considers all their works.
>
> (Ps. 33:13-15)

Yahweh individually fashions men's hearts! The Hebrew word translated by the NKJV here as *fashions* is *yatsar*, which more aptly means to *form, mould, determine, create*. It is used of God shaping the First Man Adam out of the dust of the earth (Gen. 2:7-8), and is commonly used to refer to a potter throughout the Old Testament (see, for example, 1 Chron. 4:23, Ps. 2:9; Is. 29:16; Jer. 18:1-11). Like the Creator shapes a man, or a potter a vessel, so God shapes the heart of every man after HIs own individual design! And notice that it is a present-tense, ongoing action—a continuous pottering rather than a deistic, once-for-all-time set the heart in motion and then He takes His hands off it.

Furthermore, we read, "O LORD, I know the way of man is not in himself; It is not in man who walks to direct his own steps" (Jer. 10:23). Why? Because, "The steps of a man are established by the LORD, and He delights in his way" (Psalm. 37:23 NASB). Or as Proverbs tells us, "A man's heart plans his way, but the LORD directs his steps" (Prov. 16:9). Therefore, "A man's steps are of the LORD; how then can a man understand his own way?" (Prov. 20:24).

And so we read repeatedly throughout Scripture that God fashions the hearts of men, as this small sampling shows:

• **Gen. 39:21:** "But the LORD was with Joseph and showed him mercy, and He gave him favor in the sight of the keeper of the prison."

• **Exodus 12:36:** "And the LORD had given the people favor in the sight of the Egyptians, so that they granted them what they requested. Thus they plundered the Egyptians" (see also Ex. 3:21-22).

• **1 Sam. 10:9:** "So it was, when he had turned his back to go from Samuel, that God gave him [Saul] another heart, and all those signs came to pass that day."

• **1 Sam. 10:26:** "And Saul also went home to Gibeah, and valiant men went with him, whose hearts God had touched."

• **2 Chron. 30:12:** "Also the hand of God was on Judah to give them singleness of heart to obey the command of the king and the leaders, at the word of the LORD."

• **Ezra 1:1:** "Now in the first year of Cyrus king of Persia, that the word of the LORD by the mouth of Jeremiah might be fulfilled, the LORD stirred up the spirit of Cyrus king of Persia..." (see also 2 Chron. 36:22).

• **Ezra 6:22:** "And they kept the Feast of Unleavened Bread seven days with joy; for the LORD made them joyful, and turned the heart of the king of Assyria toward them, to strengthen their hands in the work of the house of God, the God of Israel."

• **Ezra 7:27:** "Blessed be the LORD God of our fathers, who has put such a thing as this in the king's heart, to beautify the house of the LORD which is in Jerusalem."

• **Neh. 7:5:** "Then my God put it into my heart to gather the nobles, the rulers, and the people, that they might be registered by genealogy..."

• **Ps. 106:46:** "He caused them to be pitied by all those who held them captive" (ESV).

• **Jer. 51:11:** "Make the arrows bright! Gather the shields! The LORD has raised up the spirit of the kings of the Medes. For His plan is against Babylon to destroy it, Because it is the vengeance of the LORD, The vengeance for His temple."

• **Dan. 1:9:** "And God gave Daniel favor and compassion in the sight of the chief of the eunuchs" (ESV).

• **Acts 7:9-10:** "'9…But God was with him 10 and delivered him out of all his troubles, and gave him favor and wisdom in the presence of Pharaoh, king of Egypt; and he made him governor over Egypt and all his house.'"

• **2 Cor. 8:16:** "But thanks be to God who puts the same earnest care for you into the heart of Titus."

• **Phil. 2:13:** "For God is the one energizing in you both to will and to energize for the benefit of His good will" (NYLT).

• **Rev. 17:17:** "For God has put it into their hearts to fulfill His purpose, to be of one mind, and to give their kingdom to the beast, until the words of God are fulfilled."

"For it is God who works in you both to will and to do for His good pleasure" (Phil. 2:13). There is probably no better summary of God's free will superimposing itself on man's free will. God gives men the heartfelt desire—the will—to do His will. They will to do God's will because they want to do God's will. They need to do God's will. They are under an inward compulsion of the heart to do God's will. And if they could not, hypothetically, fulfill God's will, they would be frustrated, discontent, vexed, and disappointed.

Furthermore, Scripture is clear that each second of the universe is a brand new act of creation, no less miraculous then the original six twenty-four hour calendar day creation described in Genesis 1 (Jn. 1:3; 1 Cor. 8:6; Heb. 1:2-3). For "in Him [Christ] all things hold together" (Col. 1:17 ESV). Everything, therefore, that exists—everything that is said, done, or thought—is continually spoken into existence by the Word of God. Everything. You have never thought one thought, felt one emotion, said one word, or performed one deed that was not created by God. You are not the Creator. You did not speak your thought patterns into existence, your mood into being, and your words and deeds into life. There is only One who has done so according to His free will. Everything you have every thought, said, and done had to be first created for you.

Scripture, therefore, teaches unequivocally that God authors our every thought, desire, feeling, and attitude. But Scripture also teaches that we remain absolutely morally responsible for our thoughts, desires, feelings, and attitudes. For all mankind everywhere in every age freely, voluntarily, and willingly commit their sin. They do not do something they do not want to do. Rather, in the absence of any force, coercion, or fear whatsoever, they wholeheartedly desire to do their reprehensibly evil deeds. And therefore God is entirely righteous and just to hold them accountable for their actions.

There are always two wills willing everything we say, do, and think—ours and God's. We will what God wills we will, but we intend one thing by it for evil and God intends another thing by it for good (Gen. 50:20). And we are therefore unequivocally morally accountable for our evil intention, purpose, and design. We wholeheartedly do God's bidding, but we do it wholeheartedly to please ourselves rather than Him.

Admittedly, Scripture does not explain in detail the relationship between our free will and God's free will. It is a mystery (Deut. 29:29). But while we may not fully understand it this side of eternity, we must not deny one truth (God's free will) in order to maintain the other (man's free will). Both exist simultaneously, both are co-equal truths, and therefore both must be taught and embraced even if they may seem incompatible.

Perhaps, however, we can illustrate this dynamic, this seeming contradiction, with the life of Christ during His first coming. Though very God of very God, He "did not live to please Himself" (Rom. 15:2). Rather, He "...emptied Himself, having taking the form of a slave, having been made in the likeness of men" (Phil. 2:7 NYLT). Though coequal with the Father and the Spirit, He came "'down from heaven, not to do My own will but the will of Him who sent Me'" (Jn. 6:38).

He '"can of Myself do nothing'" (Jn. 5:30), but it is '"the Father who dwells in Me [who] does the works'" (14:10). Everything about Jesus' earthly life and ministry was scripted for Him by the Father from before time began (Matt. 26:56; Lk. 24:27, 32, 44-47; 1 Pet. 1:19-20; Rev. 13:8), including every word He ever spoke:

> 49 For I have not spoken on My own authority; but the Father who sent Me gave Me a command, what I should say and what I should speak. 50 And I know that His command is everlasting life. Therefore, whatever I speak, just as the Father has told Me, so I speak."
>
> (Jn. 12:49-5; see also 14:10)

And yet Jesus didn't rebel against the Father's script for HIs life. He didn't chaff. He didn't complain about what He wanted to do with HIs free will. Rather, He sought after God's will (Jn. 5:30). It was food to His soul to do His Father's bidding (4:34). His will was to "always do those things that please [God the Father]" (8:29; see also Ps. 40:7-8).

True, this analogy is not entirely adequate. It isn't a completely apples to apples comparison because God the Son co-wrote His script with His Father in eternity past, whereas such a divine right does not exist in the creature. We cannot co-write the script of our lives before our existence and give it the stamp of our approval. And yet we must never lose sight of the fact that we do, in a very real sense, co-write our lives with God in real time. For all of us are freely and voluntarily writing the script that we want. We may not like the hand we are dealt. We may not like the consequences of our choices. But there isn't a second of our lives in which we are not willingly writing the very same script that God wrote for us before the world came into being and time began to tick. All of us are doing exactly what we want to do, and we would have it no other way.

To use another analogy, the 1999 blockbuster movie *The Matrix* imagined a post-apocalyptic world in which artificial intelligence raised humans for the bioelectric energy they provided, keeping them comatose while their consciousness existed in a computer simulated pre-apocalyptic world. Assuming that the architects of this world programmed every word, deed, and thought, it is a script willingly, albeit unknowingly, followed by the human actors. They will what the architects will, they desire what the architects desire, they choose what the architects determine, and these human actors do so freely, willingly, and without any hint of coercion or fear. It is exactly what they wanted, and they would have it no other way.[4]

A similar analogy comes from the world of fiction—whether it is a novel, a movie, playing with dolls, or having an imaginary friend. Though these characters are not real, yet they come to life in the imagination of the reader, listener, or viewer. That is the point of good fiction—to make the worlds of Middle Earth, Narnia, and Calvin & Hobbes, for example, as real and tangible to the reader as their own. And in these worlds a character never says a line or commits a deed—though dictated to it from its creator— that it does not freely, voluntarily, and willingly choose to do. From the perspective of these characters, they are acting with free will in behaving exactly as they desire to do. The fact that it is all scripted and imposed upon them by the free will of their creator doesn't change the fact that they are doing exactly what they want to do and they would have it no other way.

A final analogy comes from the divine authorship of Scripture itself. We are told the all Scripture is breathed out by God (2 Tim. 3:16) as the human authors were moved or carried by the Holy Spirit (2 Pet. 1:21). In other words, God Himself was speaking through human authors as He dictated every word, tense, and sentence structure. At the same time, however, this does not mean that the human authors were so completely controlled by God when they wrote the Biblical text so as to erase all differences in personality and character. They were not mechanical mystics whose quills channeled the Holy Spirit as

---

[4] Other potential (but I think ultimately flawed) analogies from fiction are: (a) the Nazgul who were willing enslaved to the will of Sauron in *The Lord of the Rings*; and (b) the Trill, a species of symbiotic life form depicted on *Star Trek*.

they flew across the page. Neither were they merely acting as secretaries taking down dictation from God as they wrote the Holy Scriptures. All of Scripture and everything contained in Scripture are the very words of God Himself, but superintended through the agency of human actors in a mysterious way that we cannot explain but only see ample proof of on every page of the Bible. Similarly, everything we say, do, and think is dictated by God Himself, but superintended through our free will in a mysterious way that we cannot fully explain but only see ample proof of on every page of history.

Concluding Implications:

In conclusion, we have seen that God's free will is part and parcel to His Godhead. It is essential, innate to His being God, for without it He cannot be God. God must either rule, or be ruled. Governed, or be governed. Impose His will upon His creatures, or have His creatures impose their will upon Him. Either God's will is omnipotent, or the will of His creatures is. Or, to put it another way, either God is absolutely sovereign, or He stands by impotent and powerless as His creatures thwart and checkmate His will.

There is no middle ground—either God is ultimately and decisively self-determining, or man is. Either God has free will, or man does. And it is incompatible with God's Godness that there should exist any maverick wills. Any rebellious wills. Any insubordinate wills. Any nullifying wills.

God "works all things"—including our wills/desires/hearts, thoughts, actions, and words—"according to the counsel of His will" (Eph. 1:11). We are His creatures, His clay, His thread, and """Is it not lawful for [M]e to do what I wish with [M]y own things?""" (Matt. 20:15).

[8] "For My thoughts are not your thoughts,
Nor are your ways My ways," says the LORD.
[9] "For as the heavens are higher than the earth,
So are My ways higher than your ways,
And My thoughts than your thoughts."

(Is. 55:8-9)

NATHAN W. TUCKER

2 THE PURPOSE OF THE FREE WILL OF GOD

God's free will is sovereign. It is omnipotent. It is irresistible. It is infallible. For the psalmist tells us that, "Whatever the LORD pleases He does, In heaven and in earth, In the seas and in all deep places" (Ps. 135:6; see also Job 42:2; Ecc. 3:13; Lk. 1:37) as "He works all things according to the counsel of His will (Eph. 1:11).

> 9 ...For I am God, and there is no other;
> I am God, and there is none like Me,
> 10 Declaring the end from the beginning,
> And from ancient times things that are not yet done,
> Saying, 'My counsel shall stand,
> And I will do all My pleasure,'
> 11 ...Indeed I have spoken it;
> I will also bring it to pass.
> I have purposed it;
> I will also do it.
>
> (Is. 46:9-11)

He watches over His word to perform it (Jer. 1:12), and no purpose of His can be thwarted (Job 42:2; Ecc. 3:13). "But he is unchangeable, and who can turn him back? What he desires, that he does" (Job 23:13 ESV). "For the LORD of hosts has purposed, and who will annul it? His hand is stretched out, and who will turn it back?" (Job 14:27). Therefore:

> All the inhabitants of the earth are reputed as nothing; He does according to His will in the army of heaven And among the inhabitants of the earth. No one can restrain His hand Or say to Him, "What have You done?"
>
> (Dan. 4:35)

God, therefore, is the absolute sovereign Author of everything that was, is, and is to come. What He wills, He does. But to what purpose does He will? What is the goal of His acting? In other words, why does He do what He does? What motivates Him? Because God, by very definition of being God, is a law unto Himself—entirely free of any and all outside restraints. How, then, is the Governor governed? How does He regulate His behavior?

I. The Chief End of God. God's passion to maximize the display of His infinite worth is the very essence of who God is. For the chief end of God is to glorify Himself by enjoying Himself forever. Let me repeat that because it is so obnoxious to our sinful, prideful ears: the chief end of God is to glorify Himself by enjoying Himself forever.

Scripture teaches us over and over again that God only acts for the sake of His name, for the sake of His praise, for the sake of His glory, for His own sake (Is. 48:9-11; see also Ex. 14:4, 17-18, 36:22-23, 32; 1 Sam. 12:20, 22; 2 Kings 19:34, 20:6; Ps. 25:11, 106:7-8; Is. 43:6-7, 25, 49:3; Matt. 5:16; Jn. 7:18, 12:27-28, 13:31-32, 14:13, 16:14, 17:1; Rom. 3:25-26, 9:17, 15:7; Eph. 1:4-6, 12, 14; 1 Pet. 2:12). For Him to do otherwise would be to make Him less than God—an idolater who would profane His name by giving His glory to another (Is. 48:9-11; Ezek. 20:14). This universe does not exist for our sake. Eternity does not exist for our sake. We were not created to exist for our own sakes. Rather, everything was created to glorify God. To worship God. To magnify God. He is the supreme reality for which this life and the next exist.

A. God is Passionate for His Glory. Let's look at just a few examples of this principle at work in Scripture:

1. Creation. First, God is passionate for His glory in creation. Five times in Genesis 1 God calls His creation "good" (Gen. 1:4, 12, 18, 21, 25). And after God created Adam and Eve, He called it "very good" (vs. 31). When God stepped back and examined

His work of creation, therefore, He was pleased and satisfied in His creative power. Psalm 104:31 tells us that Yahweh rejoices in His works. Why? Because David tells us in Psalm 19:1 that, "The heavens declare the glory of God; and the firmament shows HIs handiwork!" In other words, God delights in His creation because, and only because, it glorifies Him.

2. Call of Israel. Secondly, look at the reason why God created the Jewish people in the first place: in Isaiah, God tells Israel that, "'You are My servant, O Israel, in whom I will be glorified'" (Is. 49:3). Or as God explains in Jeremiah:

> "For as the belt cleaves to the loins of a man, so I caused to cleave to Me the whole house of Israel and the whole house of Judah," an affirmation of Yahweh, "to be to Me for a people, and for a name, and for praise, and for beauty, but they have not heard."
>
> (Jer. 13:11 NYLT)

God called Abraham out of Ur of the Chaldeans in order to make from his loins the Jewish people for God's own renown, praise, and glory.

3. Redemption of Israel. Third, this is the reason why God redeemed His people Israel from bondage in slavery through the Exodus. The psalmist, for instance, declares that:

> [7] Our fathers in Egypt have not considered wisely Your wonders;
> They have not remembered the abundance of Your steadfast love,
> But rebel by the sea, at the Red Sea.
> [8] Yet He saves them for His name's sake,
> To make known His might.
>
> (Ps. 106:7-8)

As you read the Bible, do not read passages like a string of unrelated pearls. Rather, the Bible—some parts more than others—builds a progressively logical argument from initial premise to ultimate conclusion. Therefore, always be on the look out for how the links in the chain of argument are connected by looking for words such as *therefore*, *because*, *for*, and *that*. In this passage, for instance, verse 7 tells us that the Israelites rebelled against God at the Red Sea when in unbelief they wished they were still back in slavery in Egypt (Ex. 14:11-12).

But then verse 8 tells us that nevertheless God still saved them. Why? "To make His might known." To maximize His glory in demonstrating His mighty power God parted the Red Sea so that He rebellious people might walk through on dry ground (Ex. 14:22). God's justice demanded that He Himself strike the Israelites dead for their rebellion or, at a minimum, that He let the Egyptians serve as the executioners. But God's righteousness— i.e., the relentless pursuit of His own glory—stayed His hand so that His glory would be maximized in providing a miraculous escape for His children. We see this confirmed in 2 Samuel where King David proclaims:

> "And who is as Your people, as Israel, the one nation in the earth whom God has gone to redeem to Himself for a people, and to make for Him a name, and to do for Yourself greatness—even fearful things for Your land, in the presence of Your people whom You has redeemed to Yourself out of Egypt, the nations and their gods?
> (2 Sam 7:23 NYLT)

We see this again in Exodus, where Yahweh tells Pharaoh, "'But indeed for this purpose I have raised you up, that I may show My power in you, and that My name may be declared in all the earth'" (Ex. 9:16). God decreed exactly who would be Pharaoh during the Exodus and hardened his heart precisely to demonstrate His unrivaled power so that His name would be glorified in all the earth. God didn't need ten plagues to bring His people out of Egypt. He could have started with the tenth plague and ended it with one blow. Or He could have started with the first plague but softened Pharaoh's heart so that he would let the Israelites go.

But God hardened Pharaoh's heart and sent plague after plague on Egypt in order to make a name for Himself. And one of the consequences of God's display of His glory is that Rahab the prostitute of Jericho was saved:

> [8] Now before they lie down, she has gone up to them on the roof [9] and says to the men, "I have known that Yahweh has given you the land, and that your terror has fallen upon us, and that all the inhabitants of the land have melted at your presence. [10] For we have heard how Yahweh dried up the waters of the Red Sea at your presence, in your going out of Egypt, and that which you have done to the two kings of the Amorites who are beyond the Jordan—to Sihon and to Og—whom you devoted to destruction. [11] When we hear this, our hearts melt and there has not stood any more spirit in any man because of your presence, for Yahweh your God, He is God in the heavens above and on the earth beneath."
>
> (Josh. 2:8-11 NYLT)

As a result of God's relentless pursuit of His glory in devastating Egypt with ten plagues and parting the Red Sea, this pagan harlot was converted and hid the two spies Joshua sent out to spy out the land of Canaan. And God rewarded her faith, for she became the great-grandmother of King David from whose line was born the God-man Jesus Christ as the long-promised Messiah of Israel.

4.   Restoration of Israel.   Fourth, God's passion for the maximization of His glory led Him to exile, but not utterly destroy, Israel for their centuries-long disregard for His glory.   For in Isaiah, God tells them:

> [9] "For My name's sake I defer Mine anger,

And for My praise I restrain it for you
So as not to cut you off.
10 Behold!—I have refined you, but not as silver,
I have chosen you for a furnace of affliction.
11 For My sake, for My own sake, I do it,
For how should My name be polluted?
And My glory to another I give not.

(Is. 48:9-11 NYLT)

God's passion for His glory led Him to mercy rather than the complete annihilation of the Jewish people.

5. Predestination. Five, God's unwavering pursuit of His chief end—to glorify Himself by enjoying Himself forever—led Him to predestine certain undeserving sinners to everlasting life. Why? For His glory. For God tells us that, "'Everyone who is called by My name whom I have created for My glory—I have formed him, yes, I have made him'" (Is. 43:7). Again, three times we are told in the first chapter of Ephesians that God "predestined us to adoption as sons by Jesus Christ to Himself" (vs. 5) *for* His praise:

- **Verse 6:** "to the praise of the glory of His grace..."
- **Verse 12:** "...to the praise of His glory."
- **Verse 14:** "...to the praise of His glory."

Or as Peter tells believers: "But you are a chosen people, a royal priesthood, a holy nation, His own special people, that you may proclaim the praises of Him who called you out of darkness into His marvelous light" (1 Pet. 2:9). Our predestination to redemption, therefore, is solely "to the riches of His grace" (Eph. 1:7, 2:7). Or, to put it another way, our salvation is owing only to God's relentless pursuit of His glory.

6. Second Coming. Sixth and finally, God's passion for His glory is the reason for His second and triumphant coming, for the Apostle Paul tells us that Christ will come "in that Day to be glorified in His saints and to be admired among all those who believe" (2 Thess. 1:10). And at HIs coming the non-elect, unregenerate sinners will be deservingly cast into hell, for we are told that He predestined such vessels of wrath for destruction so "that He might make known the riches of His glory to the vessels of mercy which He had prepared beforehand for glory" (Rom. 9:23).

Conclusion: We have, therefore, seen that God is passionate for His glory in the creation of the Jewish people, redeeming them from Egypt, mercifully disciplining them, predestinating the elect unto salvation, and in His Second Coming and execution of judgment. And this is hardly an exhaustive survey of all the ways given in Scripture that God acts solely to maximize His own glory. For instance, in the book of Ezekiel alone God tells the Jewish people seventy-two times that He is acting, "so that you might known that I am Yahweh." Seventy-two times! And in ten other places in Ezekiel He simply declares, "I am Yahweh." Throughout the book of Ezekiel God promises both punishment and eventual restoration "that you may know that I am Yahweh." For instance:

- **33:29:** "'And they have known that I am Yahweh, in My making the land a desolation and an astonishment for all their abominations that they have done'" (NYLT).
- **20:44:** "'And you have known that I am Yahweh, In My dealing with you for My name's sake, not according to your evil ways nor according to your corrupt doings, O house of Israel,' an affirmation of Adonai Yahweh'" (NYLT).

To say, therefore, that God is passionate for His glory is an understatement. It would be far more accurate to say that God is jealous with a consuming fire for the fame of His name.

B. God is Jealous for His Glory. Over and over in Scripture God makes clear that He is jealous for His name, for His character, for His glory. (See generally Ps. 78:58, 79:5; Ezek. 38:19; Joel 2:18; Nahum 1:2; Zeph. 1:18, 3:8; Zech. 1:14, 8:2; 1

Cor. 10:22; James 4:5). In fact, Moses warns the Israelites that, "Yahweh your God is a consuming fire, a jealous God" (Deut. 4:24) for the reputation of His holy name (Ezek. 39:25).

Two chapters later Moses urges them to:

> 13 Yahweh your God you do fear, and Him you do serve, and by His name you do swear. 14 You do not go after other gods, of the gods of the peoples who are round about you, 15 for a zealous God is Yahweh your God in your midst, lest the anger of Yahweh your God burn against you and He has destroyed you from off the face of the ground.
>
> (Deut. 6:13-15 NYLT)

When Moses renews God's covenant with Israel at Moab, we read in Deuteronomy 29:

> 18 Lest there be among you a man or woman, or family or tribe, whose heart is turning today from Yahweh our God to go to serve the gods of those nations; lest there be in you a fruitful root of gall and wormwood. 19 Lest it has been, in hearing the words of this oath, that such a man blesses himself in his heart, saying, "I have peace, though I go on in the stubbornness of my heart." In order to end the fulness with the thirst. 20 Yahweh is not willing to be propitious to him, for then the anger and zeal of Yahweh smokes against that man. Lain down on him has all the oath which is written in this book, and Yahweh has blotted out his name from under the heavens. 21 Yahweh has separated him for evil, out of all the tribes of Israel, according to all the oaths of the covenant which is written in this Book of the Law."
>
> (Deut. 29:18-21 NYLT)

Three chapters later Moses predicts what will happen to Israel in the future:

15 And Jeshurun waxes fat and kicks: "You have been fat, you have been thick, you have been covered with fat." And he leaves God who made him and dishonors the Rock of his salvation. 16 They make Him zealous with strangers, with abominations they make Him angry...

18 You forget the Rock that begat you, and neglect the God who forms you. 19 And Yahweh sees and despises, for the provocation of His sons and His daughters. 20 And He says, "I hide My face from them, I see what is their latter end. For a froward generation they are, sons in whom is no steadfastness.

21 They have made Me zealous by what is not god. They made Me angry by their vanities. And I make them zealous by those who are not a people. By a foolish nation I make them angry."

> (Deut. 32:15-16, 18-21a NYLT; see also Ezek. 8:3-5).

Joshua, Moses' successor, warned the Israelites that:

19 And Joshua says unto the people, "You are not able to serve Yahweh, for a God most holy He is; a zealous God He is. He does not bear with your transgression and with your sins. 20 When you forsake Yahweh, and have served gods of a stranger, then He has turned back and done evil to you and consumed you after He has done good to you."

> (Josh. 24:19-20 NYLT)

Several centuries later we are told that, "Judah does evil in the eyes of Yahweh, and they make Him zealous above all that their fathers did by their sins that they have sinned" (1 Kings 14:22 NYLT). And in the book of Ezekiel, God compares Himself to a vengeful husband as He condemns the Israelites as an:

Adulterous wife! You prefer strangers to Me—your own husband! All your detestable practices and your

27

prostitution provoked me to anger with your increasing promiscuity. I turned away from you in disgust, yet you became more and more promiscuous. I will direct My jealous anger against you. I will sentence you to the punishment of women who commit adultery and who shed blood; I will bring upon you the blood vengeance of My wrath and jealous anger. I will put a stop to your prostitution, and you will no longer pay your lovers. [42] Then My wrath against you will subside and My jealous anger will turn away from you. Your lewdness and promiscuity have brought this upon you, because you lusted after the nations and defiled yourself with their idols.

      (paraphrase of Ezek. 16:22, 26, 32, 38, 41-42, 23:18-19a, 25, 29-30)

But though Israel stirred up God's jealous anger against them so that He drove them out of Palestine, His jealousy for His glory also brought them back from exile:

39 [25] Therefore, thus said Adonai Yahweh, "Now do I bring back the captivity of Jacob, and I have pitied all the house of Israel, and have been zealous for My holy name."...
36 [5] Therefore, thus said the Adonai Yahweh, "Have I not, in the fire of My jealousy, spoken against the remnant of the nations and against all Edom who—with joy of the whole heart and spite of soul—gave My land to themselves for a possession for the sake of casting it out for a prey? [6] Therefore, prophesy concerning the ground of Israel, and you said to mountains and to hills, to streams and to valleys, thus said Adonai Yahweh, 'Behold!—I, in My jealousy, and in My fury, I have spoken because the shame of nations you have borne. [7] Therefore, thus said Adonai Yahweh, "I have lifted up My hand, 'Do not the nations who are with you from round about bear their own shame?'"'"

THE FREE WILL OF GOD

(Ezek. 39:25, 36:5-7 NYLT)

II. God Behaves Righteously:

God's passion and jealously for HIs glory is the reason why He does what He does. It is the motivation for everything He decrees. The fame of His name is the purpose of all things He ordains. It is the end for which He created creation—both visible and invisible. This passion and jealously for His glory is God's righteousness. For this is how the Apostle Paul uses the term righteousness in defending God's electing purpose in the ninth chapter of Romans:

> [14] What shall we say then? Is there unrighteousness with God? Certainly not! [15] For He says to Moses, "I will have mercy on whomever I will have mercy, and I will have compassion on whomever I will have compassion." [16] So then it is not of him who wills, nor of him who runs, but of God who shows mercy. [17] For the Scripture says to the Pharaoh, "For this very purpose I have raised you up, that I may show My power in you, and that My name may be declared in all the earth." [18] Therefore He has mercy on whom He wills, and whom He wills He hardens.
>
> (Rom. 9:14-18)

Paul had just expressed his "great sorrow and continual grief" (vs. 2) for the lost and perishing among his "brethren, my countrymen according to the flesh" (vs. 3). But the fact that so many of God's chosen people are rejecting their Messiah Jesus begs the question, has "the word of God...taken no effect" (vs. 6). In other words, can God be trusted to keep His covenants of promise (Eph. 2:12; Rom. 9:4) when the apple of His eye (Ps. 17:8; Zech. 2:8) is hardened against Him? How can these new Gentile believers confidently place their hope and trust in God's promises when the majority of the Jewish people are sons of perdition (Jn. 17:12)?

And Paul's answer—using the examples of God's election of Isaac over Ishmael (vs. 7-9) and Jacob over Esau (vs. 10-12)—is that "6...they are not all Israel who are of Israel, 7 nor are they all children because they are the seed of Abraham" (vs. 6-7). Rather, the true Israel of God (Rom. 2:28-29; Gal. 6:16) are those "imputed as the seed" (Rom. 9:8 NYLT; see also 4:16-17; Gal. 4:28) of Abraham by God's electing promise (vs. 8) made while we are "not yet being born, nor having done any good or evil, [in order] that the promise of God according to election might stand, [because it is] not of [our] works but [solely] of Him who calls" (vs. 11). In other words, God's word of promise has not failed because salvation has *never* been the result of ethnic identity— "children of the flesh" (vs. 8; see also Jn. 1:13)—but solely of God's sovereign will decreed before the foundation of the earth was laid (Matt. 25:34; Eph. 1:4; Rev. 13:8).

So in verse 14 the apostle anticipates the objection: If God sovereignly elects who among fallen humanity to impute as the seed of Abraham—the children of promise—before they are born or have done anything good or evil, isn't this unrighteous? In other words, the skeptics and scoffers are asking how God could possibly be just[1] to deprive men of their free will and assign their eternal fates before they were even conceived, must less have a chance to hear and respond to the Gospel?

And what is Paul's response in verse 15? It is to quote what God told Moses in Exodus 33:19. But how is this an answer, for it just sounds like a restatement of the problem? The dilemma is: "How is it just that—before we are conceived or have done anything meriting eternal damnation—God sovereignly elects who goes to heaven and who goes to hell?" And the inspired apostle's answer is: "'I will have mercy on whomever I will have

---

[1] The same Greek word—dikaiosuné—is translated as either righteous or justice. In verse 14, the word translated *unrighteousness* by the NKJV is adikia, meaning *not* (a) and *just* or *righteous* (dike). It is translated as *injustice* by the ESV and NASB and *unjust* by the NIV84.

mercy, and I will have compassion on whomever I will have compassion'" (vs. 15).

The context of that answer is vital to understanding how it is, in fact, an answer and not merely a restatement. For Israel had just committed idolatry with the golden calf while Moses was on Mount Sinai the first time receiving the levitical law and instructions for building the tabernacle. Around 3,000 Israelites died in the plague Yahweh sent as judgment for their idol worship (Ex. 32:28). And God told Moses that His Presence "will not go up in your midst, least I consume you on the way, for you are a stiff-necked people" (33:5).

Moses, however, pleads with God to go with them, arguing, "For how then will it be known that Your people and I have found grace in Your sight, except You go with us?" (vs. 16). God agrees to Moses' request because "'you have found grace in My sight, and I know you by name'" (vs. 17). It is then that Moses asks God, "'Please, show me Your glory'" (vs. 18), to which Yahweh responds:

> [19] Then He said, "I will make all My goodness pass before you, and I will proclaim the name of the LORD before you. I will be gracious to whom I will be gracious, and I will have compassion on whom I will have compassion." [20] But He said, "You cannot see My face; for no man shall see Me, and live." [21] And the Lord said, "Here is a place by Me, and you shall stand on the rock. [22] So it shall be, while My glory passes by, that I will put you in the cleft of the rock, and will cover you with My hand while I pass by. [23] Then I will take away My hand, and you shall see My back; but My face shall not be seen."
>
> (Ex. 33:19-23)

Then in the next chapter we read of God showing Moses His glory:

5 Now the LORD descended in the cloud and stood with him there, and proclaimed the name of the LORD. 6 And the LORD passed before him and proclaimed, "The LORD, the LORD God, merciful and gracious, longsuffering, and abounding in goodness and truth, 7 keeping mercy for thousands, forgiving iniquity and transgression and sin, by no means clearing the guilty, visiting the iniquity of the fathers upon the children and the children's children to the third and the fourth generation."

(Ex. 34:5-7)

The glory that God showed Moses was not so much in what he *saw*, but rather in what he *heard*. It was in God's self-revelation of Himself. Yahweh proclaimed His name, all of His goodness, by telling Moses some of His essential and intrinsic attributes of deity. And notice how sovereign grace is found in both 33:19 and 34:6—"Yahweh, Yahweh God—I will be gracious to whom I will be gracious, and I will have compassion on whom I will have compassion." In short, much like His self-revelation in response to Moses request for His name in Exodus 3 (which we looked at in the last chapter), here God is declaring to Moses that His sovereign free will is an inherent and innate part of His Godness without which He cannot be God.

So returning to Romans 9 with this context in mind, we can now see how Exodus 33:19 is an answer to the objection raised in Romans 9:14: God is righteousness in sovereign, unilateral, monergistic election because such free will is an indispensable essence of His deity. To abdicate such electing purposes would be to abdicate His throne. God must exercise His holy attributes in accordance with His moral excellences with absolute free will or He ceases to be God.

The Apostle Paul then restates his verse 11 answer to the dilemma of verse 6 twice more in Romans 9:

• **Verse 16:** "So then it is not of him who wills, nor of him who runs, but of God who shows mercy."

- **Verse 18:** "Therefore He has mercy on whom He wills, and whom He wills He hardens."

The reason God's word of promise has not failed (vs. 6) in the damnation of so many Jews (vs. 1-5) is because they are not all elect (vs. 11, 16, 18). And God is righteous in such electing purposes because the goal of His innate free will is His own glory. God's righteousness is doing right by Himself. As R.C. Sproul explains God's righteousness in his book *The Holiness of God*, it means that, "What God does is always consistent with who God is. He always acts according to His holy character."[2] But it is much more than that. It is no less than that, but it much more than that. For notice the reasons—the goal, the end, the purpose — Paul gives for the exercise of divine free will in Romans 9:

- **Verse: 11:** To demonstrate that salvation is not of works.
- **Verse 16:** To eliminate salvation based on man's will or effort but on God's sovereign grace alone.
- **Verse 17:** To demonstrate God's power, so that His name may be declared in all the earth.
- **Verse 22:** To show God's worth and to make His power known.
- **Verse 23:** To make known the riches of His glory.
- **Verse 30-33:** To demonstrate that salvation is by faith alone and not by works of the law.

God's righteousness, therefore, isn't God merely behaving in a certain way according to His holy character, but rather a passionate pursuit of the value of His holy character.[3] It is the

---

[2] https://tabletalkmagazine.com/posts/what-was-rc-sprouls-favorite-word-2019-11/

[3] This distinction, for instance, is vital to understanding God's providence throughout redemptive history. As just one example, it explains why God did not kill Adam and Eve immediately at the Fall but rather promised a Seed who would crush Satan's head (Gen. 3:15).

maximization of His glory. God's righteousness is the infinite and perfect display of His infinite and perfect value. God, by very definition of being God, is holy—utterly set apart from anything or anyone else in His complete uniqueness. He is the most supremely valuable Being imaginable in the magisterial perfect of all His attributes—His love, mercy, grace, justice, anger, wrath, immutability (unchangeableness), faithfulness, generosity, sovereignty, omnipotence, omniscience, omnipresence, and wisdom, to name but a few. Therefore, as John Piper has explained:

> The righteousness of God...is God's unwavering allegiance to uphold the value of what is infinitely valuable, namely his own glory...Since God has no constitution or legal code outside of himself by which to measure what is right and good in his own thinking and feeling and doing, it must be measured by himself.
> What then is righteousness in God? God's righteousness is his devotion to, his allegiance to, his absolute unwavering commitment to stand or and uphold and vindicate that which is infinitely valuable: himself. That is the righteousness of God. If he for one millisecond diverted from his passionate, infinitely zealous cause of holding up his glory, he would be unrighteousness and unworthy of our worship.[4]

This sounds egotistical to our sinful ears. It sounds prideful and arrogant. It sounds unloving and selfish. For how can God be for us if He is only for Himself? But such a response by our egotistical, prideful, arrogant, unloving, and selfish hearts fails to grasp how God's righteousness is the most wonderful news in the world. For God cannot be loving if He is not first and foremost for Himself.

---

[4] https://www.desiringgod.org/messages/the-echo-and-the-insufficiency-of-hell

If He does not love, worship, treasure, and rejoice in His own infinite value and worth above all else, He is not God. By very definition, God must be the infinitely supremely valuable object imaginable. Therefore, should God stop loving, worshipping, treasuring, and rejoicing in Himself, He would be an idolater by instead bestowing His love, worship, treasuring, and rejoicing on another. He would commit blasphemy. He would deny His own infinite glory. And if God would worship something that is not god, then we, in turn, have no god worth worshipping. And if there is no god worth worshipping, then there is no god, and we might as well eat, drink, and be merry, for tomorrow we will die without hope.

But, by relentlessly pursuing His own glory above all other considerations, God is unfathomably good to us. We just saw earlier how His passion for His glory moved Him to create the universe, call out from among the nations the Jewish people, redeem them from bondage in Egypt, in mercy restoring them from exile, in predestining the elect unto salvation, and in His Second Coming. If God were not first and foremost for Himself, then none of these things would have occurred. If God did not relentlessly pursue His own glory above all else, there would have been no creation, no Cross, and no resurrection from the dead.

Or, to put it another way, God's passion for His glory means that God is passionate to display His infinite worth and value. Namely, to magnify His attributes of love, grace, mercy, patience, goodness, faithfulness, justice, wrath, etc. So when we say that God relentlessly pursues His own glory, we mean that He relentlessly pursues the display of His perfect and infinite love. Or He relentlessly pursues the display of His perfect and infinite grace. Or mercy. Or goodness. How, exactly, is that a bad thing? It would be the height of foolishness to tell God not to pursue His glory in displaying the infinite excellencies of His love. It is the epitome of insanity to tell God, "I think it is unloving that you are maximally loving."

Let's imagine, for instance, that you were a huge Celine Dion fan and spent quite a bit of money going to Los Vegas and buying

35

a ticket to hear her perform. But once she was on stage, she simply read the lyrics to the audience. In disgust, someone asks her how this was possibly loving and honoring to her fans. She replied that she became convinced that it was unloving and selfish on her part to pursue her excellence in singing so now she merely reads the lyrics in a monotone voice. She had become convicted that it was prideful and arrogant to receive praise from her adoring fans, so she had stopped singing entirely.

Or imagine that you that you were about to board a plane, undergo brain surgery, or needed your car fixed. How many of you would tell the pilot, surgeon, and car mechanic that you thought it was unloving for them to pursue a good reputation at their craft? Rather, would you not think that by pursuing their own excellence in their profession they were also loving to their customers? In fact, it was only by working hard to become experts in their fields that they were able to do their customers any good at all. If they had instead thought it was the height of arrogance to have a good reputation for excellence, they would be of no good to anyone at all, themselves included.

Similarly, therefore, it is only by treasuring Himself above everything else that God is able, in turn, to give us Himself as the greatest treasure imaginable for us to enjoy for all eternity. That is what is meant by God's righteousness.

Concluding Implications:

The point of all of creation, therefore, is to maximally display God's glory. God creates, God governs, God acts, He decrees, ordains, and wills—ongoing, present-tense—everything in order to magnify His infinite worth and supreme value. And because God is infinitely and perfectly good, omnipotent, omniscient, omnipresent, omniwise, immutable, eternal, and absolutely free, then everything He creates, governs, acts, decrees, ordains, and wills is also, likewise, infinitely and perfectly good, omnipotent, omniscient, omnipresent, omniwise, immutable, eternal, and absolutely free.

In other words, this is the best of all possible worlds.[5] Not just in general, in total, in looking at it from the big picture. But every single minute detail in every millisecond of all creation everywhere is the best of all possible scenarios. There is nothing, absolutely nothing, that occurs without God's willing it to happen in the most infinitely perfect way for the exhibition of His glory in the demonstration of the fulness of HIs attributes. And therefore, every single thing in all of creation is infinitely perfectly designed for the best possible maximization of our eternal joy in our Creator's infinite worth.

And consequently, there are no rogue characters in God's infinitely perfect novel. No maverick notes in His infinitely perfect symphony. No rebellious brush strokes in His infinitely perfect painting. His creation cannot thwart His relentless and passionate pursuit of the maximum display of His glory. His righteousness cannot be held hostage by the insubordination of His creatures. His masterpiece has never once been in doubt because His clay, His marble, His stone was unwilling to cooperate as He sculpted.

God, for instance, was not waiting on pins and needles for a Noah to appear at just the right time so He could destroy the earth in the Flood. That's blasphemous. He was not wringing His hands for just the right moon worshipper from Arabia to arrive on the scene so He could create a people group. That's scandalous. He was not waiting with bated breath for just the right kind of stupid to sit on the throne of Egypt before He could deliver His people with ten plagues. That's impiously irreverent. He wasn't pulling out His hair, hoping beyond hope that His Son would somehow be able to pull off the impossible by fulfilling all the Old Testament prophecies made about Him. That's profanely heretical.

Other examples, of course, are practically endless. No God worth worshipping leaves the execution of His plans for the manifestation of His glory up to the "free will" of HIs creatures. Such a god is weak, impotent, emasculated; a beggar, a servant,

---

[5] Ergo, there is no such thing as parallel universes.

a slave; worthless, useless, and contemptible. Such a god would be like poor little King Ahab who, "sullen and displeased" after Naboth refused to sell him his vineyard, "lay down on his bed, and turned away his face, and would eat no food" (1 Kings 21:4). Such a god would be no better than an idol made by hands:

> [1] Bel crouches; Nebo cowers.
> Idols depicting them are consigned to beasts and cattle.
> The images you carry are loaded,
> as a burden for the weary animal.
> [2] The gods cower; they crouch together;
> they are not able to rescue the burden,
> but they themselves go into captivity.
> [3] "Listen to me, house of Jacob,
> all the remnant of the house of Israel,
> who have been sustained from the womb,
> carried along since birth.
> [4] I will be the same until your old age,
> and I will bear you up when you turn gray.
> I have made you, and I will carry you;
> I will bear and rescue you.
> [5] "To whom will you compare me or make me equal?
> Who will you measure me with,
> so that we should be like each other?
> [6] Those who pour out their bags of gold
> and weigh out silver on scales—
> they hire a goldsmith and he makes it into a god.
> Then they kneel and bow down to it.
> [7] They lift it to their shoulder and bear it along;
> they set it in its place, and there it stands;
> it does not budge from its place.
> They cry out to it but it doesn't answer;
> it saves no one from his trouble.
> (Is. 46:1-7 CSB)

Notice the contrast—idols are wearily carried by those who make them (vs. 1-2, 7), but Yahweh God of Scripture sovereignly carries those He makes (vs. 3-4). Gods who are dependent upon men are a burden (vs. 1). They are powerless to rescue but instead they themselves go into captivity (vs. 2). They cower and crouch together in their impotence (vs. 2). They cannot move themselves, much less perform salvation and answer prayers (vs. 7).

A god with no sovereign free will might as well be blind, mute, deaf, unable to smell, paralyzed, and breathless for all the good he can do (Ps. 115:4-7, 135:15-18; Hab. 2:18-19). And everyone who creates such a god to protect man's vaunted "free will" will be like them—worthless (Ps. 115:8; Is. 44:9). Such a god provokes no fear, for they can do neither good nor evil (Jer. 10:5). They "are altogether dull-hearted and foolish," "a worthless doctrine" (vs. 8).

May we rightly mock such a god as Elijah did Baal on Mount Carmel:

> At noon Elijah mocked them, saying, "Shout louder, for surely he is a god! Maybe he is mulling it over? Or possibly he has turned aside to relieve himself? Or perhaps he is busy traveling on a long journey? Or is he sleeping and needs to be awakened?
>
> (1 King 18:27; author's own paraphrase)

Such a god has no voice, cannot answer, cannot pay attention (vs. 29). But in contrast, Yahweh God of Scripture is absolutely sovereign who infinitely perfectly orchestrates everything—down to the smallest, seemingly most insignificant milidetail,—for the joy of His creation in the display of His glory. God only acts for the sake of HIs name, for the sake of His praise, for the sake of His glory, for His own sake (Is. 48:9-11; see also Ex. 14:4, 17-18, 36:22-23, 32; 1 Sam. 15:20, 22; 2 Kings 19:34, 20:6; Ps. 25:11, 106:7-8; Is. 43:6-7, 25, 49:3; Matt. 5:16; Jn. 7:18, 12:27-28, 13:31-32, 14:13, 16:14, 17:1; Rom. 3:25-26, 9:17, 15:7; Eph. 1:4-6, 12, 14; 1 Pet. 2:12). For Him to do otherwise would be to make Himself an idolater—it would profane His name by giving

His glory to another (Is. 48:9-11; Ezek. 20:14). He, and only He, is a God worth worshipping.

33 Oh, the depth of the riches both of the wisdom and knowledge of God! How unsearchable are His judgments and His ways past finding out!

    34 "For who has known the mind of the Lord?
    Or who has become His counselor?"
      35 "Or who has first given to Him
    And it shall be repaid to him?"

36 *For of Him and through Him and to Him are all things*, to whom be glory forever. Amen.

        (Rom. 11:33-36; emphasis added)

NATHAN W. TUCKER

3 THE FREE WILL OF GOD IN CREATING

God creates because He is love. He creates out of the overflow of His trinitarian love for Himself. And as a result, He creates not out of need, want, or loneliness, but as the most free and absolutely sovereign Creator.

I. God is Love. In order to understand this, we first must climb the very heights of the Himalayas of Scriptural insight and peer into what may be known and deduced of the relationship of the Triune Godhead. And the key to beginning to understand this great mystery is the fact, as the Apostle John tells us, that "God is love" (1 Jn. 4:8, 16).

If you believe in a divine being, you probably have no problem agreeing with this statement. But what most people mean when they say that God is love is not what the Bible means by saying that God is love. When an unregenerate pagan says that God is love, what they really mean is that God is love to the exclusion of all His other attributes. They mean that God is love, but not just, angry, or wrathful, and thereby they not only deny the entire testimony of Scripture but the personality of God as well. And too often they equate love with God, as if love and God are identical, equal, and interchangeable. But by making an emotion god, then we are all under obligation to worship love as god, which is not only nonsensical but blasphemous.

However, when Scripture says that God is love, it simply means that love is an essential aspect of God's character, not His complete character. "God is love" simply sums up the entire Scriptural record of who God is. And the rest of that Biblical witness to God helps us define what His love is. As the twentieth century pastor and theologian A.W. Tozer wrote in his book *The Knowledge of the Holy*:

> We can know, for instance, that because God is self-existent, His love has no beginning; because He is

eternal, His love can have no end; because He is infinite, it has no limit; because He is holy, it is the quintessence of all spotless purity; because He is immense, His love is an incomprehensible, vast, bottomless, shoreless sea before which we kneel in joyful silence and from which the loftiest eloquence retreats confused and abashed.

I.A. Love Requires the Trinity. But in saying that God is love, we have a dilemma. For the Bible declares that God is the Great I Am—the uncreated, self-sufficient, self-existent, unchangeable, limitless One who has no beginning, no end, no need, and no weakness (Ex. 3:14-15; Numb. 23:19; Ps. 33:11, 102:27; Mal. 3:6; Jn. 5:26; Heb. 13:8; Jac. 1:17; Rev.1:8, 22:13). The problem we face, therefore, is how can a solitary god love if there is no one else to love? As author Jared C. Wilson explains:

> A solitary god cannot be love. He may learn to love. He may yearn for love. But he cannot in himself be love, since love requires an object. Real love requires relationship. In the doctrine of the Trinity we finally see how love is part of the fabric of creation; it's essential to the eternal, need-nothing Creator. From eternity past, the Father and the Son and the Spirit have been in community, in relationship. They have loved each other. That loving relationship is bound up in the very nature of God himself. If God were not a Trinity but merely a solitary divinity, he could neither be love nor be God.[1]

Fred Sanders, in his book entitled *The Deep Things of God: How the Trinity Changes Everything*, wrote:

> The doctrine of the Trinity expels a host of unworthy ideas about God's love. . . .God is not lonely, or bored, or selfish. . . . This is what the doctrine of the Trinity helps us learn with greater precision: that God is love. The

[1] https://www.thegospelcoalition.org/article/no-trinity-no-love/

triune God is a love that is infinitely high above you, eternally preceding you, and welcoming you in.[2]

I.B. The Triune God as Love. Scripture defines the Triune God in this way: one God, eternally existent in three Persons—God the Father, God the Son, and God the Holy Spirit. These three Persons of the Godhead are equal in every perfection, and that these three are one God, having precisely the same nature, attributes, and perfections, and worthy of precisely the same homage, confidence, and obedience (Gen. 1; Lev. 19:2; Deut. 6:4-5; Is. 5:16; 6:1-7; 40:18-31; Matt. 3:16-17; 28:19-20; Jn. 14:6-27; 1 Cor. 8:6; 2 Cor. 13:14; Gal. 4:4-6; Eph. 2:13-18; 1 Jn. 1:5; 4:8).

I.B.1. God the Father is the Deity existing, as 18th century pastor and theologian Jonathan Edwards explains, "in the prime, unoriginated, and most absolute manner, or the Deity in its direct existence." This is why He is called the *Father*. He, for instance, begot the Son. He is the One whose will Jesus obeyed and whose words Jesus spoke during His earthly ministry. He is the One who Jesus prayed to. He is the One who sends forth the Holy Spirit. God the Father is God in "the prime, unoriginated, and most absolute manner...the Deity in its direct existence."

I.B.2. God the Son, as Edwards goes on to explain, "is the Deity generated by God's understanding of Himself, and subsisting in that idea." God the Son is the self-expression of God the Father. He is God the Father's understanding of Himself so perfectly so as to become a living reproduction, or begetting, of Himself as a distinct and separate Person. God the Son has eternally existed with God the Father as the Father's image or idea of Himself.

C.S. Lewis explains it this way in his book *Mere Christianity*:

He is always, so to speak, streaming forth from the Father, like light from a lamp...or thoughts from a mind. He is the self-expression of the Father—what the Father has to say. And there was never a time when He was not saying it.

It is impossible for us as finite creatures to perfectly know ourselves, so all analogies are going to be woefully inadequate. But let's imagine that the person staring back at you in the mirror suddenly popped out of the mirror and became a living, personal human being. He would not only look like you but act like you with your personality and character. He would be your double in every way; a perfect image of yourself.

Or, let's imagine that we were able to make a complete clone of you. Not only of your genetic DNA, but we were able to somehow map your personality and character, thought patterns and memories, and upload all of that into your clone. He would be an exact, perfect carbon copy of you, but yet a distinct and separate living, volitional, and emotional person.

These illustrations are probably the closest we as mere mortals can get to grasping God the Son as the mirror image of the Father. But, like all human analogies, they are imperfect. Their biggest flaw is their inability to illustrate the singular unity of God the Son as the same essence, nature, and substance of God the Father. There is one God, consisting of three separate and distinct Persons—a mystery for which we have no real analogy for. One substance, three Persons. Not personalities or modes, but Persons. One essence, but three living, volitional, and emotional Persons.

Perhaps the closest is a three-headed man—three brains, three consciousness, three personalities, three wills, but one physical property. We may call him Robert, but each head or Person we may call Bobby, Rob, and Roberto respectively. But this analogy loses the strengths of the first two—the shared personality and character, thought patterns and memories, of the individuals. So to better complete this analogy, each person in this three-headed man would be an identical clone—mentally, emotionally, intellectually—of the others, but yet be a distinct and separate Person.

But though these illustrations are imperfect, we see the idea they represent confirmed throughout the testimony of Scripture. For instance, the Apostle Paul describes Jesus as "the image of God" (2 Cor. 4:4) and "the image of the invisible God" (Col. 1:15). The author of Hebrews describes God the Son as "the radiance of God's glory and the exact representation of His substance, sustaining all things by His powerful word" (Heb. 1:3; see also 2 Cor. 4:6). Though Christ was, "in the nature of God, [He] did not consider His equality with God to be grasped" (Phil. 2:6). Finally, as Jesus Himself declared, "'Anyone who has seen Me has seen the Father'" (Jn. 14:9).

And there was never a time before the Father begot or reproduced the Son. Nor could there be for the simple reason that God is eternally perfect. Therefore He has always had a perfect understanding of Himself eternally projected as the living and infinite God the Son. It is impossible for this Word, or image, or imprint, or thought of the Father to be even a fraction of a nanosecond less eternal than the Father Himself. You cannot have one without the other. Again, therefore, it must be stressed that using the term *begetting* simply describes relations of origin within the Godhead and not degrees of subordination or inferiority.

In short, Scripture teaches that from eternity past the eternal Father has always had:

- A perfect image of Himself (2 Cor. 4:4; Col. 1:15, 4:4).
- A perfect reflection or radiance of His glory (2 Core. 4:6; Heb. 1:3).
- A perfect nature of His essence (Phil. 2:6)
- A perfect form of His Person (Jn. 14:9)

And this perfect image, reflection, nature, and form is God the Son. As pastor and theologian John Piper put it:

Since the Son is the image of God and the reflection of God and the stamp of God and the form of God, equal with God, and indeed is God, therefore God's delight in the Son is delight in Himself. Therefore, the original, the primal, the deepest, the foundational joy of God is the joy He has in His own perfections as He sees them reflected in His Son. He loves the Son and delights in the Son and takes pleasure in the Son because the Son is God Himself.[3]

We see this in Matthew, chapter 17:

[1] And after six days Jesus takes Peter, Jacob, and John his brother, and brings them up to a high mountain by themselves, [2] and He was transfigured before them: His face shone as the sun and His garments did become white as the light. [3] And behold!—Moses and Elijah did appear to them, talking together with Him.
[4] And Peter answering said to Jesus, "Lord, it is good to us to be here. If You will, we may make here three tents: for You one, and for Moses one, and one for Elijah."
[5] While he is yet speaking, behold!—a bright cloud overshadowed them, and behold!—a voice out of the cloud, saying, "This is My Son, the Agaped, in whom I did delight. Hear Him!"
[6] And the disciples having heard, did fall upon their face, and were exceedingly afraid. [7] And Jesus, having come near, touched them and said, "Rise, be not afraid!" [8] And having lifted up their eyes, they saw no one except Jesus only.

(Matt. 17:1-8 NYLT)

There are three necessarily vital things to note in this passage. First, that God the Father gave these three Apostles a glimpse of

---

[3] https://www.desiringgod.org/messages/the-pleasure-of-god-in-his-son

Jesus' true glory as God the Son. We see this confirmed by Peter in the second chapter of his second epistle:

> For having received from God the Father honor and glory when such a voice being borne to Him by the Excellent Glory: "This is My Son, the agaped, in whom I was well pleased."
>
> (2 Pet. 1:17 NYLT)

Look at what Peter says—that on the Mount of Transfiguration God the Father bestowed upon God the Son "honor and glory." John also makes reference to Christ's transfiguration when he states that the disciples, "beheld His glory, the glory as of the only begotten of the Father" (Jn. 1:14). Christ was revealed on the mountain to be fully God—of the same essence, nature, and equality.

The second thing to note is that God the Father called Jesus His agaped Son. In the Greek language, *agape* love is the highest form, the highest kind, of love. It is an unconditional, self-giving love. Jesus is God's beloved Son. And third and finally, it is important to note that God the Father states of Christ that He is delighted, or well pleased, in Him.

He says these two things—that Christ is His agaped Son and that He is well pleased in Him—on one other occasion: at Jesus' baptism as the Father anoints Him with the Holy Spirit (Matt. 3:7; Mk. 1:11; Lk. 3:22). Therefore, God the Father finds infinite pleasure, joy, delight, and happiness in God the Son as He loves, treasures, embraces, admires, and worships Christ. And the only way it is impossible for this to constitute idolatry is if God the Son is fully and equally God.

We see this confirmed in several other places as well. Jesus testifies that, "'The Father loves the Son, and has given all things into His hand'" (Jn. 3:35). Again, Jesus tells us, "'For the Father loves the Son, and shows Himself all things that He Himself does; and He will show Him greater works than these, that you may marvel'" (Jn. 5:20). Speaking through the prophet Isaiah, God declares of the coming Messiah, "'Behold!—My Servant whom I uphold; My Elect One in whom My soul delights!"' (Is. 42:1). Once again, therefore, we see that God the Father finds infinite pleasure, joy, delight, and happiness in God the Son as He loves, treasures, embraces, admires, and worships Christ as Himself.

And Christ, in turn, finds infinite pleasure, joy, delight, and happiness in God the Father as He loves, treasures, embraces, admires, and worships the prime, unoriginated, and most absolute Deity. For the Bible tells us that this God-man Jesus Christ, though being of the very nature and essence of God, did not come to earth to seize by force equality with God (Phil. 2:6). Rather, "He emptied Himself of His divine privileges, took the form of a slave, and was made in the likeness of men" (Phil. 2:7). In other words, though He was very God of very God, Jesus "did not live to please Himself" (Rom. 15:3), but rather became the submissive and obedient love-slave of His Father. He lovingly obeyed His Father's will by humbling Himself in becoming a Man.

He further lovingly obeyed His Father by submitting to His will, telling us that, "I have come down from heaven, not to do My own will but the will of Him who sent Me" (Jn. 8:38). So in love was He with His Father that He declared to His disciples that, "My food is to do the will of Him who sent Me and to finish His work" (Jn. 4:34). Elsewhere Jesus declared, "I can of Myself do nothing...I do not seek My own will, but the will of the Father who sent Me...I always do those things that please Him" (Jn. 5:30, 6:29). Out of loving obedience, the very words Jesus said (Jn. 12:49, 17:8) and the works He performed (Jn. 5:36) were dictated to Him by God the Father from eternity past. Finally, out of loving obedience, God the Son humbled Himself to die as a propitiation for sins upon the cross of Calvary (Phil. 2:8).

God the Father and God the Son, therefore, have eternally had mutually infinite pleasure, joy, delight, and happiness in each other as They love, treasure, embrace, admire, and worship the mirror divine perfections They behold in one another.

I.B.3. This, in turn, helps us understand **God the Holy Spirit**. As Edwards explains, He is "the Deity subsisting in act, or the divine essence flowing out and breathed forth, in God's infinite love to and delight in Himself." In other words, the Holy Spirit is the love birthed out—or breathed out—of the mutual delight that has eternally existed between God the Father and God the Son. Again, the Holy Spirit was not created; He is no less eternal than the other two Persons of the Godhead. He has always existed as the Spirit of Love between the members of the Deity.

As C.S. Lewis goes on to explain in *Mere Christianity*:

> Much the most important thing to know [about the relationship between God the Father and God the Son] is that it is a relationship of love. The Father delights in the Son; the Son looks up to His Father....What the Christians mean by the statement "God is love" (1John 4:8) ... is that the living, dynamic activity of love has been going on in God forever and has created everything else....In Christianity God is not a static thing... but a dynamic, pulsating activity, a life, almost a kind of drama. Almost, if you will not think me irreverent, a kind of dance.
>
> The union between the Father and the Son is such a live concrete thing that this union itself is also a Person. I know this is almost inconceivable, but look at th[i]s. You know that among human beings, when they get together in a family, or a club, or a trade union, people talk about the "spirit" of that family, or club, or trade union. They talk about it's "spirit" because the individual members, when they are together, do really develop particular ways of talking and behaving which they would not have if they were apart. It is as if a sort of communal personality came into existence. Of course, it is not a real person: it is only rather like a person. But that is just one of the differences between God and us. What grows out of the joint life of the Father and the Son is a real Person, is in fact the Third of the three Persons who are God....this spirit of love, from all eternity, is a love going on between the Father and the Son.

I.C. The Gloriously Happy God. What this means is that God is a gloriously happy God. In fact, that is was the Apostle Paul writes in describing the Gospel in 1 Timothy 1:11—that it is the Good News of the gloriously happy God. The Greek word translated *happy* here is *makarios*, the same word translated *blessed* throughout the New Testament. The Greeks used it in reference to their gods, which they called "the blessed ones" because the Greeks believed that they had achieved a state of happiness and contentment that was beyond the cares, stress, worry, and problems of earth.

God, however, can only be infinitely happy or blessed by being entirely and completely, perfectly and eternally, self-sufficient in everything. Which means that God can only be infinitely happy or blessed in being love by being entirely and completely, perfectly and eternally, self-sufficient in His Triune love. God is infinitely happy or blessed precisely because He exists as a Triune Godhead that overflows with pleasure, joy, delight, and happiness as the three Persons love, treasure, embrace, admire, and worship each other. God's pleasure, joy, delight, happiness, love, and worship is perfect and infinite. He neither created the universe nor planned Redemption out of need, but rather out of the overflow of His infinite happiness in His eternal triune love.

No other religion in the history of the world has a Triune God. Mormons don't. Jehovah Witnesses don't. Muslims don't. Hindus don't. Native Americans don't. The ancient Greeks and Romans, Babylonians and Egyptians didn't. Only the God of the Bible is a Triune God. Which means that *only* the God of the Bible can be both love and God. A solitary god cannot have the essential attribute of love. He may long to love, but it is impossible for him to be, in and of Himself, love. He may be taught by experience how to love, but he will always and forever love finitely and imperfectly. And therefore a solitary god cannot be God—because he will always have this deficiency. This imperfection. This flaw. This weakness. And a god with a deficiency, imperfection, flaw, and weakness cannot be God. A solitary god, therefore, is a logical impossibility; even more of a myth than Big Foot, unicorns, and Santa Clause.

Imagine, however, if a god existed who was not infinitely happy in his love. He would be completely dependent on external factors for his happiness, which is the exact opposite of the Greek word for blessedness. He would be dependent on his creation to try to satisfy his longing to be happy. He would be worse then a needy, clingy boyfriend in his attempt to find love. And being imperfect, he would seek for love in all the wrong places. And failing to be fulfilled in love, he would become upset, angry, and wrathful. Such a god is not worthy of worship, love, or obedience, but only of fleeing as far away from as possible.

But because the God of the Bible is infinitely happy in His eternal Triune love, He is not dependent on anyone or anything for His happiness. He is entirely and completely, perfectly and eternally, self-sufficient in the Triune love of the Father, Son, and Holy Spirit and therefore has no needs. Consequently, He can love us without hypocrisy. Without flaw. Without pretense. Without dubious motives. His love is infinitely good and perfect, all the time; and all the time, His love is infinitely good and perfect. Therefore God can be trusted, loved, worshipped, and obeyed without reservation or hesitation.

II. The Triune God Creates Out of Love:

So we have established the God creates without compulsion. Without constraint. Without need. Without loneliness. For God declares in Psalm, chapter 50:

> 9 "I take not from your house a bull,
> Nor from your folds goats.
> 10 For Mine is every beast of the forest,
> The cattle on the hills of oxen.
> 11 I have known every bird of the mountains,
> And the wild beast of the field is with Me.
> 12 If I am hungry I will not tell you,
> For Mine is the world and its fulness.
> 13 Do I eat the flesh of bulls,
> And drink the blood of goats?

14 Sacrifice to God thanksgiving,
And complete to the Most High you vows.
15 And call upon Me in the day of adversity;
I deliver you, and you glorify Me.

(Ps. 50:9-15 NYLT)

Or as God declared in Isaiah:

15 Behold!—nations as a drop from a bucket,
And have been reckoned as small dust on the balance;
Behold!—isles are as a small thing He takes up.
16 And Lebanon is not sufficient to burn,
Nor its beasts sufficient for a burnt offering.
17 All the nations are as nothing before Him,
They have been reckoned by Him as nothing and emptiness.

(Is. 40:15-17 NYLT)

Instead, therefore, God creates only because He exists as a Triune Godhead self-sufficient in infinitely perfect love. He creates because He wants to in order to accomplish His sovereign purposes.

And what are those sovereign purposes? Why is God creating the universe? I use the word *creating* intentionally, for God did not create creation, set it in motion with certain natural laws, and then take a hands off approach to its fate. Rather, creation is an ongoing, realtime event that is being made, maintained, and upheld continuously. For the author of Hebrews tell us that:

2... His Son, whom He has appointed heir of all things, through whom also He made the worlds; 3 who being the brightness of His glory and the express image of His person, and upholding all things by the word of His power...

(Heb. 1:2-3)

We see this echoed in Colossians, chapter 1:

¹⁵ He is the image of the invisible God, the firstborn over all creation. ¹⁶ For by Him all things were created that are in heaven and that are on earth, visible and invisible, whether thrones or dominions or principalities or powers. All things were created through Him and for Him. ¹⁷ And He is before all things, and in Him all things consist.

(Col. 1:15-17)

Notice the last part of that last verse—"in Him all things hold together" (ESV). In God all the universe is held together every single second of every single day. Nothing occurs, therefore, that He did not cause. So the Word of God continually speaks creation into existence (Jn. 1:3; 1 Cor. 8:6), and should He ever fall silent the universe and everything in it would be annihilated.

But to what end is God creating? As the author of Hebrews tells us, God is the One, "for whom are all things and by whom are all things" (Heb. 2:10). God causes all things for His own glory. He is creating in order to display the manifold fulness of His divine attributes for the glory of His name. God has always been and always will be infinitely perfect in His divine attributes, but before creation He had no stage upon which to exercise them to be praised by others.

For instance, God has always been and always will be infinitely perfect in His mercy. But before creation He had no one to reveal mercy to, nor anyone to praise Him for such mercy. God has always been and always will be infinitely perfect in His justice. But before creation He had no one to demonstrate justice to, nor anyone to praise Him for such justice. The same could be said of His grace, wrath, patience, faithfulness, humility, etc.

We see something similar in Hebrews 5:8: "through being a Son, He learned obedience by the things which He suffered" (NYLT; see also 2:10). The Bible is not saying that God the Son was imperfect and had to be perfected. It is not arguing that He was disobedient and had to learn obedience. That is blasphemous in light of other passages in the book of Hebrews alone (4:15, 9:14). Rather, the point of this verse is that it was through suffering that the God-man Jesus Christ's untested yet perfect obedience to God the Father was tested and found to remain perfect. In eternity past, before the dawn of time Christ was perfectly obedient to His Father but had no opportunity to show that. The Incarnation, however, afforded Him that opportunity to display His obedience—being "obedient to the point of death, even the death of the cross" (Phil. 2:8).

Creation, therefore, is the theater for the full manifestation of God's glory. "The heavens declare the glory of God, and the sky above proclaims his handiwork" (Ps. 19:1 ESV). God Himself "rejoices in his works" (Ps. 104:31 ESV), as do the angels (Job 38:7) and the saints (Rev. 4:11). For they display His invisible attributes, eternal power, and Godhead (Rom. 1:19-20), revealing a God worthy to receive all glory, honor, and power (Rev. 4:11).

Even man himself exists for God's glory. For the Bible declares that God "created man after His own image; in the image of God He created him; male and female He created them" (Gen. 1:27). He created us in His image as rational creatures so that we might know Him (Jn. 17:3; Rom. 1:19-21a). He created us in His image as relational creatures so that we might have a relationship with Him (Rev. 21:3, 22:4-5). And He created us in His image so that we would reflect His glory! That is, after all, what images do—they are copies created to reflect the original and thereby glorify the original. As John Calvin explained, "man resembles [God] and that in him God's glory is contemplated, as in a mirror."

God makes that abundantly clear throughout Scripture. In Isaiah, for instance, He declares that mankind, "whom I formed and made," "I created for My [own] glory" (Is. 43:7). Elsewhere Scripture states that He will be glorified in His people (Is. 44:23, 49:3). In another place the Bible proclaims that God's glory will be seen upon His people (Is. 60:2); that He will plant them and they will be called oaks of righteousness in order that He might be glorified (Is. 61:1-3). All of this was made with one purpose in mind—that "'the glory of the LORD will be revealed, and all mankind together will see it'" (Is. 40:5). And in doing so, as we saw in the last chapter, He lavishes us with love by maximizing our joy in Him as we behold His glory.

III. Sovereignly Creates Every Detail:

The whole earth is Yahweh's, and everything in it (Exod. 19:5; Deut. 10:14; Job 38:4; Ps. 24:1, 50:12, 89:11; Is. 45:12). And whether through secondary causes such as the laws of nature[4] or through direct intervention, God sovereignly creates every detail of every second of the entire universe. For instance, in the eighth chapter of Luke we read that:

> 22 And it came to pass, on one of the days, that He Himself went into a boat with His disciples, and He said unto them, "We may go over to the other side of the lake." And they set forth. 23 And as they are sailing He fell asleep. And there came down a windstorm on the lake, and they were filling with water, and were in peril. 24 And having come near, they awoke Him, saying, "Master, master, we perish!" And He, having arisen, rebuked the wind and the raging of the water. And they ceased, and there came a calm. 25 But he said to them, "Where is your faith?" And they, being afraid, marveled, saying to one another, "Who, then, is this, that He commands even the winds and the water and they obey Him?"
>
> (Lk. 8:22-25 NYLT)

Jesus "rebuked the wind and the raging of the water. And they ceased, and there was calm" (vs. 24). And His disciples, "being afraid, marveled, saying to one another, 'Who, then, is this, that He commands even the winds and the water and they obey Him?'" (vs. 25).

---

[4] Scripture shows that God is free to use secondary causes (Gen. 8:22; Is. 55:10-11; Acts 27:31-44), though it also shows that He is free to work without (Hos. 1:7), above (Rom. 4:19-21), and against them (Dan. 3:17) at His pleasure.

The book of Jonah records that "Yahweh appoints a great fish to shallow up Jonah" (Jonah 1:16 NYLT) as the reluctant prophet attempted to "flee from the face of Yahweh" (vs. 3 NYLT). After being "in the bowels of the fish three days and three nights," (vs. 17 NYLT), "Yahweh speaks to the fish, and it vomits Jonah out onto dry land (2:10 NYLT). Later, we are told "Yahweh God appoints a vine and causes it to come up over Jonah, to be a shade over his head to give deliverance from his affliction" (4:6 NYTL). "But God appoints a worm at the going up of the dawn on the next day, and it smites the worm and dries it up" (vs. 7 NYLT).

In the Gospel of Matthew, the Lord Christ tells us that, though "two sparrows are sold for a penny, yet not one of them will fall to the ground apart from the will of" God (Matt. 10:29). The Bible makes clear that God is the sovereign Ruler over all nature, authoring and designing every detail of His creation, from the wind (Ps. 135:7; Lk. 8:35) to lightning (Job 36:32), earthquakes (Num. 16:30-32; Job 9:5-6; Ps. 60:2; Acts 16:26; Rev. 16:18), snow (Ps. 147:18), frogs (Ex. 8:1-15), gnats (Ex. 8:16-19), drought (1 Kings 17:1, 18:41-46; Joel 1:20); flies (Ex. 8:20-32), hail (Ps. 105:32); locusts (Ex. 10:1-12; Joel 1:4), quail (Ex. 16:6-8), worms (Jonah 4:7), fish (Jonah 2:10), sparrows (Matt. 6:26; 10:29), grass (Ps. 147:8), plants (Jonah 4:6), famine (Ps. 105:16), the sun (Josh. 10:12-13), water (Ex. 15:19; Neh. 9:11; Job 37:10; Ps. 106:9; Matt. 8:27, 14:25; Lk. 8:24), and everything else in the entire universe.

And God is absolutely sovereign over the womb as well— deciding who is born, when, to what parents, and whether they are male or female. For the very first woman Eve tells us that she had "acquired a man from the LORD" (Gen. 4:1). Later in Genesis we read, "Now Isaac pleaded with the LORD for his wife, because she was barren; and the LORD granted his plea, and Rebekah his wife conceived" (25:21). Similarly, "When the LORD saw that Leah was unloved, He opened her womb; but Rachel was barren" (29:31). Likewise, "[t]hen God remembered Rachel, and God listened to her and opened her womb" (30:22). "[T]he LORD [also] gave [Ruth] conception, and she bore a son" (Ruth 4:13). Conversely, Sarai confesses that, "'See now, the LORD

THE FREE WILL OF GOD

has restrained me from bearing children'" (Gen. 16:2). And a few
chapters later we are told that "the LORD had closed up all the
wombs of the house of Abimelech" (Gen. 20:18). Similarly, we
read of Hannah, the mother of Samuel the prophet, that "the
LORD had closed her womb" (1 Sam. 1:6; see also 2:5).

And Scripture is replete with references to God's common
grace in continually creating for the good of mankind. The
Apostle Paul tells us, for instance, that "'Nevertheless He did not
leave Himself without witness, in that He did good, gave us rain
from heaven and fruitful seasons, filling our hearts with food and
gladness'" (Acts 14:17). The psalmist praises God for His
providential provisions:

> 14 The LORD upholds all who fall,
> And raises up all who are bowed down.
> 15 The eyes of all look expectantly to You,
> And You give them their food in due season.
> 16 You open Your hand
> And satisfy the desire of every living thing.
>   (Ps. 145:15-16)

He even bestows this common grace on the righteous as well
as the wicked. Jesus tells us that, "'He makes His sun rise on the
evil and on the good, and sends rain on the just and on the
unjust'" (Matt. 5:45; see also Lk. 6:35). Finally, there is perhaps
no greater passage detailing God's everyday governance of His
universe than Psalm 104:

> 1 Bless the LORD, O my soul!
> O LORD my God, You are very great:
> You are clothed with honor and majesty,
> 2 Who cover Yourself with light as with a garment,
> Who stretch out the heavens like a curtain.
> 3 He lays the beams of His upper chambers in the waters,
> Who makes the clouds His chariot,
> Who walks on the wings of the wind,

4 Who makes His angels spirits,
His ministers a flame of fire.
5 You who laid the foundations of the earth,
So that it should not be moved forever,
6 You covered it with the deep as with a garment;
The waters stood above the mountains.
7 At Your rebuke they fled;
At the voice of Your thunder they hastened away.
8 They went up over the mountains;
They went down into the valleys,
To the place which You founded for them.
9 You have set a boundary that they may not pass over,
That they may not return to cover the earth.
10 He sends the springs into the valleys;
They flow among the hills.
11 They give drink to every beast of the field;
The wild donkeys quench their thirst.
12 By them the birds of the heavens have their home;
They sing among the branches.
13 He waters the hills from His upper chambers;
The earth is satisfied with the fruit of Your works.
14 He causes the grass to grow for the cattle,
And vegetation for the service of man,
That he may bring forth food from the earth,
15 And wine that makes glad the heart of man,
Oil to make his face shine,
And bread which strengthens man's heart.
16 The trees of the LORD are full of sap,
The cedars of Lebanon which He planted,
17 Where the birds make their nests;
The stork has her home in the fir trees.
18 The high hills are for the wild goats;
The cliffs are a refuge for the rock badgers.
19 He appointed the moon for seasons;
The sun knows its going down.
20 You make darkness, and it is night,
In which all the beasts of the forest creep about.

[21] The young lions roar after their prey,
And seek their food from God.
[22] When the sun rises, they gather together
And lie down in their dens.
[23] Man goes out to his work
And to his labor until the evening.
[24] O LORD, how manifold are Your works!
In wisdom You have made them all.
The earth is full of Your possessions—
[25] This great and wide sea,
In which are innumerable teeming things,
Living things both small and great.
[26] There the ships sail about;
There is that Leviathan
Which You have made to play there.
[27] These all wait for You,
That You may give them their food in due season.
[28] What You give them they gather in;
You open Your hand, they are filled with good.
[29] You hide Your face, they are troubled;
You take away their breath, they die and return to their dust.
[30] You send forth Your Spirit, they are created;
And You renew the face of the earth.
[31] May the glory of the LORD endure forever;
May the LORD rejoice in His works.
[32] He looks on the earth, and it trembles;
He touches the hills, and they smoke.
[33] I will sing to the LORD as long as I live;
I will sing praise to my God while I have my being.
[34] May my meditation be sweet to Him;
I will be glad in the LORD.
[35] May sinners be consumed from the earth,
And the wicked be no more.
Bless the LORD, O my soul!
Praise the LORD!

(Ps. 104)

CONCLUDING IMPLICATIONS:

This means that every single thing that happens in creation is by God's sovereign design. There are no maverick molecules. No rebellious hurricanes. No insubordinate blizzards. No insurgent tornadoes. Or lightening strikes. Or avalanches. Or mud slides. Or flooding. Or earthquakes. Or tsunamis. Or volcanoes. Or hail storms. Or wildfires. Or viruses. Or plagues. Or miscarriages. Or stillbirths. Or deaths.

There are no brainfarts of the universe. No accidents. No coincidences. No mistakes. God, in essence, tells every molecule, every atom, every cell, that they cannot exist, cannot happen, cannot do anything without His leave (Gen. 41:44). Without His permission. Without His willing it.

God is never blindsided. He is never caught unawares. He is never surprised. He is never scrambling for a backup plan. A Plan B. Or C. Or D. He is never stunned that a hurricane ripped through the wrong town. He is never flummoxed that an earthquake destroyed the wrong metropolis. He is never flabbergasted by a sudden death. He is never dumbfounded that Hitler and Stalin didn't die sooner, or that Jim Elliot and David Brainerd died so young.

For everything is by sovereign design, by God's irresistible free will, and therefore has meaning and purpose. Understanding this is essential for the Christian to bear up under sorrow and grief. For instance, Question 28 of the Heidelberg Catechism asks, "What does it benefit us to know that God has created all things and still upholds them by His providence?" The answer it provides reads:

> [So that] we can be patient in adversity, thankful in prosperity, and with a view to the future we can have a firm confidence in our faithful God and Father that no creature shall separate us from his love; for all creatures are so completely in his hand that without his will they cannot so much as move.

It is so that "we can be patient in adversity, thankful in prosperity, and with a view to the future we can have a firm confidence in our faithful God and Father." That is why understanding God's absolute free will is so important. Or as Article 13 of the Belgic Confession states:

> This doctrine affords us unspeakable consolation, since we are taught thereby that nothing can befall us by chance, but by the direction of our most gracious and heavenly Father; who watches over us with a paternal care, keeping all creatures so under His power, that not a hair of our head (for they are all numbered), nor a sparrow, can fall to the ground, without the will of our Father, in whom we do entirely trust; being persuaded, that He so restrains the devil and all our enemies, that without His will and permission, they cannot hurt us.

"This doctrine affords us unspeakable consolation" because all things happen to us, not by chance, but by the "paternal care" of "our most gracious and heavenly Father."

There is a theory called the butterfly effect, made famous a few years ago by a movie of the same name. It holds that the flap of the wings of a single butterfly, for instance, can have massive but untold repercussions (such as altering the path of a distant storm). Imagine then, if you will, all the countless ripple effects caused in just a single half second of human history the world over. And the butterfly effect is not merely limited to the physical realm, but naturally extends to all social interactions as well.

But let's apply this theory to every single event in every single second in all of human history. Either they are random, meaningless brain farts of the universe, or they are plotted down to the exactest detail by the Master Storyteller. There can be no in-between. God cannot be partially sovereign—planning, for instance, just a few events in human history here and there. For such sporadic Providence would render Him completely incapable of keeping His story from unraveling due to all the unintended butterfly effects He carelessly causes as He intervenes on an ad hoc basis in human history. God must be completely sovereign, or incompetent.

Only an absolutely sovereign God can orchestrate such seeming chaos that we see throughout the world. Therefore, the wisdom of the God of the Bible can be trusted precisely because He is the Potter rather than a blunderer. The promises of the God of the Bible can be trusted precisely because He is sovereign rather than impotent. The Providence of the God of the Bible can be trusted precisely because He is the Grand Weaver rather than a synergistic tailor. The goodness of the God of the Bible can be trusted precisely because there is no such thing as meaningless events.

That is what the doctrine of God's absolute sovereignty is all about—to anchor a hope that endures, come what may (Job 38-41).

6…"All flesh is grass,

And all its loveliness is like the flower of the field.

7 The grass withers, the flower fades,

Because the breath of the LORD blows upon it;

Surely the people are grass.

8 The grass withers, the flower fades,

But the word of our God stands forever."

9 O Zion,

You who bring good tidings,

Get up into the high mountain;

O Jerusalem,

You who bring good tidings,

Lift up your voice with strength,

Lift it up, be not afraid;

Say to the cities of Judah, "Behold your God!"

10 Behold, the LORD God shall come with a strong hand,

And His arm shall rule for Him;

Behold, His reward is with Him,

And His work before Him.

11 He will feed His flock like a shepherd;

He will gather the lambs with His arm,

And carry them in His bosom,

And gently lead those who are with young.

12 Who has measured the waters in the hollow of His hand,

Measured heaven with a span

And calculated the dust of the earth in a measure?

Weighed the mountains in scales

And the hills in a balance?

13 Who has directed the Spirit of the LORD,

Or as His counselor has taught Him?

14 With whom did He take counsel, and who instructed Him,

And taught Him in the path of justice?

Who taught Him knowledge,

And showed Him the way of understanding?

15 Behold, the nations are as a drop in a bucket,
And are counted as the small dust on the scales;
Look, He lifts up the isles as a very little thing.
16 And Lebanon is not sufficient to burn,
Nor its beasts sufficient for a burnt offering.
17 All nations before Him are as nothing,
And they are counted by Him less than nothing and worthless.
18 To whom then will you liken God?
Or what likeness will you compare to Him?
19 The workman molds an image,
The goldsmith overspreads it with gold,
And the silversmith casts silver chains.
20 Whoever is too impoverished for such a contribution
Chooses a tree that will not rot;
He seeks for himself a skillful workman
To prepare a carved image that will not totter.
21 Have you not known?
Have you not heard?
Has it not been told you from the beginning?
Have you not understood from the foundations of the earth?
22 It is He who sits above the circle of the earth,
And its inhabitants are like grasshoppers,
Who stretches out the heavens like a curtain,
And spreads them out like a tent to dwell in.
23 He brings the princes to nothing;
He makes the judges of the earth useless.
24 Scarcely shall they be planted,
Scarcely shall they be sown,
Scarcely shall their stock take root in the earth,
When He will also blow on them,
And they will wither,
And the whirlwind will take them away like stubble.
25 "To whom then will you liken Me,
Or to whom shall I be equal?" says the Holy One.

²⁶ Lift up your eyes on high,
And see who has created these things,
Who brings out their host by number;
He calls them all by name,
By the greatness of His might
And the strength of His power;
Not one is missing.
²⁷ Why do you say, O Jacob,
And speak, O Israel:
"My way is hidden from the LORD,
And my just claim is passed over by my God"?
²⁸ Have you not known?
Have you not heard?
The everlasting God, the LORD,
The Creator of the ends of the earth,
Neither faints nor is weary.
His understanding is unsearchable.
²⁹ He gives power to the weak,
And to those who have no might He increases strength.
³⁰ Even the youths shall faint and be weary,
And the young men shall utterly fall,
³¹ But those who wait on the LORD
Shall renew their strength;
They shall mount up with wings like eagles,
They shall run and not be weary,
They shall walk and not faint.

(Is. 40:6b-31)

NATHAN W. TUCKER

4 THE FREE WILL OF GOD OVER SIN

God's absolutely free will decrees all the evil and sin, all the pain and suffering, of the world. God's sovereign authorship doesn't merely extend to the natural realm that we examined in the last chapter, but it also encompasses man's behavior as well. Even to his vile wickedness and immorality. God free will not only governed the Fall of mankind in Adam, but also all other sinful actions of both men and angels. And He does so not by merely giving bare permission, but rather by the imposition of His infinitely perfect wise, good, and irresistible free will.

God's free will yields to no man. No man sins without God's superintendence. There is not a murder, a rape, a kidnapping, or a robbery that God did not will before the foundation of the world. And yet this manifold display of His determinate counsel is for His holy purposes, so that the *sinfulness* of their acts proceeds only from the creatures and not from the Creator who, being absolutely pure and sinless, cannot Himself sin or approve of sin.

I. God Wills That Sin Occur:

For God tells us that, "'Forming light and creating darkness: making peace, and creating evil: I Yahweh am doing all these things'" (Is. 45:7 NYLT). Jeremiah the prophet declares that, "Is it not from the mouth of the Most High that both evils and good go forth?" (Lam. 3:38 NYLT). In Deuteronomy God proclaims:

> "Now see that I, even I, am He,
> And there is no God besides Me;
> I kill and I make alive;
> I wound and I heal;
> Nor is there any who can deliver from My hand."
> (Deut. 32:39)

In Exodus God proclaims, "'...Who appointed a mouth for man? Or who appoints the mute or deaf, or open-eyed or blind? Is it not I, Yahweh?'" (Ex. 4:11 NYLT; see also Prov. 20:12). God, therefore, is ultimately the One who puts to death and who causes new birth, who heals and who wounds, who makes some deaf and mute, and makes some blind or able to see.

The inspired author of the book of Job tells us that it was Yahweh who "had brought" "all the evil" that had befallen Job (Job 42:11 ESV)—even though chapters 1 and 2 clearly blame Satan as the perpetrator—and yet in doing so Job did not sin (1:22, 2:10). When Naomi returns home to Bethlehem after losing her husband and two sons, she wished to be called Mara because:

> 20 ...the Almighty has dealt very bitterly with me. 21 I went out full, and the LORD has brought me home again empty. Why do you call me Naomi, since the LORD has testified against me, and the Almighty has afflicted me?"
> (Ruth 1:20-21)

She no longer desired to be called Naomi (which means *pleasant*) but Mara (which means *bitter*) because:

- **Verse 20**—"'The Almighty has dealt very bitterly with me.'"
- **Verse 21**—"'The LORD has brought me home again empty.'"
- **Verse 21**—"'The LORD has testified against me.'"
- **Verse 21**—"'The Almighty has afflicted me.'"

And in attributing this pain and suffering to God, she no more "sinn[ed] nor charge[d] God with wrong" than Job did (Job 1:22) when he declared:

> ..."Naked I came from my mother's womb,
> And naked shall I return there.
> The LORD gave, and the LORD has taken away;
> Blessed be the name of the LORD."
> (Job 1:21)

Yahweh gives and Yahweh takes away (Job 1:21), He gives good as well as evil (Job 2:10; Jn. 3:27; 1 Cor. 4:7). He even kills

THE FREE WILL OF GOD

(Lk. 12:5). Everything we experience is directly from the hand of God. Everything. The good, bad, and ugly. Scripture is clear, therefore, that God designs evil (Gen. 50:20; Ps. 105:17) and affliction (Ruth 1:20-21; Job 42:11) so that, if a calamity occurs in a city, only He has ultimately done it (Amos 3:6). Consequently, He is the absolutely sovereign governor of the barrenness of the womb (Gen. 4:1, 16:2, 20:18, 25:21, 29:31, 30:2; 1 Sam. 1:5-6, 2:5-6; Ruth 4:13), sickness of children (2 Sam. 12:15), fever (Matt. 8:15), paralysis (Lk. 5:24-25), blindness (Ex. 4:11; Lk. 18:42), deafness (Ex. 4:11; Mk. 7:37), and every other possible ailment (Matt. 4:23).

And He is the absolutely sovereign governor of man's sin as well. We could look at numerous examples in Scripture (see, for instance, Judg. 14:4; 2 Sam. 12:11-12, 16:5-8, 11, 24:1; 1 Kings 11:14, 22:23, Jonah 2:3), but time will permit us to only look at four:

A. Abimelech:

The first comes from Genesis 20, where we read that Abraham and his wife Sarah traveled to the city of Gerar:

> 1 And Abraham journeys from there toward the land of the South, and dwells between Kadesh and Shur, and sojourns in Gerar. 2 Now Abraham says concerning Sarah his wife, "She is my sister." And Abimelech king of Gerar sends and takes Sarah.
> 3 But God comes in unto Abimelech in a dream of the night, and says to him, "Behold!—you are a dead man because of the woman whom you have taken, for she is married to a husband."
> 4 But Abimelech has not drawn near unto her; and he says "Adonai, will You slay a righteous nation also? 5 Has he himself not said to me, 'She is my sister'? And she, even she herself, said, 'He is my brother.' In the integrity of my heart, and in the innocence of my hands, I have done this."

6 And God says unto him in the dream, "Yes, I have known that in the integrity of your heart you have done this, for I withhold you, even I, from sinning against Me; therefore I have not suffered you to come against her. 7 And now send back the man's wife, for he is a prophet, and he prays for you, and you shall live. But if you do not send her back, know that dying you die, you and all that you have."

(Gen. 20:1-7 NYLT)

Notice what God tells Abimelech when he protests that he was acting in "the integrity of my heart, and in the innocence of my hands" because he had innocently relied upon Abraham's deception (vs. 5 NYLT). God replied that, "Yes, I have known that in the integrity of your heart you have done this, *for I withhold you, even I, from sinning against Me; therefore I have not suffered you to come against her*" (vs. 6 NYLT; emphasis added). Let me repeat that, God told Abimelech that the only reason he did not commit the sin of adultery was because *God* restrained him from it.

And if God is able to keep Abimelech from sinning, is He not therefore able to keep everyone from sinning at all times and in all places? In fact, we know that in heaven there is no sin because God graciously enables its citizens to perfectly love Yahweh their God with all their hearts, soul, mind, and body and one another as themselves. Therefore, if God is able to keep Abimelech from sinning, and the inhabitants of heaven from sinning, then He is perfectly capable of prohibiting all sin altogether. But He doesn't. Rather, He decrees it for His holy purposes.

B. Eli's Sons:

The second example is found in the second chapter of 1 Samuel, where we are told that the aging priest Eli had two sons who "were corrupt; they did not know the LORD" (vs. 12). "Therefore," the Bible tells us, "the sin of the young men was very great before the Lord, for men abhorred the offering of the LORD" (vs. 17). As if that wasn't enough, they also wronged "all Israel" and slept with the prostitutes who sold their bodies near the tabernacle (vs. 22). So Eli rebuked his sons, saying:

> [23] ..."Why do you do such things? For I hear of your evil dealings from all the people. [24] No, my sons! For it is not a good report that I hear. You make the LORD's people transgress. [25] If one man sins against another, God will judge him. But if a man sins against the LORD, who will intercede for him?"
>
> (1 Sam. 2:23-25)

But the Bible tells us that, "Nevertheless, they did not heed the voice of their father, *because* the LORD desired to kill them" (1 Sam. 2:25; emphasis added). Let me repeat that: God desired to kill Eli's two sons for their wickedness and, therefore, He did not restrain their sinning as He did Abimelech.

C. Pharaoh:

The third example is that of Pharaoh in the Exodus account of Yahweh's deliverance of His people Israel from bondage in Egypt. Before Moses had even stepped foot in Egypt and God sent the very first plague, Yahweh told Moses:

> "When you go back to Egypt, see that you do all those wonders before Pharaoh which I have put in your hand. But *I will harden his heart*, so that he will not let the people go."
>
> (Ex. 4:21; emphasis added)

Before Moses had even told Pharaoh to let the Israelites go, God not only predicted that Pharaoh would disobey His divine will, but that Pharaoh's disobedience was caused by Yahweh Himself as He hardened Pharaoh's heart. And again, after

Pharaoh's initial refusal to let the children of Israel go (chapter 5) *but before* the first plague, we read:

> [1] So the LORD said to Moses: "See, I have made you as God to Pharaoh, and Aaron your brother shall be your prophet. [2] You shall speak all that I command you. And Aaron your brother shall tell Pharaoh to send the children of Israel out of his land. [3] *And I will harden Pharaoh's heart*, and multiply My signs and My wonders in the land of Egypt. [4] But Pharaoh will not heed you, so that I may lay My hand on Egypt and bring My armies and My people, the children of Israel, out of the land of Egypt by great judgments. [5] And the Egyptians shall know that I am the LORD, when I stretch out My hand on Egypt and bring out the children of Israel from among them."
>
> (Ex. 7:1-5; emphasis added)

Here, for the second time, God states that He will harden Pharaoh's heart (vs. 3) *so that* He could lay HIs hand on Egypt in mighty judgments (vs. 4) for the renown of His name (vs. 5).

And after Aaron's rod devoured the rods of the magicians, we are told that, "Pharaoh's heart grew hard and he did not heed them, as the LORD had said" (7:13). At first blush this verse doesn't appear to specify who hardened Pharaoh's heart, only that it was hardened. But the last five words do, in fact, tell us who hardened Pharaoh's heart—Yahweh. For the phrase, "as the LORD had said" is referring back to Yahweh's promise in 4:21 and 7:3 to harden Pharaoh's heart. God did not predict that Pharaoh would hardened his own heart. No, God vowed that *He* would harden Pharaoh's heart. We see this again after the first plague: "[22]...and Pharaoh's heart grew hard, and he did not heed them, as the LORD had said. [23]...Neither was his heart moved by this" (7:22-23).

It wasn't until after the second plague that we read that Pharaoh, "hardened his heart and did not heed them, as the LORD had said" (8:15). So Yahweh twice promises that He will harden Pharaoh's heart, and we had already been told twice that

Yahweh had in fact hardened Pharaoh's heart, and now we read that Pharaoh hardened his own heart. But, again, we are also told by that vital five word phrase "as the LORD had said" that he only did so as a consequence of Yahweh's first hardening his heart. Yahweh hardened, *then* Pharoah hardened. God willed his heart hardened, *then* he willed his heart hardened.

After the third plague we are told that, "Pharaoh's heart grew hard, and he did not heed them, just as the LORD had said" (8:19). Then after the fourth plague we read that, "Pharaoh hardened his heart at this time also; neither would he let the people go" (8:32). After the fifth plague we find that, "the heart of Pharaoh became hard, and he did not let the people go" (9:7).

Then after the sixth plague we are told that, "the LORD hardened the heart of Pharaoh, and he did not heed them, just as the LORD had spoken to Moses" (9:12). It is almost as if the author of Exodus (Moses) wants to reinforce the fact that it was first and superintendently Yahweh hardening Pharaoh's heart by reiterating it twice: "the LORD hardened the heart of Pharaoh... just as the LORD had spoken to Moses." The ancient Hebrews used repetition to highlight, to draw attention to, to emphasize something important. So here, it is as if Moses is using exclamation points to attribute Pharaoh's hardening to Yahweh— "Yahweh hardened Pharaoh's heart just as He said He would!" And why is God doing this? "But indeed for this purpose I have raised you up, that I may show My power in you, and that My name may be declared in all the earth" (9:16).

However, though it is God who is hardening his heart, Pharaoh confesses after the seventh plague that his refusal to obey God by letting the people go is, in fact, sinful, acknowledging, "'The LORD is righteous, and my people and I are wicked'" (9:27). God decreed the sin, and yet man, not God, is the sinner. And Moses, understanding that Yahweh is not through hardening Pharaoh's heart (4:21, 7:3), knows that Pharaoh's repentance isn't genuine and rebukes him, "'I know that you will not yet fear the LORD God'" (9:30). And sure enough, we are told:

> 34 And when Pharaoh saw that the rain, the hail, and the thunder had ceased, he sinned yet more; and he hardened his heart, he and his servants. 35 So the heart of Pharaoh was hard; neither would he let the children of Israel go, as the LORD had spoken by Moses.
>
> (Ex. 9:34-35)

He hardened his heart, just as He said He would harden his heart. Pharaoh willed what Yahweh first and superintendently willed. And yet Pharaoh, not God, sinned. Then in the very next verse we read:

> 1 Now the LORD said to Moses, "Go in to Pharaoh; *for I have hardened his heart and the hearts of his servants*, that I may show these signs of Mine before him, 2 and that you may tell in the hearing of your son and your son's son the mighty things I have done in Egypt, and My signs which I have done among them, that you may know that I am the LORD."
>
> (Ex. 10:1-2; emphasis added)

In response to the eighth plague, Pharaoh again confesses, "'I have sinned against the LORD your God and against you" (10:16). Again, Pharaoh, not God, is the sinner. And the divine response? "But the LORD hardened Pharaoh's heart, and he did not let the children of Israel go" (vs. 20). And after the ninth plague we read, "But the LORD hardened Pharaoh's heart, and he would not let them go" (vs. 27).

Moses then summarizes what has happened through the first nine plagues: "So Moses and Aaron did all these wonders before Pharaoh; and the LORD hardened Pharaoh's heart, and he did not let the children of Israel go out of his land" (11:10). And when Moses announces to Pharaoh the tenth and final plague (vs. 4-8) —the death of all firstborn sons— we read, "But the LORD said to Moses, 'Pharaoh will not heed you, so that My wonders may be multiplied in the land of Egypt'" (vs. 9). Why? Because "'against all the gods of Egypt I will execute judgment; I am the LORD'"

(12:12). And it happened, after the final plague, Pharaoh did just as Yahweh said he would—he drove them out with a strong hand (6:1, 11:1).

But God was not through triumphing over Pharaoh, for He tells Moses to have the Israelites camp near the Red Sea because "'Then I will harden Pharaoh's heart, so that he will pursue them; and I will gain honor over Pharaoh and over all his army, that the Egyptians may know that I am the LORD'" (14:4). And a few verses later we are told, "And the LORD hardened the heart of Pharaoh king of Egypt, and he pursued the children of Israel" (vs. 8). Yahweh then tells Moses to stretch out his hand over the sea and that it will divide so that the children of Israel can cross over on dry ground in the midst of the sea (vs. 16). But, Yahweh continues:

> 17 "And I indeed will harden the hearts of the Egyptians, and they shall follow them. So I will gain honor over Pharaoh and over all his army, his chariots, and his horsemen. 18 Then the Egyptians shall know that I am the LORD, when I have gained honor for Myself over Pharaoh, his chariots, and his horsemen."
>
> (Ex. 14:17-18)

This is not God judicially hardening Pharaoh's heart—an abandoning him to the stubbornness wickedness of his own heart. Rather, as we have just seen, Scripture is emphatic that God first vows to harden Pharaoh's heart (4:21, 7:3, 10:1, 11:9, 14:4, 17), and then God does, in fact, harden Pharaoh's heart (7:15, 22, 8:15, 19, 9:12, 35, 10:20, 27, 14:8). God first and superintendently wills the hardening of Pharaoh's heart, and Pharaoh *only* hardens it in response to God's initiative. Note, also, that God's unilateral hardening is displayed in 14:17 when He announces His intention to harden not just Pharaoh's heart, but the Egyptians in general.

Furthermore, we see that this is not judicial hardening but initiated hardening by God *for* the demonstration of His glory. The Exodus account makes this explicit:

• To multiply His signs and wonders (7:3) *in order* (a) to lay His hand on Egypt and deliver His people with great judgments (7:4) *so that* (b) "the Egyptians shall know that I am the LORD" (7:5).
• To show His power so that His name may be declared in all the earth (9:16).
• To show "these signs of Mine before him" (10:1) *so that* the Hebrews "may know that I am the LORD" and so instruct their children (vs. 2).
• To multiply His wonders in Egypt (11:9) *in order* to execute judgment on all the gods of Egypt (12:12).
• To gain honor over Pharaoh and his entire army (14:4, 17) *so that* the Egyptians "shall know that I am the LORD" (14:4, see also vs. 18).

This is purposeful, premeditated hardening planned before the creation of the universe in order to lavishly display the fame of Yahweh's name. As noted in chapter 2, God was not waiting with bated breath for just the right kind of stupid to sit on the throne of Egypt so that He finally had a chance to show off His glory and might. No! Such a notion is impiously irreverent. Rather, "that you may know that there is none like Me in all the earth" (9:14), God raised up Pharaoh and hardened his heart so that He "may show My power in you and that My name may be declared in all the earth" (vs. 16).

And Pharaoh is hardly the only individual in Holy Writ whose heart God hardened. As we saw in Exodus 14:17, God hardened the hearts of all the Egyptians so that they would pursue the Israelites. God also "hardened [the] spirit and ma[d]e [the] heart obstinate" of Sihon, king of Heshbon, so that He might defeat him (Deut. 2:30). No kingdom in the Promised Land (except the Hivites) made peace with the Israelites:

> For it was of the LORD to harden their hearts, that they should come against Israel in battle, that He might utterly destroy them, and that they might receive no mercy, but

that He might destroy them, as the LORD had commanded Moses,

(Josh. 11:20)

Centuries later as God's Chosen People rebel against their Creator, Isaiah the prophet calls them a "rebellious people" (Is. 40:9) who despise God's word (vs. 12) who refused to return and rest in Yahweh God, the Holy One of Israel (vs. 15). And therefore God shall suddenly, in an instant, break them like a potter's vessel; He will not spare (vs. 13-14). And yet, while the Jewish people are really guilty and justly condemned, Isaiah yet cries out to God, "O LORD, why have You made us stray from Your ways, and hardened our heart from Your fear? (Is. 63:17a). In other words, these people have sinned, but it was first and superintendently Yahweh who hardened their hearts.

In Romans 11 the Apostle Paul continues to elaborate on his answer to the question posed in 9:6—has God's word of promise failed because so many Jews have rejected Jesus as their Messiah? Remember that Paul explains that God has not failed because His covenant of promise was never to every child of Abraham, but only to the elect—of both Jews and Gentiles—who were imputed to be Abraham's offspring. Now in chapter 11 Paul explains that "a remnant according to the election of grace" (vs. 5)—"elect" Jews (vs. 7)—have obtained salvation while the remainder of the Israelites were blinded (vs. 7). And to buttress this point he quotes various passages from the Old Testament:

"God has given them a spirit of stupor,
Eyes that they should not see
And ears that they should not hear,
To this very day."

(Rom. 11:8)

Who gave them this spiritual blindness? This dullness of hearing? This hardness of heart? God has! God is the one who has blinded, deafened, and hardened the non-elect but has sovereignly brought spiritual life to the elect. We see the Lord Christ ell us the same thing:

> [10] And the disciples having come near, said to Him, "Why do You speak to them in parables?"   [11] And He, answering, said to them, "That to you it has been given to know the initiation mysterious of the kingdom of the heavens, but to these it has not been given.   [12] For whoever has, it shall be given to him, and he shall have overabundance; but whoever has not, even that which he has shall be taken from him.   [13] Because of this I speak to them in parables, because seeing they do not see, and hearing they do not hear, nor understand.   [14] And in them is fulfilled the prophecy of Isaiah, that says:
>
> 'With hearing you shall hear, and you shall not understand,
> And seeing you shall see, and you shall not perceive;
> [15] For the heart of this people has been made thick,
> And with the ears they heard heavily,
> And their eyes they did close,
> Lest they might see with the eyes,
> And might hear with the ears,
> And with the heart understand and turn back,
> That I might heal them.'"
> (Matt. 13:10-15 NYLT)

Jesus explained His parables to His elect because to them it had been given by God to know the mysterious of the Gospel. But to those elected to perdition, Jesus spoke to them in parables that their hearts might remain thick with fat and unresponsiveness, their ears heavy and dull, and their eyes closed in spiritual deadness *so that* they do not see and grasp the Light in penitent faith and be saved. As Moses told the children of Israel, "'Yet Yahweh has not given to you a heart to know, and eyes to see, and ears to hear, to this very day'" (Deut. 29:4 NYLT). Or as the Apostle Paul explains:

¹² Having, then, such hope, we use much freedom of speech ¹³ and are not as Moses, who was putting a veil upon his own face, for the sons of Israel could not look steadfastly at the end of that which is being made useless. ¹⁴ But their minds were hardened, for unto this day the same veil abides not unveiled at the reading of the Old Covenant, which in Messiah is being made useless. ¹⁵ And till today, when Moses is read, a veil lies upon their heart. ¹⁶ But whenever they may turn to the Lord, the veil is taken away.

(2 Cor. 3:12-16 NYLT)

God hardens, blinds, and deafens whom He wills, and gives life to hearts, eyes, and ears on whom He wills (Rom. 9:18). And in all these cases it is God who initiates the hardening, the blinding, the deafening. The non-elect may certainly harden, blind, and deafen themselves, but only in irresistible response to God's first and superintending free will. God predestines, man obeys.

D. The Crucifixion:

The fourth and final example is the crucifixion of the Lord Christ. The Bible makes clear that long before time began, in ages past before He created the world (Gen. 1-2) and the first man fell (Gen. 3), God decreed (Acts 2:23, 4:28; 1 Cor. 2:7) that He would make a name for Himself (Ezek. 38:23) by redeeming a people for Himself (Eph. 1:4; Tit. 2:14; 1 Pet. 2:9-10) by the sacrifice of Himself (Rom. 3:25) in the incarnate God-man Jesus Christ.

We see this clearly in the fourth chapter of Acts, the passage that not only made me a believer but a lover of the absolute sovereignty of God. For in it we find that God the Father decreed in eternity past when, where, how, and by whom God the Son would be killed:

²⁷ "For truly gathered together against Your holy Servant Jesus, whom You anointed, were both Herod and Pontius

81

Pilate, with the ethnic groups and peoples of Israel, 28 to do whatever Your hand and Your counsel determined beforehand to come to pass."

(Acts 4:27-28 NYLT)

Look at all the human actors responsible—yes, morally culpable before God—for the death of the Lord Christ: (a) King Herod, (b) the Roman governor Pontius Pilate, (c) the Gentile solders, and (d) the Jewish people (vs. 27). But even though these human actors are guilty of perpetrating the greatest evil in the history of the world—the crucifixion of God the Son—verse 28 tells us that they merely did "whatever Your hand and Your purpose determined beforehand to come to pass" (NYLT). In other words, God scripted this evil down to the minutest detail, and these human actors were simply executing God's will.

In the 53rd chapter of Isaiah we see even more explicitly that God the Father authored the most evil act imaginable in the crucifixion of God the Son:

3 "He is despised, and discarded of men,

A man of pains, and acquainted with suffering,

And as one hiding the face from us, He is despised, and we esteemed Him not.

4 Surely our sicknesses he has borne,

And our pains—He has carried them,

And we—we have esteemed Him plagued, smitten of God, and afflicted.

5 And He is pierced for our transgressions,

Bruised for our iniquities,

The chastisement of our peace is on Him,

And by his bruise there is healing to us.

6 All of us like sheep have wandered,

Each to his own way we have turned,

And Yahweh has laid on Him the punishment of us all.

7 He was oppressed and He was afflicted,

Yet He opens not his mouth,

As a lamb to the slaughter He is brought,

And as a sheep before its shearers is dumb,
So He opens not his mouth.
8 By restraint and by judgment He has been taken,
And of His generation who meditates—
That He has been cut off from the land of the living?
By the transgression of My people He is plagued.
9 And His grave is appointed with the wicked,
And with the rich at His death,
Because He has done no violence,
Nor is deceit in His mouth.
10 And Yahweh has delighted to bruise Him,
He has made Him suffer,
If His soul makes an offering for guilt,
He sees His seed -- He prolongs His days,
And the pleasure of Yahweh prospers in His hand.
11 Of the labor of His soul He sees—and is satisfied,
Through His knowledge the righteous One, My Servant,
gives righteousness to many,
And their iniquities He bears.
12 Therefore I give a portion to Him among the great,
And He apportions spoil with the mighty,
Because He exposed His soul to death,
And with transgressors He was numbered,
And the sin of many He has borne,
And for transgressors He intercedes."

(Is. 53:3-12 NYLT)

God the Son was smitten by God the Father and afflicted (vs. 4). It delighted God the Father to bruise the Lord Christ and to make Him suffer (vs. 10). God the Father made His one and only Son an offering for sin by laying upon Him the iniquity of His elect (vs. 6, 10). Which leads to the conclusion that, if God could decree the greatest evil imaginable and still be holy and righteous, pure and without sin, then He could He ordain all other sin in the history of the world and sill remain holy and righteous, pure and without sin.

II. The Potter's Rights:

But, "You will say to me then, 'Why does He still find fault? For who has resisted His will?'" (Rom. 9:19). And what is the inspired response?

> 20 But indeed, O man, who are you to reply against God? Will the thing formed say to him who formed it, "Why have you made me like this?" 21 Does not the potter have power over the clay, from the same lump to make one vessel for honor and another for dishonor?

(Rom. 9:20-21)

The Greek word translated here by the NKJV as *power* in verse 21 is *exousia*, which is much more accurately translated as *authority*, *right*, or *jurisdiction* (see generally Matt. 8:9, 9:6, 8, 10:1; Jn. 1:12; Acts 26:10, 12. 18). God has absolute rights over His clay, for as Isaiah the prophet proclaimed, "But now, O LORD, You are our Father; we are the clay, You are our Potter; and all we are the work of Your hand" (Is. 64:8). Or as Jeremiah the prophet reports, "Then the word of the LORD came to me: 'O house of Israel, can I not do with you as this potter does?' declares the LORD. 'Like clay in the hand of the potter, so are you in My hand, O house of Israel'" (Jer . 18:6). Clay has no rights. Period.

Understanding this, grasping this, embracing this is the key to the fear of the Lord (Ex. 9:30) and the beginning of wisdom (Prov. 9:10). Such man-humbling, man-debasing, pride-destroying understanding is essential to the proper worship of God. It is not the place of clay to talk back to its Potter. It is only the place of the clay to worship, trust, and obey.

Nevertheless, we are talking about the unexplainable. The seemingly irreconcilable. For Scripture is clear that God commands us not to sin and yet He wills sin to happen. The Bible is explicit that God wills sin and yet He is not sinful. Holy Writ is emphatic that God wills His creatures to sin and yet they, not He, are really sinful. While the Bible is mostly silent on how man is to reconcile the tension between these seemingly incompatible truths, it would be foolish to make our understanding the measure of God's mind. And the Bible does provide several interrelated principles that may shed light on how the irreconcilable is, in fact, reconcilable.

A. Characters, Not the Arthur, Are Responsible:

Dr. Wayne Grudem, in his masterful *Systematic Theology*, uses an illustration (pg. 321-322) from Shakespeare's tragedy *Macbeth* in which the title character murders King Duncan. But Grudem poses the question, who killed Duncan—Macbeth or the play's author, Shakespeare? Obviously, within the world of the play, Macbeth is legally and morally responsible for the murder of King Duncan. There can be no dispute over this point.

But is Shakespeare also a murderer? Here I disagree with Grudem, who argues that Shakespeare also killed Duncan.[1] True, Shakespeare wrote the murder into the play when he could have had it thwarted or written it out entirely. So he does absolutely bear responsibility, but only on the level of existence as a creator, not a creature. To borrow an important term from criminal law, he lacked the mens rea—the criminal intent or guilty mind—to murder Duncan. Rather, Shakespeare's will in willing the murder was to display the heinousness of evil and the righteousness of justice. And there is and never has been a sheriff, judge, or jury who would charge, arrest, and convict him of murder.

The analogy could be expanded to screenwriters of movies, television shows, and plays. Or of artists who depict a famous historic murder (Julius Caesar, for instance) or battle scene. Or a boy playing with toy soldiers or Cowboys and Indians with his friends. Creators can script murder and even the character's sinful mens rea and yet lack the necessary mens rea for murder

---

[1] Dr. John Frame also disagree with Grudem in his *Systematic Theology* (pg. 298-300).

themselves. They may rightfully be blamed as the ultimate cause of the murder, but not be *morally* blamable of the murder. Or rape. Or kidnapping. Or robbery. Or any other sin.

Why? Because creators and creations live on entirely different levels of reality. Of existence. God is transcendent, man is but a maggot and a worm (Job 25:6). God is the Potter, man but the clay. The Creator has absolute rights, the creature none. God wrote His redemptive narrative in eternity past, and then breathed His novel into life. We are real people making real choices that have real consequences in a real reality, but all scripted down to the minutest detail before the very first molecule was ever spoken into existence. We are very willing actors upon whose hearts God has written HIs script (Rev. 17:17), "For God is the one energizing in you both to will and to energize for the benefit of His good will" (Phil. 2:13 NYLT).

B. God Only Does Good:

As we have seen, Scripture is emphatic that God decrees every detail of every second of all of history in the entire universe for His glory, and it is only by doing so that He cannot sin. For the Bible makes clear that while men *will* (i.e., design, craft, intend, design, mean) sin for their own ends, God *wills* those same sins for His good purposes (1 Pet. 4:19). An act may be sinful, but also good that it happened.

Let me repeat that—an act may be evil, but also good that it happened. We all know this intuitively. For instance, as six-year-olds, we considered spankings, household chores, and going to school as evil on par with the Apocalypse. But none of those things were intended by our parents to be evil but rather good. Our parents considered them as both necessary and excellent tools to mature us, develop our character, and prepare us for adulthood.

Or, for example, the cutting and intrusive nature of surgery is the quintessential definition of felony assault, except when it is done to heal. Keeping my dog on a leash may at times seem like the greatest evil imaginable to him, but doing so actually serves to protect him from his own stupidity. In the same way, therefore, the sin of this world should not—nay, must not—be viewed from our finite human perspective but from God's perfectly infinite wisdom, goodness, and love. We must never forget that this world exists as a stage to fully manifest the myriad display of God's glorious attributes.

Let's briefly look at just three examples from Scripture. The first comes from the ninth chapter of the Gospel of John. Jesus declared to His disciples that the man was born blind in order "that the works of God should be revealed in him" (Jn. 9:3). Let that sink in for a moment—God created a man blind, and thereby a poor, destitute beggar (vs. 8), so that He might be glorified in healing him.

The second example comes a few chapters later in the story of Lazarus. The Bible clearly tells us that Jesus loved His friend Lazarus (Jn. 11:3, 5). And yet when Lazarus' sisters Mary and Martha wrote Jesus to implore Him to come quickly because their brother lay dying, the text tells us that Jesus "stayed two more days in the place where He was" (vs. 6). When Jesus finally did arrive, "He found that [Lazarus] had already been in the tomb four days" (vs. 17). Both sisters, almost accusingly, told Jesus, "[I]f you had been here, [our] brother would not have died" (vs. 21, 32).

And what is the divine response? As Jesus predicted to His disciples upon first receiving the news of Lazarus' illness, "'This sickness is...for the glory of God, that the Son of God may be glorified through it'" (vs. 4). Yet again, a few verses later, we read that Jesus, before even leaving to travel to the three siblings, told His disciples: "14 ...Lazarus is dead. 15 And I am glad for your sakes that I was not there, that you may believe'" (vs. 14b-15).

After Jesus arrived in town and had the stone rolled away from the tomb, we read that:

> 41 ...Jesus lifted up His eyes and said, "Father, I thank You that You have heard Me. 42 And I know that You always hear Me, but because of the people who are standing by I said this, that they may believe that You

sent Me." ⁴³ Now when He had said these things, He cried with a loud voice, "Lazarus, come forth!" ⁴⁴ And he who had died came out...

(Jn. 11:41-44)

But the story doesn't end there, for Jesus did not come to simply raise a dead friend from the grave but that, in doing so, those watching would believe that He was the Son of God (vs. 42). And the very next verse tells us that that goal was achieved, "Then many of the Jews who had come to Mary, and had seen the things Jesus did, believed in Him" (vs. 45). In summary, God killed His friend Lazarus and let his sisters mourn for four days in order that He might be glorified in the newfound trust of many observers.

The third and final example comes from the story of Joseph, who was sold into slavery in Egypt by his jealous brothers, where he was eventually thrown into prison for life (Gen. 37:12-36, 39:1-23). "But the LORD was with Joseph and showed him mercy" (Gen. 39:21), and he eventually became the prime minister of all of Egypt (41:39-41). In the midst of a severe famine throughout the entire region, Joseph's jealous brothers were forced to go to Egypt to buy food from him, and Joseph eventually revealed himself to them and moved his entire family to Egypt from Canaan (Gen. 42:1-47:12),

After their father died, Joseph's brothers became fearful that he would finally take revenge upon them and kill them (50:15), so they came to Joseph and lied to him and told him that their father had asked him to forgive them (vs. 16-19). Joseph, however, "wept when they spoke to him" (vs. 17) and said to them:

¹⁹ ..."Do not be afraid, for am I in the place of God? ²⁰ But as for you, you meant evil against me, but God meant it for good, in order to bring it about as it is this day, to save many people alive"

(Gen. 50:19b-20)

Or as the psalmist elaborates in Psalm 105:

[16] Moreover [God] called for a famine in the land;
He destroyed all the provision of bread.
[17] He sent a man before them—
Joseph—who was sold as a slave.
[18] They hurt his feet with fetters,
He was laid in irons.
[19] Until the time that his word came to pass,
The word of the LORD tested him.
[20] The [pharaoh] sent and released him,
The ruler of the people let him go free.
[21] He made him lord of his house,
And ruler of all his possessions,
[22] To bind his princes at his pleasure,
And teach his elders wisdom.
[23] Israel also came into Egypt,
And Jacob dwelt in the land of Ham.
[24] [God] increased His people greatly,
And made them stronger than their enemies.

(Ps. 105:16-24)

Notice the three purposes mentioned in these two passages alone for Joseph's slavery and imprisonment: (1) to test and mature Joseph (Ps. 105:19); (2) to put Joseph in a position of power to prepare ahead of time for the famine in order to save millions of lives (Gen. 50:20); and (3) and finally, to lead the Jewish people to a land where they would become a mighty nation (Ps. 105:23-24).

Scripture is clear, therefore, that God wills sin for His glory in bringing about His good purposes (1 Pet. 4:19). For instance, God wills evil for the sanctification of His children (Rom. 8:28-29) in refining their worshipful trust (Deut. 8:2-5, 16; Heb. 12:5-11) by:

1. Discipline that leads to repentance (1 Cor. 5:1-8; 2 Cor. 7:8-12; 1 Tim. 1:20);
2. Pruning that leads to abounding fruit (Jn. 15:1-8);

3. Humiliating weakness that severs our self-reliance (Deut. 8:3, 16; 2 Cor. 12:7-10; Phil. 3:7-16, 4:11-13); in order that they may:

4. Be partakers of His holiness (Heb. 12:10); and

5. Kknow Him intimately (Job 42:5).

As the old hymn *How Firm a Foundation* reminds us:

> When through fiery trials thy pathway shall lie,
> My grace, all sufficient, shall be thy supply;
> the flame shall not hurt thee; I only design
> thy dross to consume, and thy gold to refine.

Furthermore, God wills sin for His glory in reminding sinners of their mortality and thereby leading them to repentance and reconciliation with Him (Lk. 13:1-5). Finally, God also wills sin for His glory in punishing unrepentant sinners (2 Chron. 32:24; Ps. 31:10b, 38:3, 103:3; Prov. 3:7-8; Jn. 5:14, 9:2; 1 Cor. 11:30; Jas. 5:16).

Therefore, an act may be sinful, but it is also good that it happened. Or to put it another way, God does not wield sin sinfully but goodly. Or, to put it yet a third way, everything sinful in this universe, though it be evil, is in *God's* authorship good. Everything in this universe, absolutely everything, is good in the sense that God willed it for His glory in producing a myriad of good, though often hidden, results.

God "cannot be tempted by evil, nor does He Himself tempt anyone" (Jas. 1:13). Therefore, Scripture affirm that God can neither sin nor approve of or delight in sin (Gen. 18:25; Deut. 32:4; Ps. 5:4, 50:21, 145:17; Hab. 1:13; Zeph. 3:5; Rom. 3:4; Acts 4:27-28; Jas. 1:13-14, 17; 1 John 1:5, 2:16). For the Bible tells us that the Lord is unapproachable, pure light (1 Jn. 1:5; see also 1 Tim. 6:16) in whom there is no darkness of sin (1 Jn. 1:5; see also Ps. 92:15; Jn. 3:19-21).

In short, God does not sin because He lacks the intent, or guilty mind, to sin. What is sin? Scripture defines sin not by whether or to what extent an act hurts other people, but whether it blasphemes (Rom. 2:24) God by failing to treasure, love, and worship Him as the most satisfying, glorious, and beautiful Being imaginable. It is a failure to desire God as He ought to be desired. It is a failure obey the very first of the Ten Commandments—that "you shall have no other gods before [Him]" (Exodus 20:3). It is a failure to obey the Greatest Commandment—to "love the LORD your God with all your heart, and with all your soul, and with all your mind" (Matt. 22:36-38; see also Deut. 6:5, 10:12, 30:6). It is a failure to love God more than father, or mother, or son, or daughter, or anything else imaginable (Matt. 10:37).

God, obviously, cannot sin or He ceases to be God. God has only a righteous intent (see chapter 2), not a sinful intent. To be found guilty of a sin, not only the actions but also the mens rea have to be proved: deeds $(a + b + c)$ + sinful intent = crime. But when God causes sin you have deeds $(a + b + c)$ + righteous intent = good. What makes sin sinful is not its horizontal dimensions (i.e., the actions by which another is wronged), but its vertical dimensions (i.e., the rebellion of the heart against God) (Psalm. 51:4). Sin is not an assault on another, but on God's glory.[2] God, therefore, cannot sin because He cannot rebel against Himself otherwise He would become undefied (Lk. 11:17).

We see in Scripture several examples of those who sinned without sinning. If Abraham, for instance, had actually killed Isaac at God's command in Genesis 22, his intent would not have been murder but rather obedience to God by not withholding the child of promise from Him. When Phinehas the son of Eleazar killed an Israelite man and a Midianite woman in Numbers 25, he did so in cold blood—serving as sheriff, judge, jury, and executioner without due process. And yet he was not morally culpable because "'he was zealous with My zeal'" (vs. 11). In sparing the Gibeonites in Joshua 9, Joshua and the children of Israel did not intend to disobey God's direct command to kill all the inhabitants of Canaan, but rather to keep their (rash) oath in

---

[2] Horizontal sins only derive their sinfulness from the vertical sin, without which it is impossible for them to be sinful.

accordance with the third commandment. Similarly, Jephthah did not intend to murder his daughter in Judges 11, but to keep his (foolish) vow to Yahweh in obedience to the third commandment. In the same way, God can will sin and the sinful intent behind it without Himself sharing in the sin because His intent is wholly otherwise.[3]

There is one final analogy that may help shed light on this difficult subject. Imagine that God has created a living board game called *Life* and designed its rules to reflect His holy character. The characters, therefore, are responsible to act in conformance with His revealed will called His moral law. However, as the game's omnipotent author, God is free to act as He sees fit—within or without the given rules—in accordance with His holy character to maximize His glory. This is God's secret will (or purpose or plan) which the characters find irresistible, and yet they are only held to account for their obedience to His revealed will. Both wills originate in and conform to God's righteousness and therefore both are holy, and yet the object of one is man's moral responsibility and the object of the other is the display of God's glory. The one governs man's behavior, the other "governs" God's behavior (see chapter 2).[4] The one tells man

---

[3] That God can impart desires that He does not and, in fact, cannot share should become plain upon reflection. For instance, God imparts to husbands an exclusive covenantal love for their wives that He does not share for He loves all the elect the same. Or an exclusive love in parents for their children, for He loves all elect children the same. Or sexual desire in one spouse for the other, for He does not have sexual desires. Or a desire to tithe in the heart of the believer,. for God has no desire to tithe to Himself. Or the normal, healthy pride of nationalism, for God belongs to no nation. These things are certainly good, but they are completely foreign to God Himself. If, therefore, He is able to impart foreign good intentions in the hearts of men without participating in them Himself, then surely He is also able to impart foreign evil intentions without participating in them Himself.

[4] Every parent understands this seeming dichotomy in which they have different standards for their own behavior and that for

what he *should* do, the other what he *will* do. We think we're playing a simple game of checkers, while in actuality God is really playing 100^{100}-dimensional chess.

In short, therefore, a Potter—simply by nature of being a Potter—is not guilty of the sin of the clay. There are always two wills behind every sin—God's for righteousness and man's for evil (Gen. 50:20). God does all things in the worship of Himself and that is not sin. Man does all things in the worship of himself and that is sin. In the hands of the Potter, the design of the Creator, the will of God, every single sin is a good that most perfectly maximizes the eternal joy of His elect in the full display of His glory.

C. God Channels Our Evil Desires:

Man, however, has the mens rea to sin in spades.[6] It oozes out of every pore of his being. We are so completely and totally depraved that there isn't a sin that we do not want to do as often as possible, save for God's restraining hand. If it were not for God's controlling grace, each and every one of us would gladly, willingly, and joyfully make Hitler look like a choir boy. That is our fallen sin nature which we have inherited from the First Man Adam. The only reason we are not all murderers and rapists and kidnappers and robbers is not because we lack the intent or desire out of some goodness of our hearts. Rather, it is owing solely to God's suppressing grace.

---

their children. Parents often engage in behavior that they would not tolerate in their children—they stay up later, do not have nap time, don't always eat their vegetables, may have more snacks then their children, may drink alcoholic beverages, may not go to the dentist that often, they discuss matters of sexual intimacy with each other, etc.. Neither standard is wrong, it merely has different objects in view.

[6] The author readily admits that this principle does not explain the origins of the original mens rea in Lucifer's fall.

Much like a dam controls a river, or a lock a cannel, so God channels the wickedness that freely and willingly gushes out of our depraved hearts.[7] And when God releases the evil of our hearts in one direction or another, we are absolutely guilty of the sin that we willfully and gleefully embrace. He directs our hearts for good according to His pure and wise counsel, but we dumbly obey our depraved lusts out of pride and arrogance. God never forces anyone to commit a sin that they don't want to do. Rather, He restrains them from committing a host of sins that they desperately want to commit. God does not need to create or originate this mens rea in our hearts, only channel it.

For instance, let's say that a rancher in Montana has a wolf that he keeps caged in his yard. The wolf has absolutely no desire to be domesticated but, instead, is quite passionate about killing anything and everything he can get his jaws on. But the rancher never gives him that opportunity, for he always keeps him in the cage. Until one day the rancher does release him and the wolf takes off and savagely rips apart the first person it comes upon. That wolf is guilty of cold-blooded murder. But the rancher is innocent of any such mens rea for the man who was killed had just killed the rancher's family and was about to kill him.

In conclusion, there are an unsearchable number of good that God produces in but a single event that we will never see this side of eternity (Job 5:9; Ecc. 3:11, 7:23, 8:17; Rom. 11:33). But we will spend an eternity of eternities marveling at the most infinitely perfect tapestry weaved by His sovereign authorship (Prov. 8:22-31; Ecc. 3:1-8, 11; Acts 17:28; Rom. 8:28, 11:36; Col. 1:16-17; Heb. 1:3, 2:10).

Concluding Implications:

What a magnificent God we serve that He superintends and imposes His will even over the sinful acts of men! We all know

---

[7] The means of channeling our hearts may include such secondary causes as parents and family; teachers, coaches, and mentors; government, society, and culture, etc.

this intuitively, for this is how we pray.   "God, please stop the persecutor." "The abuser." "The backstabbing coworker." "The cheating spouse."   We all pray that God will interpose His will on the wicked perpetrator and restrain his hand.   If we didn't believe that, we would instead only pray that God would either uphold us by HIs grace through the trial, or that He would take us home to heaven to be with Him forever.   But we don't only pray that way because we are all Reformed when on our knees.

It is a fundamental Christian tenant that man is born totally depraved, having inherited the First Man Adam's corrupted sin nature.   It does not mean that we are utterly depraved, only pervasively depraved.   But the only reason we are not utterly depraved is by God's common grace restraining our evil hearts. We want to be as bad as we can be, but God won't let us.   He checks our wickedness, and not a single person in all of human history has ever faulted Him for doing so by claiming that He is violating man's so-called free will.   And if God can restrain or dam the flow of vileness that oozes from the human heart without violating man's vaunted free will, then certainly He can channel and guide the desires of our heart without violating our free will as well.

To hold otherwise means that sin is simply the product of happenstance or of man's volition outside outside the boundaries of God's governance.   That God is merely a helpless spectator of sin rather than its absolute sovereign.   Sadly, however, this is the view of a number of prominent theologians.   William Barkley, for instance, wrote in his *A Spiritual Autobiography*:

> I believe that pain and suffering are never the will of God
> for his children. I cannot conceive that it is the will of God
> that anyone should be run over by a driver under the
> influence of drink or that a young mother should die of
> leukemia or that someone in the first flush of youth
> should face increasingly helplessness of arteriosclerosis.

Not only is such a view unbiblical, but such a world would be untenable in its wickedness.   Unbearable in its horror.   Evil quickly unraveling into purposelessness, and therefore meaninglessness, and therefore despairing madness (Ecc. 1:2, 14, 2:1-2, 11, 17, 4:4, 12:8; 1 Thess. 4:13).   Echoing Barkley, John Sanders wrote in his book *The God Who Risks*:

> God does not have a specific, divine purpose for each and every occurrence of evil. When a two month old child contracts a painful, incurable bone cancer that means suffering and death, it is a pointless evil. The holocaust is a pointless evil. The rape and dismemberment of a young girl is a pointless evil. The accident that caused my brother's death was a tragedy. God does not have a specific purpose in mind for these occurrences. I think that is wrong.

Similarly, Greg Boyd, writing in his book *Letters from a Skeptic*, pontificates:

> When an individual inflicts pain on another individual, I do not think we can go looking for the purpose of God in the event. I know Christians frequently speak about the purpose of God in the midst of tragedy caused by someone else, but this I regard to simply be a piously confused way of thinking.

He continues in the same vein in his book *God at War*:

> Neither Jesus nor his disciples assumed that there had to be a divine purpose behind all events in history. The Bible does not assume that every particular evil has a particular godly purpose behind it.

Such views emasculate God's Godness—His providence would offer no comfort; His omnipotence would be omniimpotence; His grace would be but a broken reed of support; and His promise that "all things work together for good to those who love God" would be a lie (Rom. 8:28).[8] Death, not God, would be the only source of peace.

But thank God that is not what the Bible says! Thank God that none of the suffering and sorrow of God's elect neither rest upon chance nor upon the will of men or demons, but solely upon God's sovereign authorship—for He has appointed who shall suffer (Rev. 6:11), when they shall suffer (Jn. 7:30; Acts 18:9-10), where they shall suffer (Lk. 9:30, 13:33), and what kind of sufferings they shall experience (Mk. 9:13; Jn. 21:19; Acts 9:16, 13:29)—who among them shall die of hunger, with the sword, be lead into captivity, and be eaten up of beasts (Jer. 15:2-3). The saints of God, therefore, are immortal until their work is done (Ps. 139:16; Heb. 9:27; Jas. 4:13-16).

Consequently, suffering for the believer is a gift from God. That is what Paul told the church at Philippi: "For to you it has been granted on behalf of Christ, not only to believe in Him, but also to suffer for His sake" (Phil. 1:29). Peter boldly declares that we "suffer according to the will of God" (1 Pet. 4:19; see also 3:17). Elsewhere Peter tells us that we are called by God to suffer (1 Pet. 2:21; 3:9). Therefore, all suffering and sorrow, pain and grief is a gift from God. A calling by God. Willed by God. Why? There are more reasons to our suffering than we can presently imagine, and we will never fully know the reasons why this side of heaven.

But Scripture is clear that—with the very same love with which He loves His Son—God the Father orchestrates all of our

---

[8] Though biblically repulsive, such views are merely consistent Arminianism taken to its logical conclusion. For if God cannot govern men's will, He cannot govern the evil that men subsequently commit by both commission and omission. If God cannot control the heart, He cannot control the actions that flow out of the heart and, consequently, all the crime and all the accidents in this world are beyond His design and control. And therefore for the consistent free-wiler, it is the height of hubristic folly to try to divine divine will, meaning, and purpose behind man-caused evil in the world because it logically—in their theology—cannot exist.

suffering in order to prune us, refine us, and strip us of all but Christ. Yes, it is to make us holy (Rom. 5:1-5; Heb. 12:3-11; 2 Pet. 1:5-9). But holiness is never the end in and of itself. Rather, it is so that we might find full and lasting satisfaction in Christ as our treasure. People often say that God will never give them more than they can bear; that God entrusts them with their suffering because He knows that they can handle it. That's idolatrous.

Rather, the Christian responds as the Apostle Paul does in 2 Corinthians 12::

> 7 And that I might not be exalted overmuch by the exceeding greatness of the revelations, there was given to me a thorn in the flesh, a messenger of the Adversary, that he might buffet me, that I might not be exalted overmuch. 8 Concerning this thing I did call upon the Lord three times that it might depart from me. 9 And He said to me, "My grace is sufficient for you, for My power is perfected in infirmity." Most gladly, therefore, will I rather boast in my infirmities, that the power of the Messiah may rest on me. 10 Wherefore I am well pleased in infirmities, in mistreatments, in necessities, in persecutions, in distresses—for Christ; for whenever I am infirm, then I am powerful.
>
> (2 Cor. 12:7-10 NYLT)

God's strength is made perfect in our weakness. In our sufferings. In our pain. God is most glorified when, truly, all we have is Christ. When He is our desire. Our delight. Our joy. Our treasure. Therefore most gladly will we boast in our pain and suffering, sorrows and grief, for when we are nothing, then Christ is magnified. When Christ is more precious to us than anything life has to offer or that death can take away, then He is most glorified.

This is the secret of the Christian life—contentment in Christ. We see this illustrated in Philippians, chapter 4, beginning with verse 11:

[11] Not that I say it in respect of want, for I did learn in things in which I am to be content. [12] I have known both to be humbled and I have known to abound. In everything and in all things I have learned the initiation secret both to be full and to be hungry, both to abound and to be in want. [13] For in all things I have strength in Christ's strengthening me.

(Phil. 4:11-13 NYLT)

The key, therefore, to being "sorrowful, yet always rejoicing" (2 Cor. 6:10) is that Christ is all we have. That He is more precious than all we could ever gain. That He is more valuable than all we could ever lose. And therefore we can be content with nothing or with everything because Christ is our all in all. He is our life. The point of suffering is to drive us to Christ, to know Him intimately (Job 42:5), and therefore the more we treasure Him in our suffering, the more joy we have in our suffering. Only joy in Christ can make suffering pleasurable.

3 Blessed be the God and Father of our Lord Jesus Christ, the Father of mercies and God of all comfort, 4 who comforts us in all our tribulation, that we may be able to comfort those who are in any trouble, with the comfort with which we ourselves are comforted by God. 5 For as the sufferings of Christ abound in us, so our consolation also abounds through Christ. 6 Now if we are afflicted, it is for your consolation and salvation, which is effective for enduring the same sufferings which we also suffer. Or if we are comforted, it is for your consolation and salvation. 7 And our hope for you is steadfast, because we know that as you are partakers of the sufferings, so also you will partake of the consolation. 8 For we do not want you to be ignorant, brethren, of our trouble which came to us in Asia: that we were burdened beyond measure, above strength, so that we despaired even of life. 9 Yes, we had the sentence of death in ourselves, that we should not trust in ourselves but in God who raises the dead,

(2 Cor. 1:3-9)

NATHAN W. TUCKER

5 GOD'S FREE WILL IN DEFINITE ATONEMENT

*F*allen mankind is part of a bad tree in which we have inherited the guilt, death, and sin nature of our First Man Adam. By this inherited corruption we have received from Adam, we are utterly biased against, and disabled and antagonistic toward, God. We have, since birth, been children of lawlessness who can no more do good than an apple tree produce oranges or a Dalmatian lose its spots.

Consequently, it is impossible for us to make ourselves good enough to receive salvation. It is impossible for us to make ourselves good enough to keep salvation. It is impossible for us to have any self-righteousness before salvation. And it is impossible for us to have any self-righteousness after salvation. We cannot—in whole or in part—save ourselves. God owes us nothing for any past "good works" we may have done.

Rather, we are pure evil and wickedly corrupt and can have no hope of ever earning God's favor. Our very nature is one of sinful blasphemy against a holy and righteous God, and it cannot be atoned for by tears, resolutions, good works, legalism, or any other effort on our part. God owes us nothing but eternal damnation from the moment we were conceived, and it is the height of pompous arrogance for sinful mankind to presume that a just and pure God owes them anything.

Therefore, if we are to be saved from our spiritual deadness and eternal damnation, it must be by God's free will and God's free will alone.[1] If anyone is to be saved, it must be by God's choice and God's choice alone. For if God will not redeem us, there is no other conceivable Savior to rescue us. Not us. Not our parents or spouse. Not even the archangels of heaven are able to impart spiritual life. Only God, in showing us unearned

---

[1] For a more in-depth exegesis of Scriptural salvation, the reader is highly encouraged to refer to my book *You Must Be Born Again! An Evangelistic Exposition of John 3:1-8.*

and unmerited love, is able to save us and sanctify us. And He does so as the only effectual and decisive actor in our salvation without any contribution on our part.

For Scripture is abundantly clear that God is absolutely sovereign in the exercise of His love. That the cause of HIs love must originate in Himself and not in man, for otherwise He would cease to be God.

I. Foreloved:

Christians are those whom God foreloved before the foundation of the world. Before He had created a single molecule of matter or a single second of time. For Romans tells us that, "For whom He foreknew, He also predestined to be conformed to the image of His Son, that He might be the firstborn among many brethren" (Rom. 8:28). *Foreknew* here is another term for *chosen* or *elected*. In other words, those whom God foreknew are those whom God chose, or elected, to set His affections upon in eternity past.

Where do I get that? The Greek word translated here as *foreknew* is *proginosko—pro* (before) and *ginosko* (to know). *To know* often means something more intimate and experimental than mere intellectual knowledge. For instance, Matthew tells us that Jesus' step-father Joseph did not "know" Mary until after "she had brought forth her firstborn Son. And he called His name JESUS" (Matt. 1:25). The verse is not telling us that Joseph did not know of his betrothed fiancé until after the Lord Christ was born, but that he did not have sexual relations with her until after she had delivered the Messiah. To know in this context means, therefore, to know sexually.[2]

To know often carries connotations of familiarity, of personal acquaintance and friendship, of owning and acknowledging, of communion and fellowship. For instance, Jesus will deny

---

[2] For examples of the same meaning of *know*, see generally Gen. 4:1, 17, 25, 19:8; Num. 31:17; Judges 21:11; 1 Sam. 1:19; Lk. 1:34; etc.

knowing self-righteous Christians in Name Only (CINOs) at the final judgment, saying, "I never knew you; depart from Me" (Matt. 7:23). In contrast, however, believers "are known by God" (Gal. 4:9). Similarly, God tells us that He has "known" Abraham "in order that he may command his children and his household after him, that they keep the way of the LORD, to do righteousness and justice, that the LORD may bring to Abraham what He has spoken to him" (Gen. 18:19). Yahweh also tells the prophet Jeremiah that, "Before I formed you in the womb I knew you" (Jer. 1:5).

God's knowing is exclusive. The term doesn't mean that He doesn't know of other people and nations, but rather that He has chosen to set His favor, His love, His affections upon a specific individual or people group. For instance, Yahweh tells Israel that, "'You only have I known of all the families of the earth'" (Amos 3:2). God obviously knows all the people groups of the earth, but He chose—or elected or foreloved—only Israel. Similarly, the psalmist tells us that, "For the LORD knows the way of the righteous, but the way of the ungodly shall perish" (Ps. 1:6). Again, the verse doesn't say that God is unaware of the ungodly, but only that He favors the way of the righteous whom He loves.

Foreknowledge in Romans 8:29, therefore, means those individuals who God foreloved out of all the earth.[3] To foreknow refers to God's sovereign, electing, exclusive love which He has

---

[3] To understand foreknowledge in Romans 8:29-30 to simply refer to God's omniscience of who would eventually exercise faith in Christ fails exegetical logic, for then the verses would, in essence, read, "For whom God foreknew would have faith, He predestined to the natural and necessary fruit of said faith— namely, their sanctification...". Why would God need to predestine believers to sanctification if He already knew they were going to believe and thereby be gradually conformed to the image of His Son anyway, even in the absence of any such predestining? For a much fuller explanation of how the faith that justifies is the very same faith the sanctifies, please see my books *The Five Solas: An Expository Exhortation* and *Agape: The Essence of Saving Faith*. *Foreloved*, therefore, is the only exegetically honest and cohesive understanding of *foreknew*.

had for His elect from all eternity. God has loved His children of promise "'with an everlasting love. Therefore with lovingkindness I have drawn you'" (Jer. 31:3). We have been loved with an eternal love (Eph. 1:4) for—before we even existed in time—God has betrothed the elect to Himself as a Bride in an exclusive marriage covenant (Exek. 16:1-4; Eph. 5:25-33).

And therefore His electing love is entirely unconditional. He loves us because He chose to love us before we existed and not because of anything good or meritorious in us (Deut. 7:7-8; see also 4:37, 9:5, 10:15). The children of promise, the bride of God's covenant, were elected before they were, "born, nor had done any good or evil" (Rom. 9:11). Jacob rather than Esau was elected solely because, "As it is written, 'Jacob I have loved, but Esau I have hated'" 9:13). God freely and unconditionally loved Jacob from eternity past (vs. 13)—before he had been born or done anything good or evil (vs. 11)—and therefore elected him over his brother Esau (vs. 12).

We have thus been loved with an everlasting love solely because God freely, voluntarily, and graciously choose to do so out of the hidden counsel of His will and not for any reason to be found in us. "So then it is not of him who wills, nor of him who runs, but of God who shows mercy" (Rom. 9:16). "Therefore He has mercy on whom He wills, and whom He wills He hardens" (9:18).

Why? "[T]hat God's electing purpose might stand, not of works but of Him who calls" (Rom. 9:11 NYLT). In other words, it is not of man's works (vs. 11), willing (vs. 16), running (vs. 16), or doing good or evil (vs. 11) that he is foreloved by God, but of God and God alone in order that He and He alone might get the glory. For as the Apostle Paul explains in the second chapter of Ephesians:

> 8 For by grace you have been saved through faith. And this is not of your doing; it is the gift of God, 9 not of works, lest anyone should boast.
>
> (Eph. 2:8-9 ESV)

Or as Paul put it in Romans, chapter 4:

27 Where, then, is boasting? It is excluded. On what principle? On that of observing the law? No, but on that of faith. 28 For we maintain that a man is justified by faith apart from observing the law.

(Rom. 4:27-28 NIV84)

We see this again echoed in the first chapter of 1 Corinthians:

26 For you see your calling, brethren, that not many wise according to the flesh, not many mighty, not many noble, are called. 27 But God has chosen the foolish things of the world to put to shame the wise, and God has chosen the weak things of the world to put to shame the things which are mighty; 28 and the base things of the world and the things which are despised God has chosen, and the things which are not, to bring to nothing the things that are, 29 that no flesh should glory in His presence. 30 But of Him you are in Christ Jesus, who became for us wisdom from God—and righteousness and sanctification and redemption— 31 that, as it is written, "He who glories, let him glory in the LORD."

(1 Cor. 1:26-31)

The sole instrument of justification is penitent faith and penitent faith alone so that no one can boast before God. And the gift of such penitent faith is owing solely to God's electing love and such electing love alone so that no one can boast before God. God has designed salvation from beginning to end so that He and He alone gets the glory from His creatures and not vice versa.\

God's foreloving—or election or choosing—is often used interchangeably with the term predestination, though technically the later refers to the specific goal or end of God's election. To use an analogy, a man's decision to propose to his girlfriend is his election of her, and the predestined purpose of his proposal is to make her his one and only bride to love and to cherish till death do them part.

Scripture reveals several predestined ends or purposes for God's foreloving, such as:

- **John 15:19:** To come out of the world.
- **Romans 8:29:** To "be conformed to the image of His Son."
- **Ephesians 1:4:** That "we should be holy and without blame before Him in love."
- **Ephesians 1:5:** To "adoption as sons by Jesus Christ to Himself."
- **1 Peter 1:15:** To be holy in all our conduct.

Chapter 1 of Ephesians makes it clear in verses 4, 5, and 11 that those of us who believe were foreloved—or chosen or elected—before the foundation of the world, and verses 6-7 and 12-14 tell us that the predestined goal of our being foreloved is the praise of God's glory. God, therefore, exercises His completely and entirely sovereign, free, and unconditional will in election to maximize His own glory by removing any grounds for boasting in those who are being saved. A believer does not make himself a Christian, but rather God makes him a Christian because He choose to do so before time even began. A person is not elect by God because He foresaw that such an individual would believe; rather, he believes because he is the elect of God. Therefore, to God alone belongs the glory.

II. Particular Propitiation:

And God has purchased, not the mere possibility of a Bride, but the reality of a Bride. He has unequivocally paid her bride price in full. Not one cent of the ransom has gone unpaid. The debt has been completed repaid. He has drunk the hell of His elect. He has clothed them with His righteousness,

For every single individual is conceived with a corrupt sin nature which makes us utterly biased against, and disabled and antagonistic toward, God. For instance, the Apostle Paul tells us:

⁵ For those who are according to the flesh, *the things of the flesh they do mind*; but those who are according to the Spirit, the things of the Spirit they do mind. ⁶ For the mind of the flesh is death, but the mind of the Spirit is life and peace. ⁷ *Because the mind of the flesh is enmity to God—for it does not subject itself to the law of God, neither is it able.* ⁸ *And those who are in the flesh are not able to please God.*

(Rom. 8:5-8 NYLT; emphasis added)

James, the half-brother of Christ, admonishes us that, "Do you not know that friendship with the world is enmity with God? Whoever therefore wants to be a friend of the world is the enemy of God" (Jas. 4:4). In Galatians, Paul writes that "the flesh lusts against the Spirit, and the Spirit against the flesh; and these are contrary to one another" (Gal. 5:17). And in Philippians he warns that, "¹⁸ many live as enemies of the cross of Christ....¹⁹ Their minds are set on earthly things" (Phil. 3:18-19). Finally, in Romans 5, the apostle describes the unregenerate as enemies of God (Rom. 5:10).

From conception, therefore, we are:

- Unable to please God (Rom. 8:8).
- Unable to subject ourselves to the law of God (Rom. 8:7).
- At enmity with God (Jas. 4:4).
- Contrary to God (Gal. 5:17).
- With minds set on sin (Rom. 8:5; Phil. 3:19).
- Enemies of God (Rom. 5:10; Phil. 3:18; Jas. 4:4).

Furthermore, from the moment of conception we are children of lawlessness. For we not only sinned in our First Man Adam's sin, but we also commit our own sins every single second of every single day of our entire lives. The Bible tells us that, "'no one is good but One, that is, God'" (Mk. 10:18). The Apostle John warns that, "Whoever commits sin also commits lawlessness, and sin is lawlessness" (1 Jn. 3:4). The Apostle Paul writes:

9 ...For we have previously charged both Jews and Greeks that they are all under sin.

10 As it is written:

"There is none righteous, no, not one;

11 There is none who understands;

There is none who seeks after God.

12 They have all turned aside;

They have together become unprofitable;

There is none who does good, no, not one."...

18 "There is no fear of God before their eyes."...

23 ...all have sinned and fall short of the glory of God,

(Rom. 3:9-12, 18, 23)

From conception each and every single one of us have rejected and ridiculed God's right to govern our lives as we blasphemously declare to Him, "Not Your will be my will be done!" We are in a state of insurrection, of rebellion, in which the Bible tells us that everyone does what is right in his own eyes (Num. 15:39; Deut. 12:8; Judges 17:6, 21:25).

Consequently, all men live already judged and condemned before God (Rom. 5:17). From the moment of conception we are already "by nature children of wrath" (Eph. 2:3) who are "condemned already" (Jn. 3:18) with "the wrath of God abid[ing] on [us]" (vs. 36).

All of us, therefore, are conceived as children of hell. As spawns of Satan. For we have all fallen short of the glory of God (Rom. 3:23) and, consequently, the wages of such sin is eternal death (Rom. 6:23) in hell (Lk. 16:23-24). Hell is a furnace of fire in outer darkness where we will be wailing and gnashing our teeth (Matt. 8:12, 13:42, 50, 24:51). Jesus warns that it is the destruction of our soul (Matt. 10:28) in a fire that shall never be quenched and where our worm does not die (Mk. 9:44, 46, 48; see also Is. 66:24). Furthermore, the book of Revelation describes hell as a place of torment with burning sulfur (14:10) in a lake of fire (20:15).

The only hope any of us has of heaven and spending eternity with God is a Redeemer. A Savior. A Mediator between God and man. Someone to appease the wrath of God. Someone to live the perfect life that we could never do, and to die as the perfect sacrificial lamb that we could never be. We cannot earn our own salvation, for no one, "can say, 'I have made my heart pure; I am clean and without sin'" (Prov. 20:9; see also Job 14:4, 15:14, 25:4). "All of us," Isaiah the prophet tells us, "have become like one who is unclean, and all our righteous acts are like menstrual rages" (Is. 64:6 NYLT).

All strands of Christianity hold that Christ did something upon the cross of Calvary, but they are hardly in agreement with what, exactly, He accomplished. Most Christians believe that Christ died for every single human being—past, present, and future—in exactly the same way. That He died for the sins of all mankind. But is this, in fact, what the Scriptures teach us Christ did in His sacrificial death?

A. *What* Does Scripture Say Christ Accomplished in His Death?

The place to begin our examination of Scripture is the end of the third chapter of Romans, often called the acropolis of the Christian faith. Acropolis comes from the Greek word *akro* (*high*) and *polis* (*city*). In this context, therefore, the term implies that this passage is the fortified city or citadel of the Gospel:

> 21 But now the righteousness of God apart from the law is revealed, being witnessed by the Law and the Prophets, 22 even the righteousness of God, through faith in Jesus Christ, to all and on all who believe. For there is no difference; 23 for all have sinned and fall short of the glory of God, 24 being justified freely by His grace through the redemption that is in Christ Jesus, 25 whom God set forth as a propitiation by His blood, through faith, to demonstrate His righteousness, because in His forbearance God had passed over the sins that were previously committed, 26 to demonstrate at the present time His righteousness, that He might be just and the

justifier of the one who has faith in Jesus. [27] Where is boasting then? It is excluded. By what law? Of works? No, but by the law of faith. [28] Therefore we conclude that a man is justified by faith apart from the deeds of the law.
(Rom. 3:21-28)

We could, and will, spend an eternity plunging the depths of these verses in worship of such scandalous divine love. But at present, look with me at verse 25: "whom [Jesus Christ] God set forth as a propitiation by His blood." The term *propitiation* comes from the Greek word *hilasterion*, which means to *appease* or *turn away (propitiate)* God's divine wrath by means of an atoning sacrifice. Specifically it refers to the mercy seat—the lid of the ark of the covenant—in the Old Testament (Heb. 9:5).

Leviticus 16 gives instructions for Yom Kippur—the Jewish Day of Atonement. The high priest was first to offer a bull as a sin offering in order to "make atonement for himself and for his house" (vs. 11, see also vs. 6). Then he was to present "two kids of the goats" (vs. 5) before Yahweh at the door of the Tabernacle (vs. 7) and cast lots for them: one lot for Yahweh and the other lot for the scapegoat (vs. 8). The goat on which Yahweh's lot fell was offered as a sin offering, its blood sprinkled on and before the mercy seat (vs. 9, 15) to make atonement for the Holy Place "because of the uncleanness of the children of Israel, and because of their transgressions, for all their sins" (vs. 16). Only the high priest could enter before the mercy seat, and only on the Day of Atonement.

The live goat on which the lot fell to be the scapegoat was then presented alive before Yahweh "to make atonement upon it, and to let it go as the scapegoat into the wilderness" (vs. 10). The high priest was to "lay both his hands on the head of the live goat, confess over it all the iniquities of the children of Israel, and all their transgressions, concerning all their sins, putting them on the head of the goat, and shall send it way into the wilderness by the hand of a suitable man" (vs. 21). The goat bore "on itself all their iniquities" into the wilderness (vs. 22).

All this, of course, was symbolic (Heb. 9:9), a copy and shadow (8:5), a shadow of the final atoning sacrifice that was made in Christ Jesus (10:1). For "it is not possible that the blood of bulls and goats could take away sins" (10:4). If they could, the worshippers would have been purified and perfected with no more consciousness of sins (10:1-2) and, therefore, would not have to continually offer the same sacrifices year after year (10:1). But they could only symbolically and temporarily propitiate, and therefore sacrifices merely served as "a reminder of sins every year" (10:3).

But in the Lord Christ's death upon the cross, all these transient, ineffectual sacrifices found their fulfillment in the real thing. Calvary is our Yom Kippur, Christ our atoning goats. As He hung there upon that hideously beautiful tree, God laid both HIs hands upon His Son's head, confessed over His One and Only all the sins of the elect, imputing them upon His head so that He bore in Himself their iniquities, and slaughtering Him (Rev. 5:6, 9. 12; original Greek) to make atonement for His people by appeasing HIs fierce wrath.

Only a sin bearer can propitiate the wrath of God. Only one with actual or imputed sin can atone for sin. Jesus bore our iniquities (Is. 53:11) and sins (vs. 12). He took upon Himself our sin in the flesh so that He might condemn it in His death (Rom. 8:3). He bore our sins in His body, so that by His stripes were are healed (1 Pet. 2:24). God imputed "Him who knew no sin to be sin for us," so that we might be imputed with "the righteousness of God in Him" (2 Cor. 5:21).

He bore our curse of condemnation in order to redeem us from God's eternal wrath (Gal. 3:13). All the divine curses reserved in the Mosaic law for the disobedient were placed on Him. As God the Son hung there upon the cross, God the Father proclaimed over Him:

> [16] "Cursed shall you be in the city, and cursed shall you be in the country…
> [19] "Cursed shall you be when you come in, and cursed shall you be when you go out.

20 "The LORD will send on you cursing, confusion, and rebuke in all that you set your hand to do, until you are destroyed and until you perish quickly, because of the wickedness of your doings in which you have forsaken Me.

21 The LORD will make the plague cling to you until He has consumed you from the land which you are going to possess.

22 The LORD will strike you with consumption, with fever, with inflammation, with severe burning fever, with the sword, with scorching, and with mildew; they shall pursue you until you perish.

23 And your heavens which are over your head shall be bronze, and the earth which is under you shall be iron.

24 The LORD will change the rain of your land to powder and dust; from the heaven it shall come down on you until you are destroyed.

25 "The LORD will cause you to be defeated before your enemies; you shall go out one way against them and flee seven ways before them; and you shall become troublesome to all the kingdoms of the earth...

28 The LORD will strike you with madness and blindness and confusion of heart. 29 And you shall grope at noonday, as a blind man gropes in darkness; you shall not prosper in your ways; you shall be only oppressed and plundered continually, and no one shall save you...

33 ...you shall be only oppressed and crushed continually. 34 So you shall be driven mad because of the sight which your eyes see...

37 And you shall become an astonishment, a proverb, and a byword among all nations where the Lord will drive you...

45 "Moreover all these curses shall come upon you and pursue and overtake you, until you are destroyed, because you did not obey the voice of the LORD your God, to keep His commandments and His statutes which

He commanded you. 46 And they shall be upon you for a sign and a wonder...

(Deut. 28:16, 19-25, 28-29, 33, 37, 45-56)

It is no wonder, then, that the night before His sacrifice Jesus sweated great drops of blood (Lk. 22:44). It is no wonder that He thrice (Matt. 22:44) "offered up prayers and supplications, with vehement cries and tears to Him who was able to save Him from death" (Heb. 5:7; see also Lk. 22:44) that night in Gethsemane. It is blasphemously inconceivable that the Captain of our salvation was afraid of a Roman cross while millions of His followers have been lead to their martyrdom joyously singing in triumph. No! He wasn't trembling at the prospect of a scourging and a crown of thorns. He didn't fear the mockery of the crowds and public humiliation as He was stripped naked. He wasn't afraid of spikes being driven into His hands and feet as He died an excruciatingly painful death. No! Rather, He feared experiencing our hell for us. He feared His Father's wrath. He abhorred the thought of being forsaken by HIs Father on that cross as He bore wave after wave of infinite and perfect justice for our sins.[4]

And by serving as our propitiating (Heb. 2:17; 1 Jn. 2:2, 4:10) sin offering (Is. 53:8, 10), the Lord Christ has appeased or turned aside the wrath of His Father. God has propitiated God. God *never* acquits, clears, or exonerates the guilty. *Never!* Satisfaction is always required. Sin must be punished—either on

---

[4] Any theory of the atonement that does not include penal substitution makes a mockery of—nay, butchers—exegetical logic and entirely disparages, diminishes, and eviscerates the value and worth of the passion of the Christ. And while it is true that, generally speaking, criminal justice systems do not recognize penal substitution, Scripture is clear that God does and, therefore, we must yield to Scripture and not vice versa. Penal substitution is the entire principle on which the Old Testament sacrificial system works. It is the only one in which Christ Jesus can serve as our Second Adam. And while it is not recognized in criminal law, it is in civil law where anyone can redeem or ransom the debt of somebody else. Creditors don't care who pays the money, only that it is paid.

the cross in Christ or in hell by the sinner. But by drinking the hell of the elect for them (Ps. 75:8; Jer. 25:15; Mk. 14:36; Lk. 22:42; Rev. 14:10, 16:19), they bear no more penalty for sins. No more condemnation for iniquities. God is now able to declare over them, "Not guilty!" for He has justified us (Rom. 3:24, 26) through His blood (Rom. 5:9; Eph. 1:7; Col. 1:14). He is now able to forgive us the penalty of our sins (Jn. 1:29; 1 Jn. 1:9). By the instrumentality of penitent faith in Jesus Christ, we pass from condemnation to innocence (Rom. 5:1; Acts 13:39; Gal. 2:16; Tit. 3:7).

And by His passive and active obedience—culminating in the humble obedience "to the point of death, even the death of the cross" (Phil. 2:8)—Christ has bought for us His righteousness. As the perfect Second Adam, the elect are, by faith, united with Christ such that His righteousness becomes their righteousness (Rom. 5:19, 10:4; 1 Cor. 1:30; 2 Cor. 5:21; Phil. 3:9). He has washed (Jn. 3:5; 1 Cor. 6:11; Tit. 3:5), purified (Tit. 2:14; Heb. 1:3), and cleansed (Ezek. 36:25; Heb. 9:14; 1 Jn. 1:7), taking away the consciousness of sins (1 Tim. 1:5, 19; Heb. 9:9, 10:2, 17, 22; 1 Pet. 3:16).

On Calvary, therefore, Christ Jesus has become our mediator (1 Tim. 2:5; Heb. 8:6, 9:15, 12:24; 1 Pet. 2:5)—interceding for His Bride before His Father. Job plaintively cried out in his pain:

> 32 "For He [God] is not a man, as I am,
> That I may answer Him,
> And that we should go to court together.
> 33 Nor is there any mediator between us,
> Who may lay his hand on us both."
>
> (Job. 9:32-33)

And several thousand years later Christ answered Job's prayer by stepping forward and interposing Himself between His Bride and His Father. And by His propitiating, atoning sacrifice for sins, He also paid our ransom to His Father (Matt. 20:28; Mk. 10:45; 1 Cor. 6:20; 1 Tim. 2:6; Heb. 9:15; 1 Pet. 1:18, 20; Rev. 5:9). He became our Kinsmen Redeemer by purchasing us back to His

Father (Acts 20:28; Rom. 3:24; Gal. 3:13; Eph. 1:7; Col. 1:14; Tit. 2:14; Heb. 9:12; 1 Pet. 1:18; Rev. 1:5, 5:9). In short, He is our Savior and Deliverer (Matt. 1:21; Col. 1:13; 1 Thess. 1:10) who by His death bought us peace and reconciliation with HIs Father (Is. 53:5; Acts 10:36; Rom. 5:1, 10-11; 2 Cor. 5:18-19; Eph. 2:16; Col. 1:20).

Furthermore, by HIs blood the Lord Christ bought for us the New Covenant promised throughout the Old Testament (Jer. 31:31-34, 32:39-40; Ezek. 11:19-20, 36:26-27). The night before His sacrifice, Jesus told the disciples as they celebrated the Passover that the wine was "My blood of the new covenant" (Matt. 26:28; see also Mk. 14:24, Lk. 22:20; 1 Cor. 11:25). Calvary purchased the elect a new heart (Jer. 32:39; Ezek. 11:19, 36:26), a heart of flesh (Ezek. 36:26, 11:19), a new Spirit (Ezek. 11:19, 36:27), with God's law in their minds and written on their hearts (Jer. 31:33), a new way (Jer. 32:39) with the fear of Him in their hearts (vs. 40) that they may fear Him forever (vs. 39). Christ died so that the elect will know Yahweh (Jer. 31:34), so that, "They shall be My people, and I will be their God" (32:38), so that He, "will rejoice over them to do them good" (32:41).

Finally, Scripture tells us that by HIs sacrifice Jesus became our High Priest—"holy, harmless, undefiled, separate from sinners, and has become higher than the heavens" (Heb. 7:26). Upon His death He entered into the Most Holy Place in heaven with His own blood and is now "seated at the right hand of the throne of the Majesty in the heavens" (8:1; see also 8:2, 9:11-12, 24). There He "always lives to make intercession for" His elect (7:25; see also Rom. 8:34; 1 Jn. 2:1) "to save [them] to the uttermost" (Id.)

In summary, therefore, we have seen that with His blood shed upon the cross of Calvary, Messiah Jesus atoned for sin and thereby propitiated—or appeased or turned away—the wrath of an angry God. Sin, not in part but the whole, was nailed to that cross, no longer able to bring condemnation and hell. Christ became our righteousness and cleansed us from the power of sin and guilt. He purchased the New Covenant and the promises of a new nature, a new creation (2 Cor. 5:17), that came with it. By

117

His blood He became Propitiator, Atoner, Mediator, Redeemer, Reconciliator, Ransomer, Savior, Deliverer, and interceding High Priest.

B. For *Whom* Does Scripture Say Christ Died For?

The question remains, however, for *whom* did Christ die? For whom are these benefits of the cross attained? Can it really be that Jesus accomplished this for everyone—past, present, and future? For if the Lord died in the exact same way for all mankind, and yet not everyone is saved, then we have a monstrous injustice of universal proportions. For Scripture is clear that not everyone goes to heaven, for most will remain spiritually dead in their trespasses and sins at the time of their physical deaths and, consequently, go to an eternal hell. Jesus tells us that "many are called, but *few* are chosen" (Matt. 22:14; emphasis added). In other words, many hear the general Gospel call, but only few are chosen (elected) by God to be granted the penitent faith to savingly respond. In another place He warns us:

> 13 "Enter by the narrow gate; for wide is the gate and broad is the way that leads to destruction, *and there are many who go in by it.* 14 Because narrow is the gate and difficult is the way which leads to life, *and there are few who find it.*
>
> (Matt. 7:13-14; emphasis added)

If, therefore, the Lord Christ paid the penalty for sin for everyone who ever walked the face of the earth, and yet "many" (Matt. 7:12) reject Him and go to hell, for whose sin are they being punished for in eternal flames? If Jesus died for everyone equally, then all are under no condemnation (Rom. 8:1, 34), under no charge (8:33), with no one against them (8:31), and unable to be separated from the love of Christ (8:35).

Therefore, because Messiah Christ bore their sins, they no longer have any sins left with which to suffer everlasting torment. And it isn't as if God the Father can go to God the Son and say, in effect, "Whoops, I thought for sure that one was going to believe in You. Oh well, I'll just retake My punishment off of you and put it back on them. No hard feelings, right? I mean, it isn't as if You experienced his hell for him. Oh wait, You did. My bad…"

It doesn't work that way. Christ's accomplishment is final. Complete. Once for all. It is finished (Jn. 19:30). Jesus suffered and died for sins once for all (Rom. 6:10; Heb. 7:27; 1 Pet. 3:18). He does not offer Himself as a sacrifice over and over again (Heb. 10:11). Rather, "[12]…after He had offered one sacrifice for sins forever, [He] sat down at the right hand of God…[14] For by one offering He has perfected forever those who are being sanctified" (Heb. 10:12, 14). He "was offered once to bear the sins of many" (Heb. 9:28) and, in His sacrifice, He "once for all… obtained eternal redemption" (Heb. 9:12).

Once paid, the penalty for sin cannot be unpaid by Christ or repaid by someone else. A "Christian" cannot lose his "salvation," or else Christ would have to be recrucified each time he came back to Christ. Such heresy would make the Romish doctrine of the eucharist seem a mild blasphemy by comparison. Similarly, an unrepentant sinner cannot be punished for sins already punished as a clear violation of the legal principle of double jeopardy. If one's hell has already been drunk, it cannot be redrunk.

Furthermore, if Christ died equally for every single person past, present, and future, then every single person past, present, and future would be legally entitled to call Christ their Righteousness, Propitiator, Atoner, Mediator, Redeemer, Reconciliator, Ransomer, Savior, Deliverer, and interceding High Priest. But if He is the Righteousness, Atoner, Mediator, Redeemer, Reconciliator, Ransomer, Savior, Deliverer, and interceding High Priest[5] of all mankind, then it is inconceivable that anyone should be in hell. For then those in hell could appeal to Christ as their

---

[5] Scripture is clear that Christ only intercedes for His elect (Jn 17:9) for the simple reason that His intercession is always effectual. It must be, or He is a failure. Imperfect. Inadequate. And that, of course, is blasphemous.

mediator. They could present a defense of Christ's righteousness as their own. They could call upon Christ as their Savior. They could protest that Christ is their intercessor, pleading their case before the throne of God for all eternity.

That's blasphemy. Note that the Lord Christ is described in Scripture as a Redeemer. As *having* redeemed. A completed fact accomplished at a specific moment in time. He is not a potential Redeemer. He is not a hypothetical Redeemer. He didn't merely create the possibility of redeeming. No! He redeemed, once and for all. Similarly, He is our Deliverer. Just as Moses didn't merely create an opportunity, a potential, a hypothetical way for the ancient Hebrews to be delivered, so Christ has actually served as our Deliverer. Nor is God still angry with us because Jesus is merely a potential Propitiator, but rather we have in fact been reconciled to God and His wrath averted. In short, Christ Jesus has definitely, decisively, and effectually accomplished all that Scripture tells us He accomplished on Calvary, not merely created hypothetical potentialities.

Furthermore, if Jesus died in the exact same way for every single individual, then all have the blood-bought entitlement to be new creations (2 Cor. 5:17) enjoying the benefits of the New Covenant (Jer. 31:31-34, 32:39-40; Ezek. 11:19-20, 36:26-27), knowing God (Jer. 31:34) and having Him "rejoice over them to do them good" (32:41). And it cannot be argued that all these benefits of the atonement are only available through the instrumentality of faith, for unbelief itself would be a sin forgiven through Christ's sacrifice. In other words, lack of penitent faith in the Son of God was atoned for by the Son of God on the cross so that, if Christ in fact died for the sins of all men, such unbelief can no longer be held against anyone and we're right back to universalism.

Additionally, it cannot be stressed enough that the promises of the New Covenant are not the promises of a mere possibility of a new heart. They are not the promise of the mere generic, general offer of a new Spirit. Rather, look at all the "I will's" God pledges to perform in the book of Ezekiel when He promised a new covenant:

25 Then *I will* sprinkle clean water on you, and you shall be clean; *I will* cleanse you from all your filthiness and from all your idols. 26 *I will* give you a new heart and put a new spirit within you; *I will* take the heart of stone out of your flesh and give you a heart of flesh. 27 *I will* put My Spirit within you and [*I will*] cause you to walk in My statutes, and you will keep My judgments and do them. 28 Then you shall dwell in the land that I gave to your fathers; you shall be My people, and *I will be* your God. 29 *I will* deliver you from all your uncleannesses.

(Ezek. 36:25-29a; emphasis added)

These are the blood-bought promises of the imposition of sovereign, decisive, divine free will in creating spiritual life out of dead, hardened, and blinded corpses. This is the promise of God that He will regenerate our hearts, grant us penitent faith, justify us and cleanse us, and give us His Spirit to cause us to walk in HIs ways. And this promise was definitely fulfilled, definitely accomplished, and definitely purchased at Calvary through the death of Christ Jesus. Therefore, Jesus cannot have died for everyone in the exact same way or else everyone would benefit in the exact same way from the New Covenant. But of course, that is ridiculous. So either God is a liar in offering false promises, or He is powerless to fulfill them, or He did not die for everyone in the exact same way.

Furthermore, no one can be in hell if Christ died for everyone or else Christ shed His blood in vain. His blood would be wasted upon the hill called Calvary, scattered to the four corners of the earth by the wind to drift unused, unwanted, and rejected. God did the hardest thing imaginable in sacrificing His agaped Son so that He could freely do the much easier work (by comparison) of giving us all things (Rom. 8:32), only to have His gifts left spurned and forlorn in a backroom of His heavenly tabernacle collecting dust. The heavenly Holy of Holies must be dwarfed by all the additions the angelical carpenters have had to make to store all the shunned and forsaken gifts of such an incompetent God.

Consequently, if Christ died for everyone in the exact same way, then of logical necessity all must be saved.[6]   But since Scripture and reality deny the validity of universalism, exegetical logic requires, therefore, that Messiah Jesus died for only some. For a limited number. A definite number. We see this reflected in several passages. For instance, Isaiah tells us that Christ "bore the sin of many" (53:12). Many, by definition, logically excludes all; that there are some for whom Christ did not bear the sins of. Again, Jesus tells us that the Son of Man came "to give His life as a ransom for many" (Matt. 20:28; see also Mk. 10:45). Not all, but many. And Jesus also tells us that His blood is the "blood of the new covenant, which is shed for many for the remission of sins" (Matt. 26:28). Again, not all, but many.[7]

So who are these many if they are not everyone?   Those certain, definite, and immutable elect that God foreloved before the beginning of time.   Redemptive history is clearly supralapsarian—meaning that God foreloved His Bride before, and as the reason, He created the universe and decreed humanity's fall in Adam.   The point of everything is the magnification of the beauties of Christ in His blood-bought Bride, and like any honorable, respectable husband, He loves His Bride with an exclusive, particular, covenantal love that He does not have for anyone else. We see this clearly explained in the fifth chapter of Ephesians:

> 25 Husbands, love your wives, just as Christ also loved the church and gave Himself for her, 26 that He might sanctify and cleanse her with the washing of water by the word, 27 that He might present her to Himself a glorious church, not having spot or wrinkle or any such thing, but

6 Christ did, in a sense, die for the damned by purchasing common grace, for all grace must be blood-bought. However, as we have just seen, He clearly cannot have purchased salvific grace for the vessels prepared for wrath.

7 Please see Appendixes A & B for a more thorough discussion of the terms *world* and *all* used in Scripture.

THE FREE WILL OF GOD

that she should be holy and without blemish. 28 So husbands ought to love their own wives as their own bodies; he who loves his wife loves himself. 29 For no one ever hated his own flesh, but nourishes and cherishes it, just as the Lord does the church. 30 For we are members of His body, of His flesh and of His bones. 31 "For this reason a man shall leave his father and mother and be joined to his wife, and the two shall become one flesh." 32 This is a great mystery, but I speak concerning Christ and the church. 33 Nevertheless let each one of you in particular so love his own wife as himself, and let the wife see that she respects her husband.

(Eph. 5:25-33)

The Apostle Paul explicitly teaches in this passage that Christ loved the Church and gave Himself for her (vs. 25). Why? That He might justify and sanctify her in order to present her to Himself as a glorious Bride—holy and without blemish. O what a glorious thought that on Calvary the Lord Christ paid in full the bride-price for His foreloved Bride! Not for everyone, but for His own flesh and His bones (vs. 30). For we are members of HIs body (vs. 30), cleaved together as with an adhesive like glue (vs. 31; original Greek). Just as no honorable, respectable wife demands that her husband love everyone else with the exact same love he has for her, so we should stop demanding that of the Lover of our souls.

We also see in the tenth chapter of the Gospel of John that Jesus died for His sheep and only His sheep. "'I am the good shepherd. The good shepherd gives His life for the sheep'" (Jn. 10:11; see also vs. 15, 17-18). And notice why He lays down HIs life for His sheep (vs. 15)—because He knows His sheep (vs. 14). In other words, Messiah Jesus foreknew or foreloved HIs sheep and that is why He took on flesh and bore their sins upon Calvary's cross. These aren't random sheep He has stumbled upon. These aren't sheep of another man's flock that He is stealing. No, these are His sheep from eternity past who, at the price of Hs blood, *shall* know Him (vs. 14) and hear His voice (vs.

123

16). We see this echoed by the Apostle Paul to the Ephesian elders when he exhorts them, "to shepherd the church of God which He purchased with His own blood" (Acts 20:28).

And in the eleventh chapter of John we see that Messiah Jesus died for the children of God and only for the children of God:

> [49] And one of them, Caiaphas, being high priest that year, said to them, "You know nothing at all, [50] nor do you consider that it is expedient for us that one man should die for the people, and not that the whole nation should perish." [51] Now this he did not say on his own authority; but being high priest that year he prophesied that Jesus would die for the nation, [52] and not for that nation only, but also that He would gather together in one the children of God who were scattered abroad.
>
> (Jn. 11:49-52)

It has been argued that "the children of God" refers to the Jewish people dispersed throughout the Gentile nations as the result of the Diaspora. There are two problems with such an interpretation. The first is that the word translated *nation* in this passage by the NKJV is *ethnos*, which means *ethnic group* and not geopolitical nation states as we know them today. Therefore, under this interpretation, verse 52 would literally read, "and not for the Jewish ethnic group but also for the Jewish ethnic group scattered abroad." It is awkwardly redundant and duplicative, which is uncharacteristic of the Apostle John. John does repeat, but only in circles and not cumbersomely.

But furthermore, the phrase *children of God* in verse 52 is never used in the entire New Testament to refer to Diasporic Jews. Never. Rather, it is only ever used to refer to believers (see generally Jn. 1:12; Rom. 8:14, 16, 19, 21, 9:8; Gal. 3:26, 4:6; Phil. 2:15; 1 Jn. 3:1-2, 9-10, 5:1-2, 18-19). Consequently, verse 52 explicitly states that Christ died, not for everyone in the exact same way, but only for the children of God. Believers. His Bride. His sheep.

124

But also for His friends, for Jesus has told us that we are His friends (Jn. 15:14) and, *therefore*, He will lay down His life for us (vs. 13). By His death He only saves "His people" from their sins (Matt. 1:21). And for His elect, chosen by God the Father *in* God the Son "before the foundation of the world" (Eph. 1:4).[8] It is only for those predestined "to adoption as sons by Jesus Christ to Himself" (vs. 5) that Christ bought "redemption through His blood, the forgiveness of sins" (vs. 7). And therefore the Apostle Paul could write to believers that Christ has loved and given Himself only for the saints (5:2; see also Lk. 1:68; Jn. 13:1, 17:2; Rom. 4:25; 1 Cor. 15:3). It is why Paul could cry out, "I live by faith in the Son of God, who loved *me* and gave Himself for *me*" (Gal. 2:20; emphasis added). Not for everyone who has every walked the face of the earth, but for me as one of the elect!

III. Forehated:

Before we leave this topic, it is important to briefly note the necessary corollary to God's electing love—that He also elects to hate. Before the foundation of the world and time even began, He forehated—or chose or elected—who among fallen, depraved humanity He would not save and, consequently, predestine to just condemnation in hell. Proverbs, for instance, tells us that, "Yahweh has made all for Himself; yes, even the wicked for the day of evil" (Prov. 16:4 NYLT).

The Apostle Peter tells us that those who stumble at Christ the Chief Cornerstone do so because they disobey the word just as they were appointed to do (1 Pet. 2:8). Again, in his second epistle, he warns of false teachers who "for a long time their judgment has not been idle" (2 Pet. 2:3). Jude warns of ungodly men who "prevent the grace of our God," men "who long ago were designated for this condemnation" (Jude 4 ESV).

In Romans 9 the Apostle Paul tells us that, before the children had been born or had done anything good or evil (vs. 11), God

---

[8] God the Father has never, for one trillisecond, ever thought of you outside of Christ.

told Rebecca that, "'Jacob I have loved, but Esau I have hated'" (vs. 13; quoting Mal. 1:2-3) in order that the electing purpose of God might stand (vs. 11). Though Esau was Jacob's twin brother (Mal. 1:2), Yahweh predestined that "'They shall be called the Territory of Wickedness, and the people against whom the LORD will have indignation forever (vs. 4).

Finally, a few verses later in the ninth chapter of Romans, Paul writes:

> 22 What if God, wanting to show His wrath and to make His power known, endured with much longsuffering the vessels of wrath prepared for destruction, 23 and that He might make known the riches of His glory on the vessels of mercy, which He had prepared beforehand for glory,
>
> (Rom. 9:22-23)

Just as God prepared before the creation of the universe vessels of mercy (vs. 23), so He also prepared beforehand vessels of wrath prepared for destruction in order to demonstrate His wrath and power (vs. 22). God predestines for glory those whom He foreloves (vs. 23), just as He predestines for destruction those whom He forehates (vs. 22). This is His right as the Potter (vs. 21) in order to maximize the display of the riches of His glory (vs. 23). This is His right as God, working all things according to the counsel of His will (Eph. 1:11).

Concluding Implications:

God's free will over definite atonement provides the believer with bedrock assurance in three areas: salvation, evangelism, and heaven. First, God's free will in particular propitiation fills the believer with complete confidence in their own salvation. For this definite atonement wrought by the Lord Christ on Calvary, though limited in scope, is limitless in extent. In other words, while the benefits of atonement are limited to the elect and only the elect, the benefits are exhaustively and decisively applied to them.

Christ didn't die to merely create the possibility of salvation. He didn't die merely to freely offer, but not guarantee, salvation to all men. He didn't die to make men savable, leaving it up to them to provide the ultimate, decisive act of free will. He didn't die merely to create the potential for a new heart, a new Spirit, a new creation. He didn't die solely to create the opportunity for man to save himself.

No! He died to securely and decisively save His elect for, "Salvation belongs to the LORD!" (Ps. 3:8; see also Jonah 2:9; Rev. 7:10). O what confidence with which to swing out into vast eternity—knowing that our God has saved us and saved us completely! O what assurance to the troubled heart that the foundations of our salvation are grounded in a divine love that is eternally deep! O what boldness in knowing that our past sins and wickedness have not put us past God's power to save! O what courage in knowing that such love is unmerited and free and not owing to anything we could ever say, do, or become!

O that every believer would daily grow in their comprehension of the width and length and depth and height of God's particular love for them which passes all understanding (Eph. 3:18-19)! O that every believer would know that the Lord Christ loved them with an eternal, exclusive, covenantal love and not just as a potential, a hypothetical, a possibility! O that every believer would then know that, just as a husband would lay down his life for his bride, so Christ has laid down His life specifically, decisively, and effectually for them! We are not just some random, chance objects of God's love by our own making and will-power; not as generic, run-of-the-mill, nameless individuals who are loved by Him only because we first loved Him; but rather we are loved as His Bride whom He chose to set His affections on before time even began!

O that every believer would know, truly know, that they are safe and secure in the arms of Christ—no longer under condemnation (Rom. 8:1, 34), no longer under a charge (vs. 33), with no one against them (vs. 31), unable to be separated from the love of Christ (vs. 35), and more than conquerors in Him who loves us (vs. 37)! And these promises, these realities, are no more changeable than God is—which is to say, they are immutable.

Unfortunately, the exact opposite is taught and preached in the majority of our churches every Sunday. Humanistic, man-centered thinking permeates the Church and the gospel it proclaims. To protect man's sacrosanct free-will, the contemporary Church proclaims an impotent God who wants all men to be saved but is unable to save anyone. They preach a beggar God who is so powerless that He has no option left but to panhandle at the door of people's hearts for them to let Him in. They present to a lost and dying world a God so hapless that He sacrificed His one and only Son to redeem potentially no one. They do not preach a God who is mighty to save, but one who can only sit on the sidelines helplessly hoping that man will save himself, bless His heart.

They proclaim that everything depends on man. That man is the decisive savior of his soul. The final link in his own salvation. The one who must perform a deed (such as a sinner's prayer, raise a hand, walk an aisle, or become baptized), in order to save himself. The one whose sanctification and perseverance in the race is ultimately up to him and him alone. The one who made himself a believer by will power alone, and the one who must keep himself a believer by will power alone. The one who was smart enough to figure this whole salvation thing out, while others with less intelligence will roast in hell for all eternity. The one who has no confidence in God's affections, always fearful of stumbling and falling out of God's love and back under His wrath. Such a limited God, a limited love, a limited atonement provides him with no assurance, no security, no boldness, no confidence except what he has in his own ability to save himself. For of man, and through man, and to man—according to Arminianism—be all the glory for his salvation.

The second basis for the believer's bedrock assurance is in evangelism, knowing that if on Calvary Christ decisively atoned for an elect few—His Bride, His children, His friends, His sheep—then it is *certain* that He will have them. For Scripture guarantees that all who desire to be saved not only *can* be saved, but that they *will* be saved. Jesus, for instance, declared in John 10 that, "[O]ther sheep I have which are not of this fold; them also I am under compulsion to bring in, and they shall hear My voice; and there shall be one flock and one Shepherd" (Jn. 10:16 NYLT). There are four specific promises in this verse alone:

- That Jesus is the Good Shepherd;
- That He has other sheep not currently in the fold;
- The He is under necessity to bring them in; and, therefore,
- That they shall hear His voice and be brought in!

What confidence in evangelism, knowing that those whom God foreloved will be saved and that no one, not even them, can thwart His will! What assurance to persevere in evangelism, knowing that God's love is irresistible! For Jesus tells us, "'No one can come to Me unless the Father who sent Me irresistibly drags him; and I will raise him up at the last day'" (Jn. 6:44 NYLT). And in another place He promises us, "'And I, if I am lifted up from the earth, will irresistibly drag all My sheep to Myself'" (Jn. 12:32 NYLT).

There is boldness in fearless evangelism, knowing that there is no sin too great nor sinner so vile that God cannot forgive! And still elsewhere Jesus promises us:

> **10** 27 My sheep hear My voice, and I know them, and they follow Me. 28 And I give them eternal life, and they shall never perish; neither shall anyone snatch them out of My hand. 29 My Father, who has given them to Me, is greater than all; and no one is able to snatch them out of My Father's hand.
>
> (Jn. 10:27-29)
> **6** 37 And Jesus declares that, "All that the Father gives Me will come to Me, and whoever comes to Me I will never drive away."
>
> (Jn. 6:37 NIV84)

The Apostle John tells us that, "the Spirit and the bride say, 'Come!' And let him who hears say, 'Come!' And let him who thirsts come. *Whosoever wills*, let him take the water of life freely" (Rev. 22:17; emphasis added)). "For the Scripture says, "*Whoever* believes on Him will not be put to shame'" (Rom. 10:11; emphasis added). Christ cries out:

* "'I am the bread of life; he who comes to Me will never hunger, and he who believes in Me will never thirst'" (John 6:35).
* "'If anyone is thirsty, let him come to Me and drink. Whoever believes in Me, as the Scripture has said, streams of living water will flow from within him'" (Jn. 7:38).
* "'Whoever drinks the water I give him will never thirst. Indeed, the water I give him will become to him a spring of water welling up to eternal life'" (Jn. 4:14).
* "' 28 Come to Me, all you who labor and are heavy laden, and I will give you rest. 29 Take My yoke upon you and learn from Me, for I am gentle and lowly in heart, and you will find rest for your souls. 30 For My yoke is easy and My burden is light'" (Matt. 11:28-30).

Therefore we are able to earnestly implore sinners to come to Christ and live, having full confidence that He is able and willing to save them to the uttermost (Heb. 7:25)! Evangelism—the public proclamation of the Gospel—is the God-appointed means of saving His elect (Rom. 10:14-15, 17), and therefore we issue, without qualm or reservation of any kind, the general or universal Gospel call to any and all without distinction.

The third and final basis for the believer's bedrock assurance is the joy of heaven, knowing that God works all things according to the counsel of His will (Eph. 1:11) for the fulness of our joy in the maximum display of God's infinite worth. In other words, we have bold confidence in anticipating eternity knowing that God's forelove and particular propitiation are infinitely and perfectly designed to satisfy our souls with ever increasing manifestations of the "exceeding riches of His grace in His kindness toward us in

Christ Jesus" (Eph. 2:7). O what heaven will be like for the vessels of mercy as God lavishes upon them the riches of His glory (Rom. 9:23)! O the ecstatic worship and praise of the riches of the glory of His grace which He has made to overflow toward us in all wisdom and prudence (Eph. 1:6-7, 12, 14)! A theology-fueled doxology for an eternity of eternities! That is a heaven to look forward to; not a humanistic, man-centered paradise where believers share their glory for their salvation with God.

3 Blessed be the God and Father of our Lord Jesus Christ, who has blessed us with every spiritual blessing in the heavenly places in Christ, 4 just as He chose us in Him before the foundation of the world, that we should be holy and without blame before Him in love, 5 having predestined us to adoption as sons by Jesus Christ to Himself, according to the good pleasure of His will, 6 to the praise of the glory of His grace, by which He made us accepted in the Beloved.

7 In Him we have redemption through His blood, the forgiveness of sins, according to the riches of His grace 8 which He made to abound toward us in all wisdom and prudence, 9 having made known to us the mystery of His will, according to His good pleasure which He purposed in Himself, 10 that in the dispensation of the fullness of the times He might gather together in one all things in Christ, both which are in heaven and which are on earth—in Him. 11 In Him also we have obtained an inheritance, being predestined according to the purpose of Him who works all things according to the counsel of His will, 12 that we who first trusted in Christ should be to the praise of His glory.

13 In Him you also trusted, after you heard the word of truth, the gospel of your salvation; in whom also, having believed, you were sealed with the Holy Spirit of promise, 14 who is the guarantee of our inheritance until the redemption of the purchased possession, to the praise of His glory.

(Eph. 1:3-14)

NATHAN W. TUCKER

6 GOD'S FREE WILL IN EFFECTUATING SALVATION

*I*n the last chapter we looked at God's free will in demonstrating HIs righteousness by being both just and the justifier of His elect (Prov. 17:15; Rom. 3:26). Now in this chapter we will examine God's free will in effectuating that salvation from regeneration to glorification.

I. New Birth:

First, the New Birth is entirely, from start to finish, a supernatural birth.[1] This is clearly stated by the Lord Christ in His John 3 discourse with Nicodemus:

• **Vs. 5:** "Jesus answered, 'Amen! Amen! I say to you, if anyone may not be *born of* water and *the Spirit*, he is not able to enter into the kingdom of God'" (emphasis added).
• **Vs. 6:** "'That which has been born of the flesh is flesh, *and that which has been born of the Spirit is spirit*'" (emphasis adde).
• **Vs. 8:** "'Thus is everyone who has been *born of the Spirit*'" (emphasis added).

We also see this in the very term *born again* used in verses 3 and 7, for the Greek word for *again* (anothen) almost always means *from above*. It comes from the Greek word *ano*, which simply means *up* or *above*. And of the thirteen times it is used in the Greek New Testament, this passage is the only place where many translators have chosen to translate *anothen* as *again*. It is not necessarily wrong to describe the New Birth as being birthed again, for it is indeed a second birth. However, doing so not only loses the supernatural flavor of the New Birth, but is inconsistent

---

[1] The reader is strongly encouraged to read my book *You Must Be Born Again! An Evangelistic Exposition of John 3:1-8* for a much fuller treatment of this subject.

with the use of *anothen* elsewhere in the New Testament (see, for instance, Jn. 3:31, 19:11). It seems best to translate it here as birth *again from above* in order to convey its entire meaning.

The New Birth, therefore, is a supernatural birth. It is to be born again from above by the Holy Spirit. It is to be begotten by God. This is the hardest doctrine in the Bible for men to accept, for it chaffs our soul. It is repugnant to our self-idolatry. It is an affront to our sense of self-sufficiency. The human heart echos with every beat the last two lines of the poem *Invictus*: "I am the master of my fate, I am the captain of my soul."

And therefore the doctrine of New Birth is a slap in the face. A bucket of cold water. A reality check to man's self-absorption. For it reminds us that we are powerless, helpless, and hopeless. That we can no more save ourselves than fly to the moon or swim the Pacific. Instead, we have to be supernaturally born again from above by the Holy Spirit because, as verse 6 tells us, "'that which is born of the flesh is flesh'" (NYLT). In other words, sin nature can only beget sin nature. Sinners can only give birth to sinners. The living dead can only engender the living dead. That is what mankind hates. Mankind hates the fact that we are born spiritually dead. That we were sinners and haters of God from the moment of conception. And that we are powerless to even do one good work, much less of saving our own souls.

In the First Man Adam, from the moment of conception you are spiritually dead. In the First Man Adam, from the moment of conception your very nature is sin. In the First Man Adam, from the moment of conception not merely your actions, thoughts, or behaviors, but you yourself are sin. In the Fist Man Adam, from the moment of conception your soul is black as night and uglier than hell. In the Fist Man Adam, from the moment of conception you have been as grotesque in your evil as any demon of hell. In the First Man Adam, from the moment of conception you cannot stop sinning. In then First Man Adam, from the moment of conception you will die a physical death. In the First Man Adam, from the moment of conception we are out of the kingdom of heaven and are children of wrath (Jn. 3:18, 36; Eph. 2:3). In the

Fist Man Adam, from the moment of conception we therefore cannot save ourselves.

Let's imagine that Andre the Giant were standing here next to me. Now if he were turned into a stone statue, I could hit him, kick him, and attempt to cut him with all kinds of weapons and he won't feel a thing. I certainly would, for I would be withering in pain; but he would not have felt anything. Similarly, the Bible describes you as spiritually dead, having a heart of stone:

• **Ephesians 2:1:** "And you He made alive, *who were dead* in trespasses and sins" (emphasis added).
• **Ephesians 2:5:** "even when *we were dead* in trespasses, made us alive together with Christ (by grace you have been saved)" (emphasis added).
• **Colossians 2:13:** "*you were dead* in your sins and the uncircumcision of your sinful nature" (NIV84; emphasis added).
• **1 John 3:14:** "We know that *we have passed from death to life*, because we love the brethren. He who does not love his brother *abides in death*" (emphasis added).
• **Luke 15:24, 32:** In His parable of the Prodigal Son, Jesus describes the returning prodigal as one who "*was dead* but is alive again" (emphasis added).
• **Matthew 8:22:** "But Jesus said to him, 'Follow Me, and *let the dead bury their own dead*'" (emphasis added). In other words, let the living spiritually dead bury the physically & spiritually dead.

What we need is nothing less than a spiritual resurrection. A dead person is unable to raise itself. A dead person is unable to resuscitate their heart. A dead person is unable to jumpstart their brain waves. A dead person is unable to give sight to their eyes. A dead person is unable to give hearing to their ears. A dead person is unable to give speech to their tongue. A dead person is unable to get off the morgue table. A dead person is unable to climb out of the coffin at the funeral home. A dead person is unable to climb up out of the tomb. A dead person is, well, dead. They may be acted *upon*, but they themselves cannot *initiate* action. They are powerless. They are helpless. They are hopeless. They cannot will or do anything.

The New Birth is supernatural, therefore, because *only God can perform it*. As John 3:6 tells us, "'That which has been born of the flesh is flesh, [BUT] that which has been born of the Spirit is spirit.'" Like our first birth, our second birth is done to us. We didn't will our first birth, and we don't will our second birth. We didn't conceive ourselves the first time, and we don't conceive ourselves the second time. We didn't labor for our first birth, and we don't labor for our second birth. In both births we didn't exist, and then we existed without any will or effort on our part. In both cases we are powerless. In both cases we are helpless. In both cases we are hopeless.

Our parents, therefore, are responsible for our first birth, not us. And likewise God, not us, is responsible for our second birth. We see this pride-humbling, breath-taking truth echoed through Scripture:

- **John 1:13:** "who were born, not of bloods, nor of the will of the flesh, nor of the will of man, *but of God*" (emphasis added).
- **Ephesians 2:4-5:** "4 But God...5 even when we were dead in trespasses, *made us alive* together with Christ..." (emphasis added).
- **Colossians 2:13:** "And you, being dead in your trespasses and the uncircumcision of your flesh, *He has made alive* together with Him [Christ], having forgiven you all trespasses" (emphasis added),
- **James 1:18:** "*Of His* [God's] *will He brought* us forth..." (emphasis added).
- **1 Peter 1:3:** "Blessed be the God and Father of our Lord Jesus Christ, who according to His abundant mercy *has begotten us again* to a living hope through the resurrection of Jesus Christ from the dead" (emphasis added).
- **Titus 3:3-7:**
  3 For we were once also foolish, disobedient, led astray, serving manifold desires and pleasures, living in malice and envy, abominable in hating one another. 4 But when

the kindness and philanthropic love of God our Savior toward men did appear, 5 not by works in righteousness that we did, but according to His mercy *He did save us*, through the bathing of regeneration and the renewing of the Holy Spirit, 6 which He poured upon us richly through Jesus Messiah our Savior, 7 that having been declared righteous by His grace we may become heirs according to the hope of life age-enduring.

(Tis. 3:3-7 NYLT; emphasis added)

The New Birth is entirely of God, by God, and for God. It is of the will of God. He made us alive. He brought us forth. He has begotten us again. He saved us. To be born again from above by the Holy Spirit means, therefore, that one is a believer, a Christian, redeemed, and converted. The term *New Birth* is often used interchangeably for these other terms in Scripture:

• **1 John 2:29:** "If you know that He [God] is righteous, you know that everyone practicing righteousness is *born of Him*" (emphasis added).
• **1 John 4:7:** "Beloved, let us love one another, for love is of God; and everyone who loves is *born of God* and knows God" (emphasis added).
• **1 John 5:18:** "We know that whoever is *born of God* does not sin; but he who has been *born of God* keeps himself, and the wicked one does not touch him" (emphasis added).

God is absolutely, decisively sovereign in salvation, as in everything else. Salvation is entirely monergistic—that God alone is the only effectual actor in our salvation. God's saving grace is not synergistic—it does not depend on our will, merit, or actions for its success. Rather, God alone acts in our redemption, and He does so effectively and decisively without any contributing effort on our part. For we not only do not deserve God's grace but, left to our own desires and devices, we are incapable of cooperating with it whatsoever.

And our New Birth starts with the effectual call of God. John 3:8 tell us that: "'The Spirit blows where He wills, and you hear His voice, but you have not known where He comes and where He goes. Thus is everyone who has been born of the Spirit'" (NYLT). Only God raises the dead—spiritual and physical. We only see the result, we do not control the process:

> 1 There has been upon me the hand of Yahweh, and He takes me forth in the Spirit of Yahweh, and places me in the midst of the valley, and it is full of bones. 2 And He causes me to pass over by them, all round about, and behold!—very many are on the face of the valley, and behold!—they are very dry.
>
> 3 And He says to me, "Son of man, do these bones live?" And I say, "O Adonai Yahweh, You have known."
>
> 4 And He says to me, "Prophesy concerning these bones, and you have said unto them: 'O dry bones, hear the word of Yahweh: 5 Thus said Adonai Yahweh to these bones: "Behold!—I am bringing into you a spirit, and you have lived, 6 and I have given on you sinews, and cause flesh to come up upon you, and covered you over with skin, and given in you a spirit, and you have lived. Then you have known that I am Yahweh."'"
>
> 7 So I have prophesied as I have been commanded, and there is a noise as I am prophesying, and behold!—a shaking, and the bones draw near, bone unto its bone. 8 And I beheld, and behold!—on them are sinews, and flesh has come up, and skin covered them over; but there is no spirit in them.
>
> 9 And He says to me, "Prophesy unto the Spirit, prophesy, son of man, and you has said unto the Spirit: 'Thus said Adonai Yahweh: "From the four winds come in, O Spirit, and breathe on these slain, and they do live."'"
> 10 And I have prophesied as He commanded me, and the Spirit comes into them, and they live, and stand on their feet—a very very great force.

(Ezekiel 37:1-10 NYLT)

In Hebrew, as with Greek, the word for *Spirit—ruach—*is the same for *breath*. Most translations render *ruach* in this passage as *breath*. However, especially given that this passage is a foreshadowing of the New Birth, I believe New Young's Literal Translation is right to translate it as *Spirit*.

We see another example of God's sovereign power in giving life in John, chapter 11:

> 38 Jesus, therefore, again snorting in Himself like an angry warhorse, comes to the tomb, and it was a cave, and a stone was lying upon it. 39 Jesus says, "Take away the stone." The sister of him who has died, Martha, says to Him, "Lord, he already stinks, for it is four days." 40 Jesus says to her, "Said I not to you, that if you may believe, you shall see the glory of God?"
>
> 41 They took away, therefore, the stone where the dead was laid, and Jesus lifted His eyes upwards and said, "Father, I thank You, that You heard Me. 42 And I knew that You always do hear Me, but because of the multitude that is standing by I said it, that they may believe that You did send Me."
>
> 43 After saying these things, with a loud voice He cried out, "Lazarus, come forth!" 44 And he who died came forth, being bound feet and hands with linen strips, and his face was bound about with a sweat-cloth. Jesus says to them, "Loose him, and suffer him to go!"
>
> (Jn. 11:38-44 NYLT)

We see, therefore, that the New Birth is owing solely to God's effectual call. As with Jesus at Lazarus' tomb, it is the call of God at the moment of New Birth that creates life. It is His divine summons by which He quickens the dead. It is the effectual grace of God's Spirit making Christ irresistibly beautiful. And it always, without fail, produces everlasting life.

As we saw in the last chapter, God's foreloving—or election or choosing—is the free act of the sovereign God in which from eternity past (Eph. 1:4, 11), for reasons only known to Himself (Matt. 11:27), and apart from any foreseen faith and/or goodness found in them (Rom. 8:29-30, 9:11; 2 Tim. 1:9), He graciously chose from among the fallen mankind a people unto salvation that they might be conformed to Christ's image (Eph. 4:13). In ages past, before the creation of the world and anyone was born or had done a single deed, whether good or bad, God sovereignly, freely, and unconditionally chose from among a humanity—blind, hardened, and dead in their sinful nature—those who would receive the Gospel and thereby be undeservedly saved for all eternity and those who would remain a rebel against God and thereby be deservedly damned for all eternity.

And those whom God has sovereignly, freely, and unconditionally foreloved unto life, He effectually calls by His Word and Spirit in His appointed and accepted timing. Election means nothing unless and until God effectually draws the elect to Christ so that, by HIs grace, they are enabled to come most freely and willingly. Predestination is set in stone from before time began, but it is not effectuated until the divine summons that creates the New Birth.

Jesus tells us that, "'He who is of God hears God's words; *therefore* you do not hear *because* you are not of God'" (Jn. 8:46-47; emphasis added). Catch the connection here—if a person is chosen and predestined by God unto salvation, they will hear God's regenerating call upon their hearts. Conversely, those who do not ultimately respond to the divine summons were never predestined to begin with. A few chapters later Jesus again reiterates this principle in telling us that, "'My sheep hear my voice, and I know them, and they follow me'" (Jn. 10:27). If one is elected to be God's sheep, he *will* hear the effectual call, know Christ as supremely valuable, and obey Christ as Lord and Shepherd. If he is not, he will not.

We see the same thing over and over again in just the Gospel of John alone:

• **John 6:37:** "All that the Father does give Me will come to Me, and him who is coming unto Me I will by no means cast without" (NYLT). Only those that the Father gives can and will come; those not so predestined cannot and will not come.

• **John 6:44:** "No one is able to come unto Me if the Father who sent Me does not irresistibly drag him; and I will raise him up in the last day" (NYLT). Only those whom the Father inescapably summons will come to Christ; those not so elect are unable to come.

• **John 6:45:** "...'Everyone therefore who heard from the Father, and learned, comes to Me'" (NYLT). Only those who first hear and respond to the divine summons come to Christ; all others eternally perish in their deafness.

• **John 6:65:** "...'Because of this I have said to you—no one is able to come unto Me if it may not have been granted him from My Father'" (NYLT). One cannot come to Christ in saving faith unless and until he has first been granted the Son by the Father in eternity past as a younger brother and co-heir.

• **John 8:42:** "...'If God were your Father, you were agaping Me, for I came forth from God, and am come, for neither have I come of Myself but He sent Me'" (NYLT). No one loves God unless and until he has first been begotten by the Father in the New Birth.

In other words, only those who have been born again can love Christ; those still dead in their trespasses and sins (Eph. 2:1) cannot love Christ to accept Him, receive Him, or treasure Him. The Father gives (Jn. 6:37, 65). The Father irresistibly drags (6:44). The Father calls and teaches (6:45).

You are not the effectual and decisive agent in your salvation; God is. You did not become a Christian because you were smart enough to figure it out. You did not become a Christian because you mustered up enough faith. You did not become a Christian because you willed it and made a decision. Remember that we are spiritually dead—blind and hardened in our deadness—who are rebels against God. We have been conceived with a sin nature of inborn, spiteful rebellion against God in which we hate

Him, loath Him, flee from Him, deny Him, and want nothing to do with Him. He has no beauty to us but only serves to show us how filthy we really are (Jn. 3:19-20). As a result, the Good News of Calvary is laughable to us in our fallen state (1 Cor. 1:18-31, 2:14).

Therefore, the only reason you became a Christian is because God first foreloved you and then summoned you. As the Apostle Paul tells us: "For it is the God who commanded light to shine out of darkness [at the moment of creation], who has shone in our hearts to give the light of the glory of God in the face of Jesus Christ" (2 Cor. 4:6). In other words, just as God created the universe out of nothing, so at the moment of His calling He creates a living, fleshly, seeing heart out of a blind, hardened, dead spiritual corpse. We see this, for instance, in the description of Lydia's conversion at Philippi, where we are told that, "The Lord opened her heart to heed the things spoken by Paul" (Acts 16:14). Notice that Lydia didn't open her own heart, but that the Lord opened her heart for her (see also Matt. 16:13-17).

Like Jesus crying out, "Come forth!" in front of Lazarus' tomb and the dead man suddenly walked out (Jn. 11:43), God's effectual and decisive call regenerates or rebirths (Jn. 3:3) a spiritually dead rebel—blind and hardened in their deadness— into a new creation (2 Cor. 5:17) in which they now love the God they once hated and hate the sin they once loved. By this saving, regenerating call of God, the dead now live, the blind now see, the deaf now hear, and the unbelieving now believe.

Penitent faith is the sole instrument by which a person is justified and pardoned of sin. We see this plainly in several places in John 3, perhaps he most famous chapter in the Bible:

• **Vs. 15:** "'in order that everyone who is *believing* in Him may not perish, but may have life age-enduring'" NYLT; emphasis added).
• **Vs. 16:** "'For God so agaped the world, that His Son—the only begotten—He gave, that everyone who is *believing* in Him may not perish but may have life age-enduring'" (NYLT; emphasis added).

• **Vs. 18:** "'He who is *believing* in Him is not judged, but he who is *not believing* has been judged already, because he has not believed in the name of the only begotten Son of God'" (NYLT; emphasis added).

• **Vs. 36:** "'He who is *believing* in the Son, has life age-enduring; and he who is *not believing* the Son, shall not see life, but the wrath of God remains upon him'" (NYLT; emphasis added).

Penitent faith is the only Scriptural means by which one is joined with Christ.   And repentance and faith are inseparable; they are two sides of the same coin called conversion.   You cannot have one without the other.   If you have faith without repentance, you do not have saving faith. You merely have head knowledge without godly sorrow for your sinfulness.   And if you have repentance without faith, you do not have saving faith. Rather, you have remorse without hope; penitence without assurance.

In fact, these two terms—repentance and faith—are used interchangeably throughout the New Testament for saving faith (Mk. 1:15; Acts 20:21, 26:19-20; 1 Thess. 1:9).   Saving faith, therefore, is a turning to Christ in belief *as* one forsakes and repents of their sins. You cannot have one without the other, or you do not have saving faith.   Genuine faith, authentic faith, saving faith is a penitent faith. And penitent faith is given by God when, by His effectual call, He births you again from above into a new creation in Christ.

And there is no room for boasting on Judgment Day that you were smart enough to figure this whole justification thing out on your own.   There is no room for pride that you mustered up enough faith to believe the Gospel message.   For Jesus has explicitly excluded boasting, telling His disciples in Matthew, chapter 16, that they only believed *because* His Father graciously enabled them to:

NATHAN W. TUCKER

¹³ And Jesus, having come to the parts of Caesarea Philippi, was asking His disciples, saying, "Who do men say that I, the Son of Man, am?"

¹⁴ And they said, "Some say John the Baptist, others Elijah, and others Jeremiah or one of the prophets."

¹⁵ He said to them, "And you—who do you say that I am?"

¹⁶ And Simon Peter answering said, "You are the Messiah, the Son of the living God."

¹⁷ And Jesus answering said to him, "Blessed are you, Simon Bar-Jonah, because flesh and blood did not reveal this to you, but My Father who is in the heavens."

(Matt. 16:13-17 NYLT)

We see this in numerous other passages in Scripture. For instance, Peter writes, "To those who have obtained like precious faith with us by the righteousness of our God and Savior Jesus Christ" (2 Pet. 1:2). Peter's audience obtained their faith. They did not earn it. They did not work for it. They did not merit it in any way. It was not of themselves but given to them. That's what obtain means. And they obtained it as a gift purchased by the righteous life and death of Jesus Christ.

Similarly, Paul writes that, "...to you it has been granted on behalf of Christ, not only to believe in Him, but also to suffer for His sake" (Phil. 1:29). You do not have to be granted something that is yours. You do not have to be granted to do something that you are already perfectly capable of doing. For instance, you would not say that I granted you breakfast this morning because I had nothing whatsoever to do with your breakfast this morning. You did. But you would say that if I had everything to do with your breakfast this morning. Similarly, God grants us faith because we have nothing to do with it.

Peter makes this explicit in his sermon recorded in Acts 3, stating that, "...faith [] comes *through* Him [Jesus Christ]" (Acts 3:16; emphasis added). Not merely faith *in* Jesus Christ, which Peter does state earlier in verse 16. But that the faith to believe in Jesus Christ comes *from* Jesus Christ. It does not come from

146

human will, effort, or contribution, but as a gracious, unearned gift from God and God alone.

We find Paul echoing this point in Ephesians 2:

> 8 For by grace you have been saved through faith. And this is not of your doing; it is the gift of God, 9 not of works, lest anyone should boast.
>
> (Eph. 2:8-9 ESV)

Verse 8 makes explicit that you are saved by grace through faith, and that this faith is not of your own doing but is the gift of God. And verse 9 tells us the reason or the purpose of this is so that no one should boast before God. Or as Paul put it in Romans, chapter 4:

> 27 Where, then, is boasting? It is excluded. On what principle? On that of observing the law? No, but on that of faith. 28 For we maintain that a man is justified by faith apart from observing the law.
>
> (Rom. 4:27-28 NIV84)

Not only is the faith side of the coin called saving faith a gracious gift of God, but so is the repentance side. For we are told by Peter that God the Father has exalted Christ "to His right hand to be a Prince and Savior, *to give repentance* to Israel and the forgiveness of sins" (Acts 5:31; emphasis added). Who gives repentance and forgiveness of sins? Christ. Repentance is impossible for man apart from the regenerating work of the Holy Spirit. God grants repentance; man does not produce it.

We see this confirmed later in Acts, where we read that, "*God has also granted* to the Gentiles repentance to life" (Acts 11:18; emphasis added). Once again—God grants repentance; man does not produce it. Finally, the Apostle Paul instructs Timothy to "in humility correct[] those who are in opposition [so that] *God perhaps will grant* them repentance so that they may know the truth" (2 Tim. 2:25; emphasis added). In other words, the point of church discipline, the point of correcting false teachers, is the hope that God will grant them repentance. Again, God grants repentance; man does not produce it.

From start to finish, therefore, the New Birth is the effective and decisive work of God and God alone.

II. Persevering Sanctification:[2]

God is a jealous God. For instance, in giving the Israelites the Ten Commandments, God gave as the Second Commandment that, "You shall not make for yourself an idol in the form of anything...You shall not bow down to them or worship them..." (Ex. 20:4-5). And the basis that He gives for this commandment is that, "I, the LORD your God, am a jealous God" (Ex. 20:5).

Several chapters later, Moses asked God to, "show me Your glory" (Ex. 33:18). "And the LORD said, 'I will cause all My goodness to pass in front of you, and I will proclaim My name — the LORD — in your presence'" (Ex. 33:19, 34:5-8). And a few verses later we read, "[10] Then the LORD said, 'I am making a covenant with you. Before all your people, I will do wonders never before done in any nation in all the world. The people you live among will see how awesome is the work that I, the LORD, will do for you. [11] Obey what I command you today...[14] Do not worship any other god, for the LORD, whose name is Jealous, is a jealous God'" (Ex. 34:10-11a, 14; see also Deut. 5:8-9).

Over and over in Scripture God makes clear that He is jealous for His name, for His character, for His glory (see generally Ps. 78:58, 79:5; Ezek. 38:19; Joel 2:18; Nahum 1:2; Zeph. 1:18, 3:8; Zech. 1:14, 8:2; 1 Cor. 10:22; Jas. 4:5). Moses warns the

---

[2] At the moment of the New Birth, several steps in the *order salutis* (Latin for *order of salvation*, which refers to the stages of salvation) occur near simultaneously—first effectual calling, then regeneration/New Birth, which produces penitent faith, which results in both justification and adoption/assurance, which leads inevitably to progressive sanctification. Though the rest of this chapter will only address sanctification, those readers who desire further study are highly encouraged to meditate deeply upon *Redemption Accomplished and Applied* by John Murray.

Israelites that, "the LORD your God is a consuming fire, a jealous God" (Deut. 4:24) for the reputation of His holy name (Ezek. 39:25). In the book of Numbers, we read that God praises the future high priest Phinehas because, "'he was as zealous as I am for My honor among [the Israelites]" (Num. 25:11). Out of jealousy for the glories of His Name, God creates, disciples, and yet preserves His people (Deut. 6:13-15, 29:18-21, 32:15-16, 18-21a; Josh. 24:19-20; 1 Kings 14:22; Ezek. 8:3-5, 23:18-19a, 25, 29-30, 26:22, 26, 32, 38, 41-42, 26:5-7, 39:25).

Salvation, from start to finish, is of God, by God, and for God. For instance, God tells us He does this, however, not "'for your sake, declares the Sovereign LORD. [Rather,] [b]e ashamed and disgraced for your conduct...!'" (Ezek. 36:32). Instead, He tells us, "'For My own sake, for My own sake, I do this. For how can I let Myself be defamed? I will not yield My glory to another.'" (Is. 48:11). Therefore, the Bible tells us that, "He predestined us for adoption as sons through Jesus Christ, according to the purpose of His will, *for the praise of the glory of His grace*" (Eph. 1:5–6; emphasis added). Elsewhere God declares, "Thus says the LORD God, It is not for your sake, O house of Israel, that I [] act, *but for the sake of My holy name*...And I will vindicate the holiness of My great name ...and the nations will know that I am the LORD" (Ezek. 36:22–23, 32; emphasis added).

And yet in another place He tells us that, "I am He who blots out your transgressions for My own sake, and I will not remember your sins" (Isaiah 43:25). In the Bible God tells us that, "I will sanctify My great name, which has been profaned among the nations, which you have profaned among in their midst, and the nations shall know that I am Yahweh, Adonai Yahweh, when I am hallowed in you before their eyes" (Is. 29:23, 43:7; Ezek. 36:23; Rom. 9:23; Eph 2:12; 1 Pet. 2:9, 12).

Therefore, in order to magnify His name in the demonstration of His moral excellencies, the Bible declares to us that, "God demonstrates His own love for us in this: While we were still sinners, Christ died for us!" (Rom. 5:8). Elsewhere God tells us that—for the sake of the manifestation of His glory—"[He] so loved the world that He gave His one and only Son"—who was "stricken by God, smitten by Him, and afflicted...it was the LORD's will to crush [Christ] and cause Him to suffer [in order to] make[] His life a guilt offering" (Is. 53:4, 10)—"so that whosoever trusts in Him shall not perish but have eternal life!" (Jn. 3:16).

Therefore, the Bible tells us that, "Jesus...for the joy that was set before Him, endured the cross, despising the shame, and has sat down at the right hand of the throne of God" (Heb. 12:2). And what was the joy that was set before Him? His exaltation in the manifestation of HIs glory displayed in His redeemed and sanctified Bride (Rev. 19:6-9, 21:9). Throughout the Old Testament, for instance, God regularly refers to Himself as a bridegroom. In Isaiah, for example, God tells us that, "'Your Maker is your husband—the LORD Almighty is His name. The Holy One of Israel is your Redeemer; He is called the God of all the earth'" (Is. 54:5). Several chapters later God tells us that, "'as a bridegroom rejoices over His bride, so will your God rejoice over you!'" (Is. 62:5a).

And throughout the Gospels Jesus regularly described Himself as "the bridegroom" who temporarily leaves earth (Matt. 9:15; Mk. 2:19–20; Lk. 5:34–35), and whose return is delayed (Matt, 25:1–10). The Apostle Paul tells us that, "I am jealous for you with a godly jealously, for I have promised you to one Husband, that I might present you as a pure virgin to Christ" (1 Cor. 11:2). And in Ephesians 5 Paul exhorts:

> 25 Husbands, love your wives, just as Christ also loved the church and gave Himself for her, 26 that He might sanctify and cleanse her with the washing of water by the word, 27 that He might present her to Himself a glorious church, not having spot or wrinkle or any such thing, but that she should be holy and without blemish.
>
> (Eph. 5:25-27)

So Christ loves the worldwide body of believers as His Bride whom He has purchased by His blood. But notice in Ephesians 5 that Paul continues to build upon this bride analogy. Quoting Genesis 2:24, Paul writes that a marriage union is formed when "a man shall leave his father and mother and be joined with his wife, and the two shall become one flesh" (Eph. 5:31). In calling this union a "great mystery" (vs. 32), Paul states that this is what has happened between Christ and His Bride—that we have become "members of His body, of His flesh and of His bones" (vs. 30). Therefore, because we are His body (1 Cor. 12:27; Eph. 1:22-23, 5:22; Col. 1:18, 24)—flesh of His flesh and bone of His bone— He "nourishes and cherishes [us]" (Eph. 5:29) whom He "gave Himself for" (vs. 25).

And God has commanded His Bride to be holy—*set apart, consecrated, made sacred*—as He is holy in that all their affections, thoughts, and actions should be in beautiful harmony with His infinite worth:

> 33 And having heard, the multitudes were astonished at His teaching. 34 And the Pharisees, having heard that He silenced the Sadducees, were gathered together unto Him. 35 And one of them, a lawyer, questioned, tempting Him, and saying, 36 "Teacher, which is the great command in the Law?" 37 And Jesus said to him, "'You shall agape the LORD your God with all your heart, and with all your soul, and with all your understanding.' 38 This is a first and great command. 39 And the second is like to it, 'You shall agape your neighbor as yourself.' 40 On these two commands hang all the law and the prophets."
>
> (Matt. 22:33-40 NYLT)

Holiness is savoring and trusting the beautifies of God in the person of Christ as the supremely and infinitely satisfyingly joyous treasure that is far more valuable than anything life can give or death can take away (Matt. 13:44; Jn. 4:10, 13-14, 7:37-39; Phil. 1:20-21, 3:7-16; Heb. 11:25-26). The opposite of holiness is sin—disdaining God as being less beautiful than what He is (Jer. 2:10-13). For the essence of sin is falling short of, or lacking, the glory of God by not treating it for what it really is—the most valuable reality and the most joyously satisfying treasure in the universe (Rom. 1:23, 2:23, 3:23).

Consequently, the grand imperative of the sanctified life of the regenerate is to be holy as God is holy (Lev. 11:44-45, 19:2, 20:7, 22:32). As the Apostle Peter exhorts us in his first epistle:

> 13 Therefore, having girded up the loins of your mind, being sober-minded, hope perfectly upon the grace that is being brought to you in the revelation of Jesus Messiah; 14 as obedient children, not fashioning yourselves to the former desires as in your ignorance, 15 but according as He who did call you is holy, you also become holy in all behavior, 16 because it has been written, "Become holy, because I am holy!"
>
> (1 Pet. 1:13-16 NYLT)

The author of Hebrews likewise commands us to "earnestly pursue peace with all, and holiness" (Heb. 12:14 NYLT). Why? For, "apart from which no one shall see the Lord." Failure, therefore, to be holy results in dire consequences—eternal damnation separated from God. Either you will be separated *unto* God in this life, or you will be separated *from* God in the next life. You can have either one or the other, but not both.

Our sanctification is the very basis (or reason, purpose, end) of our election: "according as He [God the Father] *did choose* us in Him [God the Son] before the foundation of the world—*for* our being holy and unblemished before Him in agape" (Eph. 1:4 NYLT emphasis added). We see this echoed in Romans, chapter 8: "Because whom He did foreknow, He also *predestined* to be conformed to the image of His Son, that He might be the firstborn among many brethren" (Rom. 8:29 NYLT emphasis added).

And Jesus Christ died in order to effectuate this predestined purpose:

> 21 And you—being once alienated, and enemies in the mind and in the evil works—yet now He reconciled 22 in

the body of His flesh through death, *to* present you holy and unblemished and unblameable before Himself.

(Col. 1:22 NYLT; emphasis added)

Or as the Apostle Paul explains elsewhere:

25 Husbands, agape your own wives, as also the Messiah agaped the assembly and gave Himself for her, 26 that He might sanctify her, having cleansed her with the bathing of the water by the word,27 that He might present her to Himself an assembly in glory, not having spot or wrinkle or any of such things, but that she may be holy and unblemished.

(Eph. 5:25-27 NYLT)

Look at the four reasons Paul gives for why Christ died for His Bride:

- **Verse 26:** That He might sanctify her.
- **Verse 27:** That He might present her as glorious.
- **Verse 27:** That she might not have any spot or wrinkle or any such thing.
- **Verse 27:** That she might be holy and without blemish.

So we have seen that holiness is essential; that it is our predestinated goal. To that end, therefore, God has given us the Spirit of holiness (Rom. 1:4) and called us to be holy ones (vs. 7), sanctifying us wholly unto Himself (Num. 8:16; Lk. 1:75) from the fleshly lusts which war against the soul, in order that we should be:

9 ...a choice offspring, a royal priesthood, a holy people group, a people acquired, that you might fully herald the excellences of Him who called you out of darkness into His marvelous light; 10 who were once not a people, and now are the people of God, who had not found mercy, and now have found mercy.

(1 Pet. 2:9-10 NYLT; see also Num. 8:16; Is. 29:23,
43:17; Ezek. 36:23; Rom. 9:23; Eph. 1:6, 2:12)

The following are but four reasons why the elect will ultimately
persevere in this race—this pursuit—of holiness:[3]

A. Being What We Are—Holy:

First, because God—out of jealously for the fame of His Name
—created a Bride for His Son, He has sovereignly and decisively
sanctified her by forensically justifying His Bride and imputing to
His saints His righteousness.   This is the basis of our
sanctification, for the battle for sanctification is being what we
truly already are in Christ—holy. There is no other basis for our
victory in the quest for godliness, for all other ground is sinking
sand—a quagmire of self-effort, self-reliance, and self-worship
which, ultimately, leads to self-defeat resulting in self-loathing.

We see the principle of "already but not yet" in Paul's salutation
of his first epistle to the Corinthians as follows:

> To the assembly of God that is in Corinth, to those having
> been sanctified in Messiah Jesus, called holy ones, with
> all those calling upon the name of our Lord Jesus
> Messiah in every place, both theirs and ours.
>
> (1 Cor. 1:2 NYLT)

Notice how the Apostle describes the Corinthian church—as
"those having been sanctified...called   holy ones" (or saints).
They have, past tense, been sanctified and, therefore, are called
holy ones.   There are few, if any, pastors who would dare risk
public scorn and ridicule as hypocrites by addressing their
churches as saints who have already been sanctified. But that is
precisely what all Christians in every place at all times are in
Christ.

---

[3] Please refer to Appendix D for a more thorough exposition of
those verses that appear to deny the perseverance of the saints.

Forensically—in a legal sense—God has already declared us at the moment of justification to be holy and righteous, pure and spotless, in the Second Adam Jesus Christ. We see this clearly in Romans, chapter 5, verses 12-19:

(1) by the *very same* obedience of the Second Adam Jesus Christ, all who are found in Him are made—or imputed—to have committed the same obedience as well (vs. 19); and therefore

(2) all who are found in Christ are imputed with His righteousness (vs. 19) and consequently declared forensically justified without fear of condemnation (vs. 16, 18; see also Rom. 8:1); which

(3) results in their eternal life (vs. 15, 17; see also 1 Cor. 15:45-49).

The regenerate cannot become more righteous than we are right now because our righteousness is not our own but Christ's, who is infinitely and perfectly righteous. We cannot become less righteous than we are right now because, again, our righteousness is not our own but Christ's, who is infinitely and perfectly righteous. Therefore we cannot become any more or less justified, or saved, than we are right now because our righteousness is not our own but Christ's, who is infinitely and perfectly righteous. And consequently we cannot become any more or less loved by God than we are right now because our righteousness is not our own but Christ's, who is infinitely and perfectly righteous.

Those planted into Christ (Jn. 15:1-8; Rom. 6:5 (original Greek)) by faith at the moment of the New Birth have been freed from the presence and power of sin, for look at how the Apostle Paul's describes the New Birth in Romans:

6 6 This knowing, that our old man was crucified with Him [Messiah], so that the body of sin may be rendered inoperative, that no longer are we slaving under sin— 7 for he who has died has been set free from sin!...[11] So you also, reckon yourselves to be dead indeed to sin, and living to God in Jesus Messiah our Lord....[14] For sin shall not have lordship over you, for you are not under law but under grace...[17] But thanks be to God that, though you were slaves of sin, yet you were obedient from the heart to the form of teaching to which you were delivered up to. [18] And having been freed from sin, you became slaves to righteousness!...[20] For when you were slaves of sin, you were free from righteousness. [21] What fruit, therefore, were you having then in the things of which you are now ashamed? For the end of those is death. [22] But now, having been freed from sin, and having become slaves to God, you have your fruit— to sanctification, to the end—life age-enduring!

8 [2] For the law of the Spirit of life in Messiah Jesus did set me free from the law of sin and death!

(Rom. 6:6-7, 11, 14, 17-18, 20, 22, 8:2 NYLT)

Look at all the past-tense realities of the Christian life detailed in this passage:

- **Verse 6:** Our old man *was* crucified with Christ!
- **Verse 6:** We are *no longer* slaving under sin!
- **Verse 7:** We *have died* with Christ!
- **Verse 18:** We *have been freed* from sin and *have already become slaves* of righteousness!
- **Verse 22:** We *have been freed* from sin and *have already become* slaves of God!
- **Verse 8:2:** We *have already been set free* from the law of sinning and death!

This is not simply the normal Christian life. Nor is this the exceptional Christian life of a "saint." Rather, this is the *only* Christian life. At the moment of New Birth one has become a new creation (2 Cor. 5:17) in which Christ is formed in him (Gal. 4:19; Col. 1:27b-28). Those in Christ, therefore, have:

• Already (past-tense) clothed themselves with Christ (Gal. 3:27).
• Already (past-tense) clothed themselves with the new man (Col. 3:10).
• Already (past-tense) stripped off the old man (Col. 3:9).
• Already (past-tense) crucified the flesh with its passions and desires (Gal. 5:24).

But Scripture is equally clear that while we are already *positionally* holy in Christ, we must strive to become holy in *practice*:

• We are commanded to keep clothing ourselves with Christ (Rom. 13:14).
• We are commanded to keep clothing ourselves with the new man (Eph. 4:24).
• We are commanded to keep putting off the old man (Eph. 4:22).
• We are commanded to put to death our fleshly members which are of the world (Col. 3:5).

This is why the Apostle Paul exhorts:

> [11] So you also, reckon yourselves to be dead indeed to sin, and living to God in Jesus Messiah our Lord. [12] Let not, therefore, sin reign in your mortal body, to obey it in its desires. [13] Neither present your members as weapons of unrighteousness to sin, but rather present yourselves to God as living out of the dead, and your members as weapons of righteousness to God. [14] For sin shall not have lordship over you, for you are not under law but under grace.
>
> (Rom. 6:11-14 NYLT)

Catch the imperative of verse 11: we are to *reckon* ourselves to be what he told us in verses 6 and 7 we already are—dead with Christ to sin. Seeing the two verses back-to-back helps make the connection impossible to miss: "This *knowing*, that our old man was crucified with Him" (vs. 6; emphasis added)..."so you also *reckon* yourselves to be dead indeed to sin, and living to God in Jesus Messiah our Lord" (vs. 11; emphasis added). In other words, we are to daily appropriate by faith—to present in full confidence the title dead—of what we already are—alive in Christ and dead to sin. Our death is no less real, no less effectual, no less potent that Christ's death, for when He died on the hill called Calvary, we died just as definitively in Him. It is finished, and therefore we are to act out by faith in God's future grace the miracle of what we are in the Second Adam.

And having reckoned what we know, the Apostle Paul then commands the regenerate in Romans 6 to *fight*:

- **Verse 12**: Stop sin from reigning.
- **Verse 12:** Resist sin's desires.
- **Verse 13:** Present yourselves to God as spiritually alive from the deadness of sin.
- **Verse 13:**   Present your members as weapons of righteousness to God rather than weapons of unrighteousness to the slave master sin.
- **Verse 14:** Fight for the lordship of grace rather than sin over your heart.

He goes on to conclude two chapters later, "for if according to the flesh you do live, you are about to die; but if by the Spirit you put to death the deeds of the body, you shall live" (Rom. 8;13 NYLT). This struggle to be what we already are is a matter of everlasting life and death to the Born Again man. This is no small battle. This is not an optional war. The war is already upon us. We were born again into it. And, unless we fight it, we shall perish eternally.

The path towards sanctification, therefore, is one of continual warfare and vigilance—constantly fighting to be what we already are in Christ. We are to resist, in striving against sin, to the point of shedding our own blood (Heb. 12: 4) lest, after we have testified to others of the Good News of the Gospel of Jesus

Messiah, we should fail at the Judgment Seat to prove ourselves to be, in fact, born again (1 Cor. 9:27).

B. Saving Faith Sanctifies:

Secondly, because God—out of jealously for the fame of His Name—created a Bride for His Son, He not only has sovereignly and decisively given her the gift of penitent saving faith, but such penitent saving faith will persevere in sanctification unto death. Saving faith is when one sees God as holy and righteous as He truly is, himself as sinful and vile as he truly is, and Christ's blood and righteousness as precious and beautiful as it truly is.   Like the angels before the throne of God, he cries out, "Holy, Holy, Holy is Yahweh Sabaoth!" (Is. 6:3 NYLT).   Like Isaiah the prophet who saw such a vision, he cries out, "Woe is me, for I am a man with an unclean heart!" (Is. 6:5).   And like the crowds at Pentecost, he cries out, "What must I do to be saved?!" (Acts 2:37). And God points him to the cross and tells him to look unto Jesus as the initiator and consummator of his faith (Heb. 12:2).

Saving faith, therefore, naturally and necessarily also sanctifies for three reasons. First, saving faith is a coming to and receiving the Lord Christ as one's supreme treasure (Matt. 13:44-46; Phil. 3:7-9), one' supreme love (1 Cor. 16:22); one's supreme delight (1 Pet. 1:8); and one's supreme satisfaction (Jn. 4:14, 6:35, 51, 7:37-38). And therefore saving faith—in embracing the superior pleasure of Christ—kills sin.   We see this clearly in Hebrews, chapter 11:

> [24] By faith Moses, having become great, refused to be called a son of the daughter of Pharaoh, [25] having chosen rather to be afflicted with the people of God than to have sin's pleasure for a season,[26] having reckoned the reproach of the Messiah greater wealth than the treasures in Egypt, for he was fixed upon the recompense of reward.
>
> (Heb. 11:24-26 NYLT)

Verse 26 tells us that Moses valued Christ more than all the riches of Egypt, and, therefore, verse 25 tells us that he rejected the fleeting pleasures of sin. A Christian doesn't gain victory over sin by simply saying "no" to it. The allure of sin is the pleasure it appears to offer. No one ever sins out of duty. Rather, we sin because we think it will bring us greater happiness than not sinning. We lie, cheat, steal, gossip, gamble, fornicate, complain, and much more because we think it will make us happy.

Simply denying ourselves the happiness of sin sanctifies no one. Rather, as Thomas Chalmers put it, only "the expulsive power of a new affection" will sanctify a believer. Saving faith sees Christ as vastly superior to any other affection, and it is on the basis of that "expulsive power" that a born-again man loses his desire for sin. Saving faith embraces Christ as infinitely more satisfying than all the fleeting happiness that an eternity of sin could bring him. As Jim Elliot famously stated, "He is no full who gives up what he cannot keep to gain what he cannot lose." A born-again believer has counted the cost, and found Christ far superior to anything this side of eternity (Matt. 10:32-39, 26:24-26; Lk. 14:25-33).

In other words, a born-again man—out of joy—forsakes all else for the sake of Christ. He abandons job, reputation, freedom, family, friends, financial security, nation, tribe, and traditions because of the superior pleasure of Christ. He flees pride, envy, covetousness, anger, bitterness, lust, and all other forms of sin for the superior pleasure of Christ. Justification is by faith alone, but the faith the justifies is never alone. The same faith that justifies also sanctifies because it receives as one's superior treasure all that God is in Christ for them in order to make much of God. Saving faith loves God supremely and others sacrificially.

Faith that still loves sin cannot be saving faith. Therefore, the evidence that you once repented and believed unto salvation is that you continue to repent and believe. The evidence that you once loved God is that you continue to love God. The evidence that you once hated your sin (Rom. 6-8; 1 Jn.) is that you continue to hate your sin. The evidence that you once "tasted and s[aw] that the LORD is good" (Ps. 24:8; see also 1 Pet. 2:3) is that you continue to "taste and see that the LORD is good." The evidence that you once found Christ irresistibly beautiful (2 Cor. 3:8, 4:4, 6) is that you continue to find Him irresistibly beautiful. The evidence that you once found in God the all-satisfying fount for your soul's thirst (Matt. 13:45-46; Jn. 4:10-14; 6:27-58; 7:7:37-39; Phil. 3:7-16) is that you continue to find Him to be the all-satisfying fount for your soul's thirst.

Secondly, saving faith naturally and necessarily also sanctifies because it embraces all of Christ in all His roles. It doesn't accept Him as Savior without accepting Him as Lord (Rom. 10:9; 1 Jn. 3:23). Saving faith does not divide Christ but accepts Him as Creator (Jn. 1:1-3), Sustainer (Col. 1:17; Heb. 1:3), Savior (Lk. 2:11), Teacher (Jn. 13:13), Guide (Acts 16:7), Comforter (Jn. 14:18, 27; 2 Cor. 1:5)), Helper (Phil. 1:19); Friend (Jn. 15:13-15); Advocate (1 Jn. 2:1); Protector (2 Thess. 3:3); and Lord (Rom. 10:9).

Saving faith sanctifies, therefore, because obedience is the natural and necessary result of loving all of Him (Jn. 14:15, 21, 23-24) with the love that He first loved us (Rom. 5:5, 8; 1 Jn. 4:7-10, 5:1-5). Saving faith sanctifies because it purposefully seizes—by receiving through grace—in persistent, resilient, and contending penitent trust all that God in Christ is for us. It is experiencing the exchanged life ("not I, but Christ" (Gal. 2:20, 6:14; Phil. 1:21)) of abiding in the Vine so that one's joy, pleasure, delight, desire, affection, enjoyment, jubilation, glory, boast, hope, and peace are so extravagantly and supremely grounded, secured, satisfied, dependent, fulfilled, and completed in Christ.

And this saving satisfaction in Christ leads to being seized, gripped, mastered, possessed, and controlled by the Spirit-infused passionate, exclusive, intentional, disciplined, relational, and experimental: (a) worship, adoration, awe, and praise of; and (b) meditating and marinating upon; and (c) communion and intimacy with God.

This hedonistic pursuit of all of Christ results in a continually, daily renewed, transformed, and sanctified Christ-like mind that compelling bursts into a continuously and ever-increasing overflowing:

161

(a) surrendered, consecrated, yielded, obedient, rejoicing in trials and tribulations, and fruit-bearing agape for God; and

(b) radical, sacrificial, self-emptying, humble, patient, forgiving, keeping no record of wrong, returning love for evil, blessing those who prosecute me, rejoicing in prosecution, and earnestly evangelistic agape for others.

And the heartfelt desire of such a joy-drenched Christian hedonist is to reproduce disciples of the same in order that God would be glorified in, by, and through all.

The third and final reason that saving faith naturally and necessarily sanctifies is that it does not merely trust Christ for salvation and stop there. No! Saving faith embraces all of God's promises to us based on that salvation. It trusts not only that we are forgiven and declared righteous through Christ, but goes even further and trusts, based on that reconciliation with God, all His other promises to us contained in Scripture (1 Cor. 1:20; 2 Cor. 3:21-23; 2 Pet. 1:2-4). Saving faith, therefore, claims— substantiates, foretastes, realizes—all the promises of God in Christ for future grace in persevering sanctification in the full expectation that they will be fulfilled. In short, saving faith sanctifies because it trusts God to keep him (1 Pet. 1:5).

C. Grafted with Imperishable Seed into the Good Tree Christ:

Third, because God—out of jealously for the fame of His Name —created a Bride for His Son, He has sovereignly and decisively resurrected Her to eternal life with imperishable Seed. For the Apostle Peter tells us that we have "been born again, not of perishable seed, but of imperishable" (1 Pet. 1:23 ESV)—"the precious blood of Christ, like that of a lamb without blemish or spot" (vs. 19 ESV).

And therefore we have passed from death to life, for Jesus tells us that "'Most assuredly I say to you, he who hears My word and believes in Him who sent Me *has* everlasting life, and shall not come into judgment, but *has passed* from death to life!'" (Jn. 5:24;

emphasis added). The Born Again man has *already* passed from death to life, from eternal damnation to eternal resurrection. The Apostle John echoes this in his first epistle, "We know that we *have* passed from death to life..." (1 Jn. 3:14; emphasis added). Have, past-tense, passed from death to life. "These things I have written to you who believe in the name of the Son of God, that you may know that you *have* eternal life..." (1 Jn. 5:24; emphasis added). Have, past-tense, already possessed eternal life. We have died to spiritual death, and our life is now "hidden with Christ in God" (Col. 3:3). Because Christ, "who is our life," can never die, we can never again die spiritually and *will* therefore "appear with Him in glory" at His coming (vs. 4).

Imperishable Seed will always result in eternal life. Always. Imperishable Seed never produces perishable life. It is a spiritual impossibility. And along the way it will result in branches that bear much fruit. For we are thereby grafted into the Good Tree of Jesus Christ—"'I am the vine, you are the branches. He who abides in Me, and I in him, bears much fruit; for without Me you can do nothing'" (Jn. 15:5). Therefore we will know who are His disciples by their fruit (vs. 8):

> 16 "From their fruits you shall know them. Do men gather from thorns grapes, or from thistles figs? 17 So every good tree yields good fruits, but the bad tree yields evil fruits. 18 A good tree is not able to yield evil fruits, nor a bad tree to yield good fruits. 19 Every tree not yielding good fruit is cut down and is cast into fire. 20 Therefore from their fruits you shall know them.
>
> (Matt. 7:16-20 NYLT)

Twice the Lord Christ tells us that by our fruit we shall be known (vs. 16, 20). Why? Because just as it is impossible for a bad tree to bear good fruit, so it is impossible for a good tree to bear evil fruit (vs. 18). It is a genetic impossibility both in the natural world and in the spiritual world. And every bad tree, evidenced by its evil fruit, will be cast into hell fire (vs. 19). A few chapters later in the same gospel Jesus warns:

33 "Either make the tree good and its fruit good, or make the tree bad and its fruit bad; for from the fruit the tree is known. 34 Brood of vipers! How are you able, being evil, to speak good things? For out of the abundance of the heart the mouth speaks. 35 The good man out of the good treasure of the heart puts forth good things, and the evil man out of the evil treasure puts forth evil things. 36 And I say to you, that every idle word that men may speak, they shall give a word for it in the day of judgment. 37 For from your words you shalt be declared righteous, and from your words you shalt be declared unrighteous."

(Matt. 12:33-37 NYLT)

Out of the abundance of the heart a person thinks, acts, and says. A believer born again into eternal life by imperishable Seed will, out of the goodness of his regenerated heart, bring forth good; but an unregenerate man, out of the evil of his dead, hardened, and blind heart, brings forth evil. This is a law of spiritual reality just as real, firm, and unchangeable as the laws of gravity or thermodynamics in the physical realm.

As we have already seen, sanctification is a blood-bought guarantee purchased on the cross of Calvary, for look at all the "I will's" God pledges to perform in the book of Ezekiel when He promised the New Birth:

25 Then *I will* sprinkle clean water on you, and you shall be clean; *I will* cleanse you from all your filthiness and from all your idols. 26 *I will* give you a new heart and put a new spirit within you; *I will* take the heart of stone out of your flesh and give you a heart of flesh. 27 *I will* put My Spirit within you and [*I will*] cause you to walk in My statutes, and you will keep My judgments and do them. 28 Then you shall dwell in the land that I gave to your fathers; you shall be My people, and *I will be* your God. 29 *I will* deliver you from all your uncleannesses.

(Ezek. 36:25-29a; emphasis added)

Sanctification isn't optional. It isn't a wishful daydream. It *shall* be accomplished, because God is jealous for the fame of His Name. Therefore, because God is neither a liar nor impotent, there can be no such thing as a "carnal Christian"—an individual who professes faith in Jesus Christ, lives in sin as the world lives, but still goes to heaven. It is a spiritual impossibility for such a person to have been genuinely born again by the Spirit into Christ, for God will not—out of jealousy for the glory of His name —beget a child only to have him defame it (Heb. 6:10).

There is no such thing as evolution in the New Birth. There are no missing links. One does not evolve from a sinner into a saint; from death to life; from rebel to love-slave; from bad tree to good tree. There is no such thing as a half-baked Christian. Of a carnal Christian still mired in a lifestyle of sin. For there are only two kinds of people in the world: the unregenerate who are dead *in* their sins and the regenerate who are dead *to* their sins (Rom. 6:1-7, 11, 7:1-6).

You cannot be simultaneously both Christlike and unChristlike, holy and unholy, pure and impure, dead and alive, slave and free, a new creation and an old creation, a new man and an old man (Jas. 3:11-12). The Bible declares that, "[n]o one can serve two masters, for either he will hate the one and love the other, or else he will be loyal to one and despise the other. You cannot serve God and [yourself]" (Matt. 6:24).

Or, to put it another way, you cannot be a branch on two trees —you must either belong to the Good Tree of Christ or the Bad Tree of Adam (Matt. 7:16-18, 12:33; Jas. 3:12). Similarly, the Bible tells us that fresh water and salt water cannot flow from the same spring—fresh water only comes from a fresh water spring and salt water only comes from a salt water spring (Jas. 3:11-12). Finally, Jesus tells us that a heart cannot produce both good and bad things, but only one or the other (Matt. 12:34b-35).

The Bible declares that the law of the Spirit of life has emancipated us from the law of sinning (Rom. 8:2). The law of sinning—our sin nature—is like the law of gravity in that it occurs without fail. That is, it did in the old man of sinful flesh imputed from the First Man Adam. But the law of the Spirit of life has severed or suspended (i.e., annulled) that law of sinning, much like the law of gravity is suspended by the law of weightlessness (zero G-force). Weightlessness does not mean the absence of weight, but the absence of stress or force acting upon the weight.

Similarly, the law of sinning is still there, of course, but it has been rendered inoperative over the new man found in the Second Adam Jesus Christ. Those found in Christ has been emancipated form sinning! The Bible does not teach sinless perfection. The Bible does not teach that it is impossible for a believer to sin (1 Jn. 1:8, 10), but it does teach that it is impossible for the believer to continue to sin willfully. As Pastor Leonard Ravenhill loved to say, "The greatest miracle that God can do today is to take an unholy man out of an unholy world and make him holy, then put him back into that unholy world and keep him holy in it."

A believer may still sin impulsively, instinctively, without premeditation, or in ignorance (1 Jn. 1:8), though he always repents (1 Jn. 1:9). A believer may even commit a willful sin, an unspeakable sin even, (2 Sam. 11:1-27; 1 Cor. 5:1-13), though he always repents (2 Sam. 12:1-23; 2 Cor. 2:3-11). But a believer *cannot* continue in a lifestyle of deliberate sinning. It is impossible. Rather, we have been planted with Christ (Rom. 6:5); He is our vine, we are the branches (Jn. 15:5). Apart from Him we can do nothing (Jn. 15:5), but with His life, grace, and victory flowing through us like sap we bear much fruit (Jn. 15:2, 4-5) to holiness (Rom. 6:22).

Our First Man Adam was our federal head who was defeated, and consequently his progeny inherited his guilt and corrupt nature. But Christ Jesus, our Second Adam, has become our federal head who conquered the law of sinning and death and as a result our victory is secure in Him. For the Bible tells us that, "having stripped the principalities and the authorities, he [Messiah] made a public spectacle of them, leading them as His prisoner in triumphal procession" (Col. 2:15 NYLT)!

This life in Christ is not always in a straight, uphill line towards perfection. Far from it. The longer one is a believer, the more they see themselves as a sinner and the more precious Christ's

THE FREE WILL OF GOD

blood and righteousness become. But like a jealous husband, God's jealous love and grace will surround you, nourish you, protect you, and always preserve you as His own. For the sake of His name, for the sake of His praise, for the sake of His glory, for His own sake, you *will* bear His fruit. You *will* bear His aroma to the world around you. You *have been* freed from the law of sinning and death (Rom. 8:2), and therefore you *cannot continue sinning* or you are not His (1 Jn. 3:7-9)!

There is no such thing as a "carnal Christian;" you are either carnal or you are a Christian. "Do not be deceived, God is not mocked" (Gal. 6:7). Therefore the Bible warns you that:

> 26 For we, if willfully sinning after the receiving the full knowledge of the truth, there remains no more a sacrifice for sins, 27 but a certain terrifying anticipation of judgment and fiery zeal about to devour the opposers. 28 Anyone who did set aside the law of Moses dies without mercies by two or three witnesses. 29 Of how much worse punishment shall he be counted worthy who trampled on the Son of God, and counted as a common thing the blood of the covenant by which he was sanctified, and insulted the Spirit of grace? 30 For we have known Him who is saying, "Vengeance is Mine, I will recompense," says the Lord. And again, "The LORD shall judge His people.'" 31 Fearful is the falling into the hands of the living God.
>
> (Heb. 10:26-31 NYLT)

D. God Disciplines, Not Divorces, His Bride:

Fourth, because God—out of jealously for the fame of His Name—created a Bride for His Son, He has sovereignly and decisively betrothed His Bride to Himself. Look again at our union with Christ described in the fifth chapter of Ephesians:

> 28 So husbands ought to love their own wives as their own bodies; he who loves his wife loves himself. 29 For

no one ever hated his own flesh, but nourishes and cherishes it, just as the Lord does the church. 30 For we are members of His body, of His flesh and of His bones. 31 "For this reason a man shall leave his father and mother and be joined to his wife, and the two shall become one flesh." 32 This is a great mystery, but I speak concerning Christ and the church. 33 Nevertheless let each one of you in particular so love his own wife as himself, and let the wife see that she respects her husband.

(Eph. 5:28-33)

"We are members of His body, of His flesh and of His bones" (vs. 30). This is "great mystery"—that we have become one flesh with Christ (vs. 31). The Greek word translated in verse 31 by the NKJV as *joined to* is *proskollao*, which literally means *towards* (pros) and *to glue* (kollao). We are cleaved to Christ, joined to Him, glued to Him with a permanent adhesive, for "what God has joined together" (Matt. 19:6) is not divorceable.[4] The Greek word here for *joined together* is *suzeugnumi*, which literally means *together* (syn) and *yoked* (zeugas). As with a marriage union, we are yoked together with Christ in an indissoluble body.

God has loved His Bride (Ezek. 16:1-4; Eph. 5:25-33) "'with an everlasting love. Therefore with lovingkindness I have drawn you'" (Jer. 31:3). We have been loved with an eternal love (Eph. 1:4), led with "cords of kindness, with the bands of love" (Hosea 11:4). He caused us to live (Ezek. 16:6) and grow (vs. 7), and He "spread My wing over you and covered your nakedness. Yes, I swore an oath to you and entered into a covenant" (vs. 8; see also Ruth 3:8). And He is making a name for Himself among the nations through our holiness, because of our "'beauty, for it was

---

[4] It is true that in Jeremiah God states that He gave Israel a certificate of divorce (3:8). But the remainder of the chapter promises the restoration of Israel because God is Her Husband (vs. 14).

perfect through My splendor which I had bestowed on you,' says the LORD God" (vs. 14).

God never divorces His Bride. He certainly disciplines her, but He never divorces her. Look with me at the story of Hosea the prophet. Yahweh God told him to take for himself "a wife of harlotry" as an illustration of His relationship with Israel. So Hosea married Gomer (Hosea 1:2-3), and she bore Hosea three children. God instructed him to name the middle child, a daughter, Lo-Ruhamah—which means *no mercy*—"For I will no longer have mercy on the house of Israel" (vs. 6). And God commanded him to name the youngest child, a son, Lo-Ammi—which means *no people*—"For you are not My people, and I will not be your God (vs. 9)"

And just as Gomer committed adultery with lover after lover (3:1), so Israel "went after her lovers; but Me she forgot" (2:13). Therefore, because Israel "has played the harlot" and "behaved shamefully" (2:5), Yahweh God declares that, "she is not My Wife, nor am I her Husband!" (2:2; see also Jer. 3:8). And God vows that He "will punish her" (2:13) and that "no one shall deliver her from My hand" (2:10).

And yet, when God commanded Hosea to redeem back his adulteress wife who was being auctioned off as a slave by her lovers, he "bought her for myself for fifteen shekels of silver, and one and one-half homers of barley" (3:2). In the same way, God promised Israel that, after her years of punishment, He "will allure her, and bring her into the wilderness, and speak tenderly to her" (2:14 ESV):

> **2** 16 "And it shall be, in that day,"
> Says the LORD,
> "That you will call Me 'My Husband,'
> And no longer call Me 'My Master,'...
> 19 "I will betroth you to Me forever;
> Yes, I will betroth you to Me
> In righteousness and justice,
> In lovingkindness and mercy;

20 I will betroth you to Me in faithfulness,
And you shall know the LORD...
23 Then I will sow her for Myself in the earth,
And I will have mercy on her who had not obtained mercy;
Then I will say to those who were not My people,
'You are My people!'
And they shall say, 'You are my God!' "
1 10 "Yet the number of the children of Israel
Shall be as the sand of the sea,
Which cannot be measured or numbered.
And it shall come to pass
In the place where it was said to them,
'You are not My people,'
There it shall be said to them,
'You are sons of the living God.'
2 1 Say to your brethren, 'My people,'
And to your sisters, 'Mercy is shown.'

(Hos. 1:10, 2:1, 16, 19-20, 23)

God's marriage covenant with His Bride— the elect—is immutable because He has sworn His vows by Himself for there is no one greater (Heb. 6:13). God's gifts (including that of penitent faith) and calling (including election and irresistible grace) are irrevocable (Rom. 11:29). He has made "an *everlasting* covenant with them, that I will not turn away from doing them good; but I will put My fear in their hearts *so that they will not depart from Me*" (Jer. 32:40; emphasis added). For He has, by His propitiating atoning sacrifice, "*perfected forever* those who are being sanctified" (Heb. 10:14; emphasis added). We who are born again into Christ are once for all clothed with His righteousness and justified for all time; there are no dropouts in the golden chain of God's electing forelove:

29 For whom He foreknew, He also predestined to be conformed to the image of His Son, that He might be the firstborn among many brethren. 30 Moreover whom He

predestined, these He also called; whom He called, these He also justified; and whom He justified, these He also glorified.

(Rom. 8:29-30)

Sanctification, however, is never accomplished apart from divine discipline, for as Moses warns, "...as a man disciplines his son, Yahweh your God is disciplining you" (Deut. 8:5 NYLT). In the book of Revelation, Jesus tells us that, "'As many as I brotherly love, I do convict and chasten. Be zealous, then, and repent!'" (Rev. 3:19 NYLT). In the book of Job we read, "Blessed is the man who God corrects, so do not despite the discipline of the Almighty. For He wounds but He also binds up; He injures, but His hands also heal" (Job. 5:17-18 NIV84). The psalmist echoes this by proclaiming, "Blessed is the man you discipline, O LORD, the man You teach from Your law" (Ps. 94:12 NIV84). King Solomon instructs us, "[11] Despise not the discipline of Yahweh, my son, and be not resentful of His rebuke. [12] For whom Yahweh loves He reproves, even as a father the son He is pleased with" (Prov. 3:11-12 NYLT).

The author of Hebrews explains:

[3] For consider again Him who endured such dispute from sinners against Himself, that you may not be wearied in your souls, being faint. [4] Not yet unto bloodshed did you resist in striving with sin, [5] and you have forgotten the exhortation that speaks fully to you as to sons:
"My son, be not despising the
chastening of the LORD,
Nor be faint, being reproved by Him,
[6] For whom the LORD agapes He chastens,
And He scourges every son whom He receives."
[7] If you endure chastening, God bears with you as with sons, for who is a son whom a father does not chasten? [8] If, however, you are without chastening, of which all have become partakers, then you are bastards and not sons. [9] Furthermore, indeed, we have had our fathers in

the flesh—correctors—and we were respecting them. Shall we not much rather be subject to the Father of the spirits and live?   10 For they, indeed, for a few days—according to what seemed good to them—were chastening, but He for our profit—to be partakers of His holiness,   11 Now all chastening for the present, indeed, does not seem to be of joy but of sorrow, yet afterward it yields the peaceable fruit of righteousness to those nakedly trained through it.

(Heb. 12:4-11 NYLT)

But though He may, for a time, discipline His Bride in love, God will keep her and preserve her until the end. For "those who are called [are] sanctified by God the Father, and preserved in Jesus Christ" (Jude 1). Because our God is faithful (1 Cor. 1:9), He will "confirm you to the end, that you may be blameless in the day of our Lord Jesus Christ" (vs. 8).   Because He who calls us is faithful (1 Thess. 5:24), therefore He will sanctify us completely and preserve our whole spirit, soul, and body blameless to the coming of our Lord Jesus Christ (vs. 23).

Because our Bridegroom is faithful, we are "confident of this very thing, that He who has begun a good work in you will complete it until the day of Jesus Christ" (Phil. 1:6). Because our Bridegroom is faithful, He is both absolutely able and willing to "keep you from stumbling, and to present you faultless before the presence of His glory with exceeding joy" (Jude 24).   Because our Bridegroom is faithful, He will immutably (Heb. 6:17) lead us "in the paths of righteousness *for His name's sake*" (Ps. 23:3b; emphasis added).

Because our Bridegroom is faithful, we can unashamedly "hold fast the confession of our hope without wavering" (Heb. 10:23), for we know whom we have believed and am persuaded that He is able to keep what we have committed to Him until that Day (2 Tim. 1:12).   Because our Bridegroom is faithful, He will never divorce or desert His Bride:

27 My sheep hear My voice, and I know them, and they follow Me. 28 And I give them eternal life, and they shall never perish; neither shall anyone snatch them out of My hand. 29 My Father, who has given them to Me, is greater than all; and no one is able to snatch them out of My Father's hand. 30 I and My Father are one."

(Jn. 10:27-30)

Because our Bridegroom is faithful, "'everyone who sees the Son and believes in Him may have everlasting life; and I will raise him up at the last day'" (Jn. 6:40). Because our Bridegroom is faithful, He will "lose nothing" of all that the Father has given Him, "but should raise it up at the last day" (vs. 39). Because our Bridegroom is faithful, He "will deliver me from every evil work and preserve me for His heavenly kingdom" (2 Tim. 4:18). Because our Bridegroom is faithful, He will "save to the uttermost those who come to God through Him" because "He always lives to make intercession for them" (Heb. 7:25). Because our Bridegroom is faithful, He effectually prays for us (Jn. 17:9-11) so that we will not be tempted beyond what we are able, "but with the temptation will also make the way of escape, that you may be able to bear it" (1 Cor. 10:13). We may stumble, but because our Bridegroom is faithful He will always bring us back (Lk. 22:32).

Because our Bridegroom is faithful, His vows never fail:

15 "Can a woman forget her nursing child,
And not have compassion on the son of her womb?
Surely they may forget,
Yet I will not forget you.
16 See, I have inscribed you on the palms of My hands"…

(Is. 49:15-16a)

Because our Bridegroom is faithful, nothing—absolutely nothing—can remove us from His love:

31 What then shall we say to these things? If God is for us, who can be against us? 32 He who did not spare His

173

own Son, but delivered Him up for us all, how shall He not with Him also freely give us all things? 33 Who shall bring a charge against God's elect? It is God who justifies. 34 Who is he who condemns? It is Christ who died, and furthermore is also risen, who is even at the right hand of God, who also makes intercession for us. 35 Who shall separate us from the love of Christ? Shall tribulation, or distress, or persecution, or famine, or nakedness, or peril, or sword? 36 As it is written:

"For Your sake we are killed all day long;
We are accounted as sheep for the slaughter."

37 Yet in all these things we are more than conquerors through Him who loved us. 38 For I am persuaded that neither death nor life, nor angels nor principalities nor powers, nor things present nor things to come, 39 nor height nor depth, nor any other created thing, shall be able to separate us from the love of God which is in Christ Jesus our Lord.

(Rom. 8:31-39)

Praise God, therefore, for:

3 Blessed be the God and Father of our Lord Jesus Christ, who according to His abundant mercy has begotten us again to a living hope through the resurrection of Jesus Christ from the dead, 4 to an *inheritance incorruptible and undefiled* and that *does not fade away, reserved* in heaven for you, 5 who are *kept by the power of God* through faith for salvation ready to be revealed in the last time.

(1 Pet. 1:3-5; emphasis added)

THE FREE WILL OF GOD

Concluding Implications:

We have seen in Scripture that, for anyone to be saved, God must first birth them from above by the Holy Spirit into spiritual life with a new heart which He then empowers to exercise penitent faith in receiving the Lord Christ. And not only is regeneration monergistic, but we have also seen that so is the perseverance of the saints. For it is only by the imposition of God's sovereign and decisive free will that we are kept for salvation at the Judgment Seat of Christ (1 Pet. 1:5) because:

• The sovereign and decisive gift of Christ's righteousness is the only grounds for our fight for sanctification.
• The sovereign and decisive gift of saving penitent faith must genetically mature into sanctification.
• The sovereign and decisive gift of being birthed into eternal life by imperishable Seed, which thereby grafts us into the Good Tree of Christ, must genetically yield much fruit.
• God is faithful and will not—nay, cannot—divorce His bride. Rather, out of jealousy for the sake of the fame of His name, He will sovereignly and decisively keep her.

In short, the saints will persevere in their salvation with fear and trembling (Phil. 2:12) because, and only because, it is God who "is the one" sovereignly and decisively "energizing in you both to will and to energize for the benefit of His good will" (vs. 13 NYLT). The reason we wake up each morning still a believer is not because of our will power, our decisive self-will, our determination. Rather, the sole reason we continue to believe is because God sovereignly and decisively wills it.

The doctrines of sovereign grace are the Gospel in full bloom, but sadly most of our churches offer only the wilted flowers of humanistic, man-centered idolatry. They tell sinners that they must be Born Again, but from what? If man is completely capable of deciding for Christ, coming to Christ, and accepting Christ, by the exercise of his own decisive, self-determining free will, then why, exactly, does he need to be born again? Why does he need a new heart, a new spirit, and a new will if he can exercise penitent faith *before* the New Birth? If he is capable of initially choosing God and pursing paths of righteousness without the regenerating power of the Holy Spirit, then why does He need the sanctifying power of the Holy Spirit after New Birth?

And while most churches tell sinners that they are sinners, they do not tell them that they are *dead* in their trespasses and sins. That they are dead, hardened, and blinded in their sins, enemies of God, and entirely incapable of reconciling themselves to Him. That their very nature is sin and that is why they sin and cannot stop sinning. That they deserve hell and nothing but hell from a holy and righteous God from the moment they were conceived.

Our "converts" have no idea how vile they are because they have no idea how holy God is. Their sins are merely bad decisions, their salvation a New Year's resolution, and their sanctification merely a 12-step self-help program. They are not humbled and stripped of their self-righteousness. They are not desperate for forgiveness and reconciliation with God; they merely want to keep their sin but go to heaven. The god they worship is a self-help guru, a genie in a bottle, a kindly grandfather who forgives and forgets and empathizes.

They have no understanding of grace and mercy because they have no understanding of their desperate straits, and therefore they cannot grasp the depth of God's condescension in pitying us. They think that God saves us because He needs us. Because He's lonely. And poor God, pinning away on HIs throne, hoping against hope that someone will take Him up on HIs offer of salvation. That someone will be with Him in heaven. That someone will take pity on His poor crucified Son. They are told that they must help God help them; that they must save God in His attempt to save them.

And when you ask them how they became saved, they will point you to a specific date and time (often written in their dust-covered Bibles) when they said a prayer, or walked an aisle, or raised a hand. When you ask them how they know they were saved, their evidence will be to point you back to those works. Their "salvation" is most emphatically based on works—on something they did, on faith they mustered up, on a righteousness they performed. Their conversion is external and nothing more; mere window dressing on a corpse.

When you ask them why they became a "believer" and not their family or friends, they will say it was because they were smart enough to figure this whole salvation thing out while others are just stubborn. They will never answer that it is because these individuals cannot come to Christ on their own power, but only that they don't want to. And if you press them why they came to Christ, they will admit—not that they saw Him as infinitely beautiful in HIs own right—but that they wanted His supposed gifts of a guilt free life of pleasure.

And this whole mentality shapes the way we do evangelism and missions. We don't preach sinners hopeless and helpless before a holy and righteous and angry God because of their wickedness. We don't preach sinners unable to turn to God because they are spiritually dead with a hardened and blinded heart. We don't preach a merciful and gracious God who—at the sacrifice of Himself—propitiated His own wrath, redeemed for Himself a Bride, and reconciled Her unto Himself as pure and spotless. We don't preach a God mighty to save and preserve by His power alone.

And we don't preach holiness, without which no one will see the Lord. We don't desire God, pursue God, and satisfy ourselves in God. We don't trust Him for the grace to endure. Rather, our average "believer" will talk of his sanctification as he does his "conversion"—an act of will-power, rule keeping, legalism, and moral reform. And so he will measure his holiness as he does his "conversion"—not by love for God, but by self-righteousness. Doing more "dos" and less "dont's." Obeying commands. By self-improvement.

And so we dilute what it means to be a Christian. We teach easy-believism; salvation by will power and self-improvement. We issue appeals based on man's need for entertainment, pleasure, security, and self-esteem rather than on His need for a Savior, a Redeemer, a Deliverer. We have rock bands lead our worship, TED talks from our pulpits, and entertainment to make church fun and cool, convenient and easy, all while Ichabod is written over the door.

And so we weaken, nay, emasculate, the Gospel and have filled our churches with wolves rather than sheep. With self-deluded, self-righteous Christians in Name Only (CINOs) rather than humbled saints stripped of any grounds for boasting. With those who worship a god after their own hearts rather than the most supremely valuable Being imaginable. With those practicing a salvation of works, or self-will, of moralizing rather than of sovereign and decisive grace alone, through the gift of penitent faith alone, wrought by the New Birth's Spirit-entranced view of Christ alone.

All these woes of the contemporary Church, certainly, cannot be laid entirely at the doorstep of Arminianism, but until we see a genuine, lasting revival of Reformed theology this inevitable fruit of free-willism will only continue and abound. We cannot fully understand the doctrine of regeneration apart from TULIP. One may certainly be a Christian without being a Calvinist, but one would be a severally handicapped Christian leaning on the broken reed of Arminianism. What assurance the doctrines of grace give the believer of God's unfailing, electing, particular love for them! What comfort it gives the saint to persevere unto sanctification in the midst of trials and tribulations! What confidence to know that our salvation—from eternity past to eternity future—is secured by an omnipotent power not our own. The Lord Christ came to save and save decisively, once-for-all—that is a Gospel worth believing, living, and sharing!

[1] Again the word of the LORD came to me, saying, [2] "Son of man, cause Jerusalem to know her abominations, [3] and say, 'Thus says the LORD God to Jerusalem: "Your birth and your nativity are from the land of Canaan; your father was an Amorite and your mother a Hittite. [4] As for your nativity, on the day you were born your navel cord was not cut, nor were you washed in water to cleanse you; you were not rubbed with salt nor wrapped in swaddling cloths. [5] No eye pitied you, to do any of these things for you, to have compassion on you; but you were thrown out into the open field, when you yourself were loathed on the day you were born.

[6] "And when I passed by you and saw you struggling in your own blood, I said to you in your blood, 'Live!' Yes, I said to you in your blood, 'Live!' [7] I made you thrive like a plant in the field; and you grew, matured, and became very beautiful. Your breasts were formed, your hair grew, but you were naked and bare.

[8] "When I passed by you again and looked upon you, indeed your time was the time of love; so I spread My wing over you and covered your nakedness. Yes, I swore an oath to you and entered into a covenant with you, and you became Mine," says the LORD God.

[9] "Then I washed you in water; yes, I thoroughly washed off your blood, and I anointed you with oil. [10] I clothed you in embroidered cloth and gave you sandals of badger skin; I clothed you with fine linen and covered you with silk. [11] I adorned you with ornaments, put bracelets on your wrists, and a chain on your neck. [12] And I put a jewel in your nose, earrings in your ears, and a beautiful crown on your head. [13] Thus you were adorned with gold and silver, and your clothing was of fine linen, silk, and embroidered cloth. You ate pastry of fine flour, honey, and oil. You were exceedingly beautiful, and succeeded to royalty. [14] Your fame went out among the nations because of your beauty, for it was perfect through My

splendor which I had bestowed on you," says the LORD God.

(Ezek. 16:1-14)

7 GOD'S FREE WILL IN REIGNING

We have looked at God's free will in creation, in providence, in providing for salvation, and in applying that salvation to the elect. Now we will examine God's free will in reigning by looking at His sovereign pleasure in answering prayer, in evangelism and missions, over so-called "gods," and in the Final Judgment.

God has, is, and will forever reign omnipotently as an absolute sovereign over the affairs of this world, for "The LORD has established His throne in heaven, And His kingdom rules over all" (Ps. 103:19). He reigns in, through, and over the opposition of men and demons, for "All the inhabitants of the earth are reputed as nothing; He does according to His will in the army of heaven and among the inhabitants of the earth. No one can restrain His hand or say to Him, 'What have You done?'" (Dan. 4:35).

The Kingdom of Christ (Rom. 14:17) has been inaugurated at His first coming (Matt. 3:2, 12:28, 28:18; Lk. 1:15, 11:20, 17:21). But it is not yet fully manifested (Lk. 19:11) with every foe utterly vanquished, which is why we are to pray in this manner:

> 9 ...Our Father in heaven,
> Hallowed be Your name.
> 10 Your kingdom come.
> Your will be done
> On earth as it is in heaven...
> 13 For Yours is the kingdom and the power and the glory forever. Amen.

(Matt. 6:9-10, 13b)

Notice that verse 13 grounds the basis, the hope, that the petitions will be answered in the fact that "the kingdom and the power and the glory forever" already belong to God. But yet verse 10 asks that His kingdom and will be completely consummated here on earth as it is in heaven. The kingdom of God, therefore, is here but not-yet. HIs reign, though autocratic, remains hidden until HIs second (and final) coming as pretenders to the throne still seek to deceive His subjects.

It is for this reason that the devil is called the prince of this world (Jn. 12:31; see also Matt. 4:8-9; Lk. 4:6; Jn. 14:30) who, seemingly, holds the world under his power (1 Jn. 5:19). He is "the prince of the power of the air" who "works in the sons of disobedience" (Eph. 2:2), blinding them to the Gospel 2 Cor. 4:4). He continually prowls about like a roaring lion who must be resisted as he looks for prey to devour (Eph. 6:12; 1 Pet. 5:8).

But Satan has already been condemned (Jn. 16:11; see also Jn. 12:31; Heb. 2:14) and his works destroyed (1 Jn. 3:8). Christ has already "disarmed principalities and power" and "made a public spectacle of them, triumphing over them in it" (Col. 2:15). The original Greek is even stronger—"He is triumphing over them by parading them as a defeated enemy before the world." But at the same time Satan will not be fully disarmed and judged until the Second Coming (Rev. 20:10) when Christ's kingdom will be fully manifested:

> [9] Therefore God also has highly exalted Him and given Him the name which is above every name, [10] that at the name of Jesus every knee should bow, of those in heaven, and of those on earth, and of those under the earth, [11] and that every tongue should confess that Jesus Christ is Lord, to the glory of God the Father.
>
> (Phil. 2:8-9; see also Eph. 1:20-22)

> [24] Then comes the end, when He delivers the kingdom to God the Father, when He puts an end to all rule and all authority and power. [25] For He must reign till He has put all enemies under His feet. [26] The last enemy that will be destroyed is death. [27] For "He has put all things under His feet." But when He says "all things are put under Him," it is evident that He who put all things under Him is excepted. [28] Now when all things are made subject to Him, then the Son Himself will also be subject to Him who put all things under Him, that God may be all in all.

THE FREE WILL OF GOD IN REIGNING

(1 Cor. 15:24-28; see also Ps. 2:8-9)

So let us look at the exercise of God's sovereign free will in His inaugurated but not yet consummated kingdom during this present Church Age:

I. The Free Will of God in Prayer:

A common objection to the absolute sovereignty of God's free will is that it removes any incentive to pray. "Why pray," so the argument goes, "if it doesn't change anything? If God has already orchestrated every minute detail of every second of human history, praying simply becomes a waste of time." But the exact opposite is true—God's absolute sovereignty is the only basis for praying.

Before we examine the interplay of God's sovereignty and the causality of prayer, we must first understand what prayer is. For the underlying assumption of the objection is that prayer is merely bringing a list of demands—I mean, requests—before God. Prayer is certainly the offering of heartfelt petitions before the throne of God in humble supplication. But prayer is much more than that. Prayer is not sitting on Santa's lap with your wish list, or rubbing the bottle of a genie (Jas. 4:3). Rather, it is worshipful fellowship.

So even if, arguendo, prayer did not affect a single outcome in our lives, the Born Again believer should still crave to be with his God in worshipful communion. For like the psalmist, the regenerate man cries out, "As a deer pants for flowing streams, so pants my soul for you, O God. My soul thirsts for God, for the living God. When shall I come and meet before God?" (Ps. 42:1-2 ESV).

Only death should keep us from our knees:

> [1] O God, you are my God; earnestly I seek you; my soul thirsts for you; my flesh faints for you, as in a dry and weary land where there is no water...[3] Because your

steadfast love is better than life, my lips will praise you...[8]
My soul clings to you; your right hand upholds me.

(Ps. 63, 1, 3, & 8 ESV)

[25] Whom have I in heaven but you? And there is nothing on earth that I desire besides you. [26] My flesh and my heart may fail, but God is the strength of my heart and my portion forever...[28] But for me it is good to be near God; I have made the Lord GOD my refuge, that I may tell of all your works.

(Ps. 73:25-26, 28 ESV)

Prayer does not change God, but it does change us. In fact, the most common word used in the Greek New Testament for prayer is *proseuchomai*, which means *towards* or *exchange* (*pros*) and *wishes* (*euxomai*). In other words, prayer is an exchange of wishes—trading in your desires for God's. The heartbeat of a believer's prayer is, "Your kingdom come, Your will be done, on earth, and in my life and heart, as it is in heaven" (Matt. 6:10; Lk. 11:2). It is asking the Lord to hallow His name in your life; to orchestrate everything in your life in such a way as to bring Him the most glory.

Prayer is the willingness to consider all we could ever ask for to be rubbish (Phil. 3:7-8) in comparison with seeking first the kingdom of God in our hearts and in our lives (Matt. 6:33). True prayer, genuine prayer, praying in pray (Jas. 5:17; original Greek), is not less than crying out to God, "Not my will but Your will be done!" (Matt. 26:38-42; Lk. 22:42), though it is more than that. It is also praise and thanksgiving (Psalm. 1104; 1 Cor. 1:4-9; Phil. 1:3-6, 4:6b; Col. 1:3-4; 1 Thess. 5:18; 2 Thess. 1:3-4). It is confession of sins (Psalm. 66:18; Is. 59:2; Matt. 5:23-24, 6:12; Mk. 11:25-26; Lk. 11:4; 1 Pet. 3:7).

And, yes, prayer is certainly about bringing our needs before God. In fact, we are commanded to "cast[] all our cares upon Him, for He cares for you" (1 Pet. 5:7). We are not to be anxious about anything for we are to bring everything before Him with prayer and urgent, heartfelt supplications (Phil. 4:6; original

Greek). We are to cast our burden upon Yahweh (Ps. 55:22) and roll our way unto Him (Ps. 37:5; original Hebrew). And not only our needs, but also (and perhaps more so) the needs of others (Rom. 1:9-10; Eph. 3:14-21; Phil. 1:3-11; Col. 1:9-14). In short, prayer is the verbal expression of faith—acknowledging in our creaturely weakness our utter dependence on God's faithful providence (Matt. 6:8).

And prayer moves the hand of God. Let me restate that in order to be unmistakably, unequivocally clear—God acts in response to prayer and doesn't act when prayer is neglected. Or, to put it another way, prayer causes things to happen in this world that otherwise would not happen in in the absence of prayer. In other words, prayer produces results, while not praying changes nothing. For James is explicitly clear that, "you do not have because you do not ask" (Jas. 4:2). We do not receive answers to prayer because we do not pray. But if we pray, then we receive answers to prayer. God's intervention in this world is conditional upon the petitions of His elect. If we pray, He acts. If we don't, He doesn't.

However, let me be equally clear that prayer does not change God's mind (Heb. 6:17). It doesn't persuade Him to change His plans (Eph. 1:11). It doesn't convince Him to do something that He hadn't already purposed in eternity past to do (Is. 46:10). Prayer never changes God. *Never* (Deut. 3:26; Jer. 15:1)! Rather, God not only sovereignly decrees the ends, but also the means by which those ends are accomplished (Lk. 22:32). For instance, if God decreed the salvation of one of your parents (the end), He also decreed the means—prayer and the sharing of the Gospel—by which that end is accomplished.

Everything that God does in response to the prayers of His saints He has already foreordained to do by the means of their foreordained prayers. And everything that God does not do in the absence of prayer He had already foreordained not to do by the means of foreordained neglected prayers. So if God decreed before the world began to answer prayer, He also decreed before the world began that the prayer would be offered.

God is immutable, unchangeable, constant, and permanent. His free will is sovereign, absolute, supreme, and omnipotent. He is not an impotent God who is dependent upon our prayers to act. He is not a beggar God, hoping like a lonely genie that we will show Him some attention. He is not a servant God, beholden to do what we ask Him to in our prayers. His is not an emasculated God whose free will is subservient to our own. He is not an indecisive God, able to be persuaded by the best, or more persistent, arguer. No! Rather, our God has "no variation or shadow of turning" (Jas. 1:17) as He reigns "in heaven [and] does whatever He pleases" (Psalm. 115:3)!

O what assurance this gives us to boldly approach the throne of grace for the well-timed help we need (Heb. 4:16; original Greek)! From eternity past God has infinitely perfectly designed every detail of every second of the entire universe throughout all of history, and His absolute sovereign free will cannot and will not be thwarted or held hostage by our prayers (or lack of them). What confidence that God's infinitely perfect loving kindness cannot be prevented! What boldness in knowing that God's infinitely perfect goodness and wisdom will triumph and prevail! "Prayer," Martin Luther once wrote, "is not overcoming God's reluctance, but laying hold of His willingness."

It is with exactly this kind of assurance, therefore, that the Apostle John exhorts us:

> 14 Now this is the confidence that we have in Him, *that if we ask anything according to His will, He hears us*. 15 And if we know that He hears us, whatever we ask, we know that we have the petitions that we have asked of Him.
>
> (1 Jn. 5:14-15; emphasis added)

We obviously do not know what God's secret will (or will of decree) is, but we do know what His revealed will (or will of command) is. And how do we know what God's revealed will is? Through His Word, for Jesus tells us that, "'If you abide in Me, *and My words abide in you*, you will ask what you desire, and it shall be done for you'" (Jn. 15:7; emphasis added). It is through His Word, therefore, that we are "transformed by the renewing of []our mind, [so] that [we] may prove what is that good and acceptable and perfect will of God" (Rom. 12:2).

And the following are just a few of the things we are commanded by God's revealed will to pray for because, apart from Christ, we can do nothing (Jn. 15:5):

- Avoid temptation (Matt. 6:13, 26:41; 1 Cor. 10:13).
- Glorify the Father (Matt. 6:9).
- Advance God's kingdom (Matt. 6:10).
- For Him to cast forth Gospel laborers (Matt. 9:38; Lk. 10:2).
- Provision of our daily bread (Matt. 6:11; Phil 419).
- Forgiveness of sins (Matt. 6:12; 1 Jn. 1:9).
- Being "filled with the knowledge of God's will in all wisdom and spiritual understanding" (Col. 1:9).
- That we "may walk worthy of the Lord, fully pleasing Him, being fruitful in every good work and increasing in the knowledge of God" (Co. 1:10).
- Our enemies (Matt. 5:44).
- Bold Gospel witness (Acts 4:29; Eph. 6:18-19).
- Church leaders (Heb. 13:7).
- Governing authorities (1 Tim. 2:1-4).
- Church unity (Jn. 17:20-21).
- Healing (Jas. 5:14-16).
- Wisdom (Jas. 1:5).

Our job is not to try to divine what the divine secret will of decree is. That's none of our business. Rather, we are to pray according to God's revealed, known will by having a mind saturated with His Word. God will always answer in the affirmative the prayers of His elect that pray Scripture—especially the prayers and HIs promises—back to Him. Why? So that we might bear fruit to His glory (Jn. 15:16). That is the reason for prayer:

7 If you abide in Me, and My words abide in you, you will ask what you desire, and it shall be done for you. 8 By this My Father is glorified, that you bear much fruit; so you will be My disciples.

(Jn. 15:7-8)

And while every prayer uttered by our hearts must be, "Not my will but Yours be done," this is not a license for resigned passivity, for fatalism, in prayer. Certainly we must always pray in humility —asking the Lord to do whatever it takes to be most glorified in and through us. And our specific requests must be but an extension of this one singular cry of our hearts; our petitions must the means by which we sincerely believe in our fallible wisdom that God would be most glorified. However, we must always be willing to yield to God's absolutely sovereign free will in His pursuit of the magnification of His glory, even if that means answering our prayers the exact opposite of what we had petitioned.

But while our heart beats with the fundamental request that God's will, not our will, be done, we are exhorted in Scripture to pray with specificity. Not, "Your will be done, it doesn't matter what I want." Not, "let fate be fate. Amen." Not, "I don't care because You are going to do what You want to do anyway." No! Rather, we are to bring our needs before God with specificity, letting Him know exactly how we want Him to be glorified in our lives for such definite faith honors Him. Simply having an obvious need and crying out, "'Have mercy on us, O Lord, Son of David!'" (Matt. 20:30-31) doesn't honor Him so much believing that He can address your specific need (vs. 32; see also Jn. 5:6).

Furthermore, we are to be boldly persistent—nay, shamelessly importune—in our prayers because it shows our desperate dependance upon Him (Lk. 11:5-8). We are to ask, and keep on asking; seek, and keep on seeking; knock, and keep on knocking (Lk. 11:9-13; see also Matt. 7:7-11). We are not heard on account of our many words (Matt. 6:7). Rather, God is honored by faith that does not give up (Matt. 15:21-28; Mk. 7:24-30; see also Gen. 18:16-33; Ex. 17:8-16; 1 Kings 17:17-24, 18:41-46; 2

Kings 13:14-19); that in its blood earnest wrestling (Gen. 32:22-32) nearly gives Him a black eye (Lk. 18:1-8; original Greek). Such tenacious, persevering faith is exactly the type of faith Christ longs to see at His return (Lk. 18:8).

And such travailing prayer is often sown with tears (Ps. 39:12; Heb. 5:7), like Hannah who, in bitterness of soul, "prayed to the LORD and wept in anguish (1 Sam. 1:10). Finally, such prevailing prayer must believe without a doubting heart that we have already received the answers sought (Mk. 11:22-24; see also Matt. 17:20, 21:17-22; Mk. 9:14-29; Jn. 14:13-14, 15:7-8, 16b, 16:23b-24; Heb. 11:1, 6).

In short, such prayer offered in Jesus' name—in His character, for His glory, according to His will—will always be answered by God in the affirmative (Jn. 14:23, 16:23-24; 2 Cor. 1:20). The answer may not be in the timing or manner we asked for, and in fact may be the exact opposite of what we specifically asked for, like Mary and Martha who sought healing for their dying brother Lazarus (Jn. 11:3, 21) and the Apostle Paul who asked for the removal of his thorn in the flesh (2 Cor. 12:8). But if we truly bring our needs before God in a humble, submissive, yielded spirit, leave them on the altar, and ask Him to solve them according to His infinitely perfect will, He will absolutely do so.

God's absolutely sovereign free will in answering our petitions is the only confidence, the only motive, the only grounds for persevering faith in our prayers. We all know this intuitively, for we are all Calvinists on our knees. We don't pray for God to provide help after a tsunami; we pray that He stops the tsunami. We don't pray that God will gently nudge our spouse to believe unto salvation; we pray that He makes and keeps him a Christian. We don't pray for aid before the persecution even begins; we pray that God will prevent the persecution from starting in the first place. We pray that God would heal the disease completely, not merely that He would give the grace to endure. Those who believe in man's free will have no reason to pray; rather, the fact that God can and will answer our prayers is the sole anchor for our faith in boldly approaching His throne.

2. The Free Will of God in Evangelism & Missions:

Another common objection to the absolute sovereignty of God's free will is that it removes any incentive to evangelize. However, evangelism—especially preaching—is the God-decreed means of accomplishing missions, and without it no one hears the Gospel and, consequently, no one is ever saved:

> 13 For "whoever calls on the name of the LORD shall be saved."
> 14 How then shall they call on Him in whom they have not believed? And how shall they believe in Him of whom they have not heard? And how shall they hear without a preacher? 15 And how shall they preach unless they are sent? As it is written:
> "How beautiful are the feet of those who preach the
> gospel of peace,
> Who bring glad tidings of good things!"
> 17 So then faith comes by hearing, and hearing by the word of God.

(Rom. 10:13-15, 17)

Furthermore, as we just saw with prayer, the opposite of the objection is in fact true—confidence in God's absolutely sovereign free will compels missions. For earlier in Chapter 5 we saw that the success of the Gospel has been guaranteed by no less than the Author of our salvation, for Jesus declared in John 10 that, "[O]ther sheep I have which are not of this fold; them also I am under compulsion to bring in, and they shall hear My voice; and there shall be one flock and one Shepherd" (Jn. 10:16 NYLT). There are four specific promises in this verse alone:

- That Jesus is the Good Shepherd;
- That He has other sheep not currently in the fold;
- The He is under necessity to bring them in; and, therefore,
- That they shall hear His voice and be brought in!

What confidence for those with beautiful feet (Rom. 10:15), knowing that God must and will save His sheep! What assurance to persevere in evangelism, knowing that God's sovereign free will in election is irresistible!   For Jesus tells us, "'No one can come to Me unless the Father who sent Me irresistibly drags him; and I will raise him up at the last day'" (Jn. 6:44 NYLT).   And in another place He promises us, "'And I, if I am lifted up from the earth, will irresistibly drag all My sheep to Myself'" (Jn. 12:32 NYLT).

We see in Scripture, therefore, promise after promise that the Lamb who was slain shall have the full reward of His sufferings throughout the world:

• **Ps. 2:8:** "'Ask of Me, and I will give You the nations for Your inheritance, and the ends of the earth for Your possession.'"

• **Ps. 22:27-28:** "All the ends of the world shall remember and turn to the LORD.   And all the families of the nations shall worship before You! For the kingdom is the LORD's, and He rules over the nations."

• **Ps. 66:4:** "All the earth shall worship You and sing praises to You! They shall sing praises to Your name! Selah."

• **Ps. 72:17:** "His name shall endure forever! His name shall continue as long as the sun! And men shall be blessed in Him! All nations shall call Him blessed!"

• **Ps. 86:9:** "All the nations whom You have made shall come and worship before You, O LORD!"

• **Is. 49:6b:** "'I will also give You as a light unto the Gentiles, that You should be My salvation to the ends of the earth!'"

• **Is. 59:17a:** "So they shall fear the name of the LORD from the west, and His glory from the rising of the sun..."

• **Hab. 2:14:** "For the earth will be filled with the knowledge of the glory of the LORD as the waters cover the sea!"

• **Zeph. 2:11:** "The LORD will be awesome to them for He will reduce to nothing all the gods of the earth!   People shall worship Him, each one from his place! Indeed, all the shores of the nations!"

NATHAN W. TUCKER

- **Rev. 5:9:** "'For You...have redeemed us to God by Your blood out of every tribe and tongue and people and nation!'" (see also Rev. 7:9, 11:15)

And all these promises and assurances are grounded in the absoluteness of Christ's reign—"'All authority has been given to Me in heaven and on earth!'" (Matt. 28:18). All authority. Not some authority. Not partial authority. Not maybe a little authority. But *all* authority. And God's omnipotence effectuates and secures His absolutely sovereign free will in electing grace. God will have His sheep, His Bride, His people, and no one can thwart His will.

Therefore, the Church has no need to ever rely on the arm of the flesh, nor catering to the carnal appetites of the lost, in doing missions (1 Cor. 1:18-2:16; 2 Cor. 3:18, 4:4, 6; Phil. 3:3). Rather, by Spirit-empowering grace, our strategy should merely be one of prayer, preaching, and patience. It is to be faithful in simple obedience to the strategy found in the New Testament. Not pragmatism, "felt-needs," contextualization, cultural sensitivity, insider movements, anthropology, sociology, psychology, or any other convenient but ultimately destructive missional strategy, but Scripture alone.

First, we should be continually devoted to prayer and fasting (Is. 56:7; Matt. 21:13; Mk. 11:17; Lk. 19:46; Acts 1:14, 24, 2:42, 4:23-31, 6:4, 12:5, 13:2-3, 14:23, 20:36, 21:5), for apart from God we can do nothing (Jn. 15:5; 2 Cor. 3:18, 4:4, 6). We should endeavor to be a praying people that cause Satan and his demons to tremble (Acts 19:15) as we "weep before the porch and the altar" (Joel 2:17; see also 1:13, 2:12; Ezek. 9:4) for God's glory in the salvation and sanctification of many souls—echoing John Knox in crying out to God, "Give us this region or this people group or we die!" (Gen. 30:1)—trusting that He alone will pull down the strongholds (2 Cor. 10:4), principalities, and powers of the darkness of this age (Eph. 6:12). Prayer is the visible engine of the Church.

Secondly, we as the Church must be submitted to the authority and sufficiency of Scripture (Acts 2:42; 17:11; 1 Tim. 3:15) and

192

committed to the centrality and primacy of the faithful proclamation of God's Word in a demonstration of the Spirit and of power (1 Cor. 2:5; see also Mk. 16:20; Acts 4:33, 14:3; Rom. 15:19; 1 Thess. 1:5; Heb. 2:4; 1 Pet. 1:12; see furthermore Matt. 7:28-29, 13:54, 22:33; Mk. 1:22, 6:2, 11:18; Lk. 2:47, 4:32; Jn. 7:15, 46; Acts 4:13, 6:10, 14:1).

Third, our missional strategy much be the centrality, supremacy, and exclusivity of Yahweh—the God of the Bible— who is not a generic deity but a specific Person who is God of all other so-called "gods," Lord of all lords, and King of all kings (Josh. 22:22; Ps. 82:1, 86:8, 95:3, 96:4-5, 97:7, 9, 135:5, 136:1-3; Dan. 2:47, 11:36; 1 Tim. 6:15; Rev. 17:14, 19:16), including over the "gods" of false religions—whether Allah, Wakanda, Zeus, Jupiter, the thousands of Hindu gods, or any other so-called god—who are really demons (Ps. 106:35-39; 1 Cor. 10:18-22).

Fourth, the Church must be committed to the centrality and primacy of the public proclamation of the Good News as the primary method (1 Cor. 1:21) commanded and modeled in Scripture for the fulfilling of the Great Commission: "Go into all the world and preach the gospel to every creature" (Mk. 16:15). Jesus Himself not only modeled this itinerant heralding of faith and repentance (Matt. 4:17; Mk. 1:14-15; Lk. 4:14-15), but He instructed both the Twelve and the Seventy-Two disciples to do likewise during His earthly ministry (Matt. 10:5-15; Mk. 6:7-13; Lk. 9:1-6, 10:1-12). This proclamation method is exemplified elsewhere in the New Testament by John the Baptist (Matt. 3:12-; Mk. 1:4; Lk. 3:3); Peter (Acts 2:14-41, 3:11-16, 8:6-8, 10:27, 34), Philip (Acts 8:6-8, 40); Paul (Acts 9:20, 29, 13:44-52, 17:17, 17:19-34, 18:27-28, 19:9-10, 20:20, 21:40), and Apollos (Acts 18:27-28). And it was the primary method of warning of impending judgment in the Old Testament (Ezra 10:9-14; Neh. 8:1-8; Is. 5:29; Jer. 7:1-3; Ezek. 3:1-5; Amos 5:10; 2 Pet. 2:5).

Fifth, the Church must proclaim the centrality of the offense of Christ crucified (1 Cor. 1:23), including the supremacy and exclusivity of the Lord Jesus Christ, God the Son, as the only means of forgiveness of sins and eternal life (Jn. 14:6; Acts 4:12; Phil. 2:9-10).

Sixth, the Church must unapologetically proclaim the New Birth whereby a man is regenerated into a new man by the Holy Spirit and therefore has the power, freedom, and victory over the presence and power of sin and cannot remain enslaved to habitual, premeditated sins such as alcohol, drugs, and sexual immorality (Jn. 3:1-8; Rom. 6, 8; 2 Cor. 5:17; Gal. 3:27; Col. 3:9-10). Additionally, the Church must emphasize the necessity of daily picking up one's cross, dying to self, and forsaking all—including family, culture, and people—(Matt. 10:34-39, 16:24-27; Mk. 8:34-38; Lk. 9:23-26, 14:25-35) in the pursuit of Christ as a hidden treasure (Matt. 13:44) and a pearl of great price (Matt. 13:45-46; see also Phil. 3:7-14).

Seventh, individual churches (corporately) must not busy themselves with social outreach—AA/NA meetings and addiction recovery/counseling services, support groups, soup kitchen, thrift stores, "work and witness" mission trips, medical aid services, after-school programs and daycares, ESL/tutoring/education, arts and crafts, sports, etc. While these things *may* not necessarily be wrong in and of themselves, the sole province of the Church is the salvation and sanctification of souls. Period. We serve the lost by preaching Christ to them. Period. Individual believers may certainly participate in these activities, but the church institutionally must not become sidetracked in its mission. If you want feel-good busyness, join the Peace Corp rather than the Church.

Eighth and finally, the Church must repeat this strategy until a harvest is reaped or the Lord calls us home, in which case others will reap the harvest only by using the same means.

Any other means, any other strategy, will overwhelmingly produce Christians in Name Only (CINOs) in pseudo churches. Carnal means only produce carnal CINOs; fleshly strategies only produce fleshly CINOs; but following the pattern on the mount (Ex. 25:9, 40; Acts 7:44; Heb. 8:5) produces Born Again believers. Genuine fruit, real fruit, authentic fruit, is only harvested in the power of the Spirit using Scriptural methods.

In conclusion, therefore, nothing can thwart God's effectual will in evangelizing the world. Neither Satan and his hordes, nor dictators and persecutions, nor the Church and Her failings, nor man and his so-called free will. God is saving precisely who He wants to save, where He wants to save them, when He wants to save them.

But what about those who die without ever hearing the name of Christ?[1] The Bible is emphatically clear that apart from personal penitent faith in the Jewish Messiah Jesus Christ there is no salvation. For God declares that, "Nor is there salvation in any other, for there is no other name under heaven given among men by which we must be saved" (Acts 4:12). As Jesus Himself declared, "'I [alone] am the [only] way, the [only] truth, and the [only] life. [Absolutely] [n]o one comes to [God] the Father except through Me'" (Jn. 14:6). The Bible describes Jesus as the one, only, and final sacrifice for sins, of which no other can either be offered to nor accepted by God (Heb. 7:27; see also Rom. 6:10; 1 Pet. 3:18).

As we saw earlier this chapter in Romans 10, apart from this personal faith—received from hearing—in the God-man Jesus Christ, there is no salvation. And in another place the Bible tells us that:

> [9] God has highly exalted Christ and given Him the name which is above every name, [10] that at the name of Jesus every knee should bow...[11] and that every tongue should confess that Jesus Christ is Lord, to the glory of God the Father.
>
> (Phil. 2:9-11)

Not Allah, nor Buddha, nor any other so-called "god." Rather, forgiveness of sins and peace with God is only possible through the imputation of Christ's blood and righteousness alone that comes through penitent faith birthed by the hearing of the Gospel (Jn. 1:12, 3:17-18, 5:24, 6:40, 47, 11:25-26; Acts 16:31; Rom.

---

[1] For a fuller treatment of the exclusivity of Christ, please refer to chapter 7 of my book: *The Five Solas: An Expository Exhortation*.

10:13; 1 Cor. 1:21; Heb. 9:26, 28). Therefore, if one never hears the Gospel of Christ, he will not believe in Christ, and if He does not believe in Christ in penitent faith, he will not be saved. Period. No exceptions.

But before we leave this topic, however, it is essential to note that the premise of this objection is entirely man-centered narcissism dressed up as a question of fairness or equity. It puts God, rather than man, on the docket. It is a feeble attempt to annul God's judgments and condemn Him that we may be justified (Job 41:8).

The Bible responds to such pompous arrogance by commanding "Silence!", for "who are you, O man, to talk back to God?! Shall what is formed say to Him who formed it, 'Why did You make me like this?' Does not the potter have the right to make out of the same lump of clay some pottery for noble purposes and some for common use?" (Rom. 9:20). The questioner neither knows how righteous and holy God is, nor how sinful and vile he is!

For as we have already seen, the Bible declares us to be evil personified without any defense or justification before God. We are not good. We are not innocent. We have no self-righteousness. We are a moral monster who is just as grotesque in our hideous treason against God as any devil of hell. We are unlovable—nay, repulsively disgusting—in God's eyes with the rightful judgment of eternal hell hanging over our heads. We are the walking scum of a creation that will one day applaud God's justice of ridding the universe of our wickedness.

And the only thing God owes us is eternal damnation from the moment we were conceived. Just as God was under no obligation to save the demons of hell, so He is under no obligation to save us. God owes us no pity, no mercy, no charity, and the only reason we remain out of hell with a chance to repent and believe the gospel is owed solely to His divine, unfathomable, unexplainable grace.

God owes us nothing for any past good works we may have done. We are pure evil and wickedly corrupt and can have no hope of earning God's favor. Our sin against a holy and righteous

God cannot be atoned for by tears, resolutions, good works, legalism, or any other effort on our part. Salvation is not of works but only of God who calls (Rom. 9:11). It is not of man who wills, nor of the man who runs, but only of God who shows mercy (Rom. 9:16; see also Jn. 1:13). God will have mercy on whom He will have mercy, and hardens whom He will harden (Rom. 9:18). We are completely hopeless and helpless before God (Eph. 2:12), Who alone decides whether and when to save us. And if He does save us, it isn't because He is making much of us, but rather it is so that we might make much of Him.

In conclusion, therefore, God doesn't have to save anyone. He would be perfectly righteous and just if He only saved 1,000 souls in all of human history. Or 100 souls. Or 10 souls. Or 1 soul. Or none at all. We have absolutely no moral claim on God for anything whatsoever.

If, for instance, Warren Buffet came to your church on Sunday and gave ten of you $10 million dollars, everyone in the media would be praising him for such extravagant generosity and benevolence. Only the most arrogant, self-righteous pompous fool would suggest that it was unfair of Mr. Buffet for not giving everyone in the room—past, present, and future—$10 million. Only the most narcissistic among you would argue that Mr. Buffet also owed you $10 million simply for also being in church.

Be stunned into silent worship, therefore, that God has graciously taken it upon Himself to save anyone by the sacrifice of Himself! For the Bible calls salvation an act of God's grace from start to finish, for we are "justified freely *by His grace* through the redemption that came by Jesus Christ" (Rom. 3:24; emphasis added). For the Bible declares that, "it is by grace you have been saved through faith—and this not of yourselves, it is a gift of God—not of works so that no one can boast" (Eph. 2:8). And in another place the Scriptures make clear:

> [27] Where then is boasting? It is excluded. On what principle? On that of observing the law? No, but on that of faith. [28] For we maintain that a man is justified by faith apart from observing the law.

197

(Rom. 3:27-28; see also Gal. 2:16; 3:11)

Be astounded at such extravagant grace! At such scandalous love! For in order to magnify His name in the demonstration of His moral excellencies, the Bible declares to us that "God demonstrates His own love for us in this: While we were still sinners, Christ died for us!" (Rom. 5:8). Elsewhere God tells us that: "[He] so loved the world that He gave His one and only Son" — who was "stricken by God, smitten by Him, and afflicted...it was the LORD's will to crush [Christ] and cause Him to suffer [in order to] make[] His life a guilt offering" (Is. 53:4, 10)—so that whosoever trusts in Him shall not perish but have eternal life!" (Jn. 3:16).

The reason why the God-man Jesus Christ is the exclusive way of salvation is because our sin is so vile, hell is so real, but God's love is so great that He did the unthinkable in crucifying His one and only Son in order to save His lost sheep!

But then why take so long to evangelize the world? Why doesn't God just simply speed up the rate of conversions? Why didn't He simply continue the revival of the first 30 years of the Church, or extend the Great Awakening, or prolong the Second Great Awakening? Why are there still thousands of people groups who remain unreached and unengaged?

We must remember, however, that God only acts for the sake of His name, for the sake of His praise, for the sake of His glory, for His own sake (Is. 48:9-11; see also Ex. 14:4, 17-18, 36:22-23, 32; 1 Sam. 12:20, 22; 2 Kings 19:34, 20:6; Ps. 25:11, 106:7-8; Is. 43:6-7, 25, 49:3; Matt. 5:16; Jn. 7:18, 12:27-28, 13:31-32, 14:13, 16:14, 17:1; Rom. 3:25-26, 9:17, 15:7; Eph. 1:4-6, 12, 14; 1 Pet. 2:12). Isaiah 40:5 declares that God created the world with one purpose in mind—that "'the glory of the LORD will be revealed, and all mankind together will see it.'" Or as the Apostle Paul proclaims in Colossians 1, "All things were created through Him and for Him...that in all things He may have the preeminence" (Col. 1:16, 18).

All creation, therefore, has but one purpose—the worship of God. This universe does not exist for our sake. Eternity does not exist for our sake. Redemptive history was not written for our sake. We were not created to exist for our own sakes. Rather, everything God does is to glorify Himself. For the worship of Himself. For the magnification of His glory. He is the supreme reality for which this life and the next exist.

So why didn't God covert the entire world on Pentecost Sunday A.D. 33? Because He is writing redemptive history in such a way as to infinitely perfectly magnify the fame of His Name. This world, and everything about it, is the most perfect world imaginable from the standpoint of magnifying God's glory. We certainly may not understand it fully this side of eternity, but that doesn't change the truth of its reality. God is writing the most amazingly wonderful love story every conceived in which He is the knight in shining armor, the Prince Charming, undertaking the most unthinkably selfless sacrifice out of scandalous love for His most undeserving Betrothed. And as with any love story, the more undeserving and unfaithful she is, and the more difficult—nay, impossible—His feat, the more glory He wins for Himself. The evangelization of the world, therefore, is taking place at precisely the right pace—no more and no less—to perfectly magnify His worth.

3. The Free Will of God over "gods":

God is the ultimate and eternal Supreme Being of which nothing greater can be conceived. There cannot be two or more Supreme Beings for the simple reason that neither one of them would therefore be supreme. There can only be one Great I Am —the uncreated, self-sufficient, self-existent, unchangeable, limitless One who has no beginning, no end, no need, and no weakness (Ex. 3:14-15; Numb. 23:19; Ps. 33:11, 102:27; Mal. 3:6; Jn. 5:26; Heb. 13:8; Jas. 1:17; Rev.1:8, 22:13). He is the uncreated source of all created things who does not owe His existence to anyone or anything else.

And because God is the all-powerful sovereign of the universe, He has no rival. Period. For the Bible declares, "Know therefore today, and take it to your heart, that the LORD, He is

199

God and there is no other besides Him" (Deut. 4:39; see also Deut. 4:35, 6:4-5, 32:39a; 2 Kings 5:16; Is. 45:22; Joel 2:27). All angels and demons, spirits and so-called "gods," have beginnings, are bound by physical locations, and have their power limited by some outside constraint. Even the devil himself is not God's co-equal but merely one of His creatures who can do nothing without God's permission (Job 1:12, 2:6; Mk. 1:27; Lk. 4:6, 22:31-32, 53).

And Scripture is clear that God uses demonic powers to accomplish His will; they are the means of achieving His ends: the trials of Job (Job 1:12-19, 2:6-7); the lying spirit who deceived Ahab to engage in the battle that resulted in his death (1 Kings 22:23); and the betrayal of the Lord Christ by Judas (Lk. 22:3-4; Acts 2:23). God has not yet consigned them to hell, not because He is powerless to do so, but because He is more glorified through their continued "freedom." And when He does cast them into hell, they will not be its jailers, as is so often depicted in secular cartoons, but rather among its most tormented prisoners.

Furthermore, the Bible tells us that God delights in bringing temporal judgment upon them as well. In Exodus, for instance, God declared that He had judged all the gods of Egypt by killing all of the firstborn—whether of man or of beast—in the land (Ex. 12:12). When the Philistines captured the Ark of the Covenant, God caused the statue of the Philistine god Dagon to fall on its face before the Ark with its head and hands broken off (1 Sam. 5:1-5). In the book of Isaiah God mocks His backsliding people Israel for seeking after other gods, saying, "'When you cry out, let your collection of idols deliver you. But the wind will carry them all away; a breath will take them'" (Is. 57:13). In contrast, however, the Bible declares, "Blessed are all those who put their trust in [God]" (Ps. 2:12).

On Mount Carmel, 450 prophets of Baal and 400 prophets of Asherah "called on Baal from morning till noon...[as] they danced around the altar they had made," pleading with their god to send down fire upon their sacrifice (1 Kings 18:19, 26). But when no response came, Elijah, the prophet of Yahweh, began to mock them: "Shout louder!" he said, "Surely he is a god! Perhaps he is deep in thought, or on the toilet, or traveling. Maybe he is sleeping and must be awakened" (vs. 27; author's paraphrase). So they shouted louder and slashed themselves with swords and spears until their blood flowed. Midday passed, and still they continued their frantic prophesying (vs. 28-39).

But the Bible is clear that, "there was no response; no one answered; no one paid attention" (vs. 29). But the story doesn't end there, for:

> [30] Then Elijah said to all the people, "Come near to me." So all the people came near to him. And he repaired the altar of the LORD that was broken down. [31] And Elijah took twelve stones, according to the number of the tribes of the sons of Jacob, to whom the word of the LORD had come, saying, "Israel shall be your name." [32] Then with the stones he built an altar in the name of the LORD; and he made a trench around the altar large enough to hold two [measures] of seed. [33] And he put the wood in order, cut the bull in pieces, and laid it on the wood, and said, "Fill four waterpots with water, and pour it on the burnt sacrifice and on the wood." [34] Then he said, "Do it a second time," and they did it a second time; and he said, "Do it a third time," and they did it a third time. [35] So the water ran all around the altar; and he also filled the trench with water.
>
> [36] And it came to pass, at the time of the offering of the evening sacrifice, that Elijah the prophet came near and said, "LORD God of Abraham, Isaac, and Israel, let it be known this day that You are God in Israel and I am Your servant, and that I have done all these things at Your word. [37] Hear me, O LORD, hear me, that this people may know that You are the LORD God, and that You have turned their hearts back to You again."
>
> [38] Then the fire of the LORD fell and consumed the burnt sacrifice, and the wood and the stones and the dust, and it licked up the water that was in the trench. [39] Now when

all the people saw it, they fell on their faces; and they said, "The LORD, He is God! The LORD, He is God!"

(1 Kings 18:30-39)

4. The Free Will of God in Judgment & Eternity:

God is not mocked (Gal. 6:7). He will not strive with His enemies forever (Gen. 6:3). For the Day is coming when "the Lord Himself will descend from heaven with a shout, with the voice of an archangel, and with the trumpet of God" (1 Thess. 4:16), and "in flaming fire taking vengeance on those who do not know God, and on those who do not obey the gospel of [the] Lord Jesus Christ" (2 Thess. 1:8).

For the psalmist tells us that "It is God who judges" (Ps. 75:7; see also 50:6). The author of Hebrews tells us that "God is the Judge of all" (Heb. 12:23), and in another place he states, "Nothing in all creation is hidden from God's sight. Everything is uncovered and laid bare before the eyes of Him to whom we must give an account" (4:13). Abraham called Him, "the Judge of all the earth" (Gen. 18:25). Isaiah the prophet declares that, "the LORD is our judge" (Is. 33:22), and Hannah proclaimed that, "the LORD will judge the ends of the earth" (1 Sam. 2:10).

Christ alone is the "judge of the living and the dead" (Acts 10:41, 17:31; 2 Tim. 4:1; 1 Pet. 4:5)—the final judge of all men's actions and arbitrator of their eternal fates. Christ Himself tells us that, "the Son of Man is going to come in His Father's glory with His angels, and then He will reward each person according to what he has done" (Matt. 16:27). Again, in another place, He states, "Moreover, the Father judges no one, but has entrusted all judgement to the Son that all may honor the Son just as they honor the Father" (Jn. 5:22-23). The Apostle Paul declares, "God will judge men's secrets through Jesus Christ, as my Gospel declares" (Rom. 2:16), and, in another place, that "Christ Jesus will judge the living and the dead" (2 Tim. 4:1). Again, Christ tells us that:

When the Son of Man comes in His glory, and all the angels with Him, He will sit on His throne in heavenly glory. All the nations will be gathered before Him, and He will separate the people one from another as a shepherd separates the sheep from the goats. He will put the sheep on His right and the goats on His left.

Then the King will say to those on His right, "Come, you who are blessed by My Father, take your inheritance— the kingdom prepared for you since the creation of the world."

Then He will say to those on His left, "Depart from Me, you who are cursed, into the eternal fire prepared for the devil and his angels"..

Then they will go away to eternal punishment, but the righteous to eternal life.

(Matt. 25:31-34, 41, 46)

The Apostle John states that on the Day of Judgment, Christ will take His seat upon "a great white throne" and "earth and sky will flee from His presence" (Rev. 20:11):

And I saw the dead, great and small, standing before the throne, and books were opened. Another book was opened, which is the book of life. The dead were judged according to what they had done as recorded in the books...each person was judged according to what he had done.

(Rev. 20:12-13)

The Apostle Paul tells us in Romans that, "God will give to each person according to what he has done...for those who are self-seeking and who reject the truth and follow evil, there will be wrath and anger. There will be trouble and distress for every human being who does evil" (Rom. 2:6-9).

And how will God judge? The psalmist tells us that, "the LORD...will judge the world in righteousness, and His peoples in His truth" (Ps. 96:13), and, in another place, "Righteousness and justice are the foundation of [His] throne" (89:14). The Apostle Paul declares "the Lord" as "the righteous Judge" (2 Tim. 4:8; see also Ps. 7:11). The Apostle Peter proclaims that He, "judges each man's work impartially" (1 Pet. 1:17). Jesus Himself states that, "I judge only as I hear, and My judgment is just, for I seek not to please Myself but Him who sent Me" (Jn. 5:30).

And the first to be judged will be the devil and his hordes, who will be "cast into the lake of fire and brimstone" and "they will be tormented day and night forever and ever" (Rev. 20:10). They will be followed by all the damned who have rejected Christ as Savior and therefore remain dead in their trespass and sins. And Jesus tells us that hell is an everlasting "furnace of fire in outer darkness [where you] will be wailing and gnashing [your] teeth" (Matt. 8:12, 13:42, 50, 24:51). It is the eternal destruction of your soul (Matt. 10:28) in "fire that shall never be quenched, where '[your] worm does not die'" (Mk. 9:44, 46, 48; see also Is. 66:24). The Bible warns you that you "shall also drink of the wine of the wrath of God, which is poured out in full strength into the tormented with fire and brimstone in the presence of the holy angels and in the presence of the Lamb. And the smoke of [your] torment [will] ascend forever and ever; and [you will] have no rest day or night" (Rev. 14:10-11).

In contrast, however, "[16]...the dead in Christ will rise first. [17] Then we who are alive and remain shall be caught up together with them in the clouds to meet the Lord in the air. And thus we shall always be with the Lord" (1 Thess. 4:16b-17). We shall tabernacle with the Lord Christ in the new heaven and the new earth (Rev. 21:1) with our resurrected bodies (1 Cor. 15:35-58).

In short, God's absolutely sovereign free will will always have the last word.

34 And at the end of the time I, Nebuchadnezzar, lifted my eyes to heaven, and my understanding returned to me; and I blessed the Most High and praised and honored Him who lives forever:

For His dominion is an everlasting dominion,
And His kingdom is from generation to generation.
35 All the inhabitants of the earth are reputed as nothing;
He does according to His will in the army of heaven
And among the inhabitants of the earth.
No one can restrain His hand
Or say to Him, "What have You done?"

36 At the same time my reason returned to me, and for the glory of my kingdom, my honor and splendor returned to me. My counselors and nobles resorted to me, I was restored to my kingdom, and excellent majesty was added to me. 37 Now I, Nebuchadnezzar, praise and extol and honor the King of heaven, all of whose works are truth, and His ways justice. And those who walk in pride He is able to put down.

(Dan. 4:34-37)

8 CONCLUSION—THE GOOD NEWS OF GOD'S FREE WILL

I was not raised Reformed. Rather, I was raised the son of a Wesleyan Arminian preacher who himself was the son of a Wesleyan Arminian preacher. I did not become Reformed until much later in life at the age of forty. In the hubris of my youth, I maintained that an absolutely sovereign God was a heresy, not because He was not the God portrayed in Scripture (which He most emphatically is), but because I could not make sense of it philosophically. As with many throughout the centuries, my objections to Reformed thought—or, more accurately, to biblical theology—were based on moral reasoning, not biblical reasoning. I even went so far as to describe a God with absolutely sovereign free will as:

• God is power—his sovereignty trumps all his other attributes/ characteristics.
• God is unjust—punishing man not as he deserves but as he has predestined him. Man is not responsible for his behavior, god is.
• God is sinful—for since nothing can contradict god's will, therefore sin is god's will. Consequently, god is the author of sin; he is the author of evil in the world.
• Evangelism and discipleship are unnecessary.
• Human life has no meaning, sanctity, or preciousness but is expendable according to god's arbitrary and despotic will.

In my stubborn, unbelieving sinfulness, I made Scripture submit to my worldview rather than my worldview submit to Scripture. I failed to understand that if two seemingly contradictory truths are taught by Scripture, my reason, not Scripture, must be faulty. For both truths must be uncontradictorily true, even if we will never fully understand how this side of eternity. We don't fully understand the three Persons yet one God of the Trinity, but we still believe it and teach it as essential to Christian thought. We don't fully understand the hypostatic union of the Lord Christ as 100% God and 100% man, but we sill believe it and teach it as essential to Christian thought.

That is one of the most fundamental lessons of Reformed theology—meekness before God, humbly acknowledging that, "'The secret things belong to the LORD our God, but those things which are revealed belong to us and to our children forever, that we may do all the words of this law'" (Deut. 29:29). In this life we only know in part, as through a glass dimly, awaiting in patient faith for a fuller understanding in heaven (1 Cor. 13:12).

It was over Christmas of 2018 that I came, by God's grace, to see that a God with absolutely sovereign free will is not the moral monster I once thought He was. Not in the least. And it is my earnest hope and prayer that this book has demonstrated how only such a God is worthy to be called God. Worthy of all our worship. Worthy of all our trust. Worthy of all our sacrifice.

God's sovereignty doesn't trump all His other attributes, but secures them. His infinitely perfect loving kindness is guaranteed by HIs absolutely sovereign free will. His infinitely perfect goodness and wisdom is anchored by His absolutely sovereign free will. His faithfulness and immutability can be trusted precisely because of His absolutely sovereign free will. The only reason human life has any sacredness is because it mirrors the infinite worth and glory of a God who reigns with absolutely sovereign free will. And the joy of the clay is not in molding itself, but in being fashioned by an infinitely valuable God with absolutely sovereign free will. In short, therefore, if God did not have absolutely sovereign free will, life would be random meaninglessness, salvation a fool's dream, and man's free will would be divine.

The implications of man-debasing, God-exalting Reformed theology are profound and far-reaching. The first is that it produces a God-besotted vision of all things. It is theology on fire that results in life-transforming doxology. It is shocked that the world ignores God. That section A of every newspaper doesn't daily proclaim His marvelous works. That there aren't 24/7 news channels declaring His greatness. For everything relates to God

THE FREE WILL OF GOD

—for of Him and to Him and through Him are all things (Rom. 11:36)! The weight of God's glory hangs too lightly upon the world—both believer and nonbeliever alike. We don't know God. Reformed theology, however, crowns God with all the glory due His name and seeks to submit every aspect of life to His lordship.

Secondly, Reformed theology prevents reversing roles with God. Modern culture is permeated with self-idolatrous men who have the audacity to judge God. As C.S. Lewis put it:

> The ancient man approached God . . . as the accused person approaches his judge. For the modern man the roles are reversed. He is the judge: God is in the dock. He is quite a kindly judge: if God should have a reasonable defence for being the god who permits war, poverty and disease, he is ready to listen to it. The trial may even end in God's acquittal. But the important thing is that man is on the Bench and God in the Dock.[1]

We are too prone to find unrighteousness with God (Rom. 9:14). To question Him and rebuke Him and second-guess Him for all the evil and sorrow in this life (Job 38:2; Rom. 11:34), and to argue with Him that we cannot be responsible moral agents if He is absolutely sovereign (Rom. 9:19-20). But Reformed theology reminds us that the Potter has absolute authority over the clay and is absolutely free to make from the very same lump one vessel for glory and another vessel for perdition (Rom. 9:22). It humbles us and puts us in our place, much like Job was humbled before Yahweh:

40 [1] Moreover the LORD answered Job, and said:

---

[1] "God in the Dock," in Lesley Walmsley, ed., C.S. Lewis: Essay Collection and Other Short Pieces [London: HarperCollins Publishers, 2000], p. 36.

2 "Shall the one who contends with the Almighty correct Him?

He who rebukes God, let him answer it."

3 Then Job answered the LORD and said:

4 "Behold, I am vile;

What shall I answer You?

I lay my hand over my mouth.

5 Once I have spoken, but I will not answer;

Yes, twice, but I will proceed no further."

6 Then the LORD answered Job out of the whirlwind, and said:

7 "Now prepare yourself like a man;

I will question you, and you shall answer Me:

8 "Would you indeed annul My judgment?

Would you condemn Me that you may be justified?...

42 1 Then Job answered the LORD and said:

2 "I know that You can do everything,

And that no purpose of Yours can be withheld from You.

3 You asked, 'Who is this who hides counsel without knowledge?'

Therefore I have uttered what I did not understand,

Things too wonderful for me, which I did not know.

4 Listen, please, and let me speak;

You said, 'I will question you, and you shall answer Me.'

5 "I have heard of You by the hearing of the ear,

But now my eye sees You.

6 Therefore I abhor myself,

And repent in dust and ashes."

(Job 40:1-8, 42:1-6)

In short, Reformed theology keeps us from playing God. From thinking that we know best. That we know it all. That we are the center of the universe. That everything is for our benefit. That He must give an account to us. Rather, it humbles and abases us before the absolute Monarch of the universe.

Third and relatedly, this humility and meekness before God, if genuine, must progressively translate into humility and meekness before men. We should be slow to anger. Slow to judge. Slow to condemn. In recognizing how little we actually are, how sinful we really are, and how loving, gracious, and holy God truly is, we should treat others as we wish to be treated (Matt. 7:12; Lk. 6:31). In recognizing how much we have been forgiven (Lk. 7:47), we should love others as we love ourselves (Matt. 22:39; Mk. 12:31; Lk. 10:27; Jas. 2:8). This resultant humility in marriages, in raising children, in church leadership, and in places of employment produces a loving, patient, and forgiving Bride for the glory of Christ.

Fourth, Reformed theology has a preservative effect in keeping one biblically orthodox. Those who are Reformed tend to "bleed biblime," as Charles Spurgeon once said of John Bunyan. They endeavor to faithfully exegete Scripture as they apply it to every aspect of life. They don't want to rest theological conclusions based on man's opinion or human logic, but only those drawn from *sola Scriptura*. They want chapter and verse, not pontification. And this inherent regulator serves to prevent one's descent down the slippery slope of egalitarianism, evolutionism, wokism, open theism, universalism, unitarianism, liberalism, and anglo-catholicism.

Fifth and relatedly, Reformed theology accentuates the pattern on the mount (Ex. 25:9, 40; Acts 7:44; Heb. 8:5). On doing ecclesiology and missions God's way, not man's way. It stands fast on Scriptural teaching in regards to church eldership and deacons, in missions as the province of the local church, in the regulative principle in governing worship, in the administration of church discipline, etc. In maintaining the self-sufficiency of Scripture, it rejects Saul's armor. In despising pride and arrogance and the preoccupation they breed with numbers and efficiency, it refuses the arm of the flesh. In desiring to be faithful rather than popular, it shuns the use of carnal methods.

Sixth, by stressing the reality of the New Birth, Reformed theology prevents and weeds out Christians in Name Only (CINOs). In rejecting altar calls and easy believism in favor of the supernatural, radical nature of regeneration, it emphasizes faith and repentance and the work of the Holy Spirit in birthing a new creation that must inevitably bear fruit unto holiness. Reformed theology doesn't care about numbers. It doesn't publicize how many professed faith. It doesn't preoccupy itself with manufacturing a response by its audience. Rather, in humble, earnest prayer it recognizes its dependence upon God alone.

Seventh and finally, Reformed theology's absorption with God's absolutely sovereign providence is an inexhaustible source of resolute, serious joy, come what may. It gives peace for those suffering, and comfort for those grieving. It provides hope for those in hard marriages and for those struggling with difficult children. It engenders confidence in congregations that church discipline will produce repentance and reconciliation. It begets risk-taking perseverance in missions and evangelism knowing that God will have His lost sheep, despite the challenges. It results in a bold, shamelessly importune prayer life, knowing that God can and will answer prayer. And it creates faith that progressively sanctifies as it endures in lovingly looking unto Jesus until we see Him face-to-face one day.

But I must end on a cautionary note. Reformed theology has a tendency, because of its strong appeal to those with an intellectual bent, to worship ideas about God rather than the God behind those ideas. To love theology rather than the God of theology. To worship an image, a painting, an idol rather than He who it purports to represent. If theology does not produce doxology, it is but a sounding gong and a clanging cymbal (1 Cor. 13:1). As Shai Linne has put it:

> Theology is the study of God and it's very important;
> Doxology is an expression of praise to God
>
> So, the point here is that all theology should ultimately lead to doxology
> If theology doesn't lead to doxology, then we've actually missed the point of theology
>
> So if you have theology without doxology, you just have dead, cold orthodoxy;

Which is horrible, right?

On the other side, we have people who say: "Ugh! Forget theology; I just wanna praise!" Right?

But, if we have doxology without theology, we actually have idolatry!

Because it's just a random expression of praise; but it's not actually informed by the Truth of who God is

So, God is concerned with both!

He's concerned with an accurate understanding of Him;

And that accurate understanding of Him, leading to a response of praise, adoration and worship towards Him[2]

Or as John Piper has explained:

Sam Crabtree said to me once, "The danger of the contemporary worship awakening is that we love loving God more than we love God." That was very profound. And you might love thinking about God more than you love God. Or arguing for God more than you love God. Or defending God more than you love God. Or writing about God more than you love God. Or preaching more than you love God. Or evangelizing more than you love God.[3]

Reformed theology must produce the "Oh!" which concludes Romans 9-11, or it is but dead orthodoxy and cold intellectualism:

[33] Oh, the depth of the riches both of the wisdom and knowledge of God! How unsearchable are His judgments and His ways past finding out!

---

[2] "Doxology Intro" from Shai Linne's "Lyrical Theology, Pt. 2: Doxology"

[3] https://www.desiringgod.org/interviews/what-cautions-do-you-have-for-the-new-reformed-movement

34 "For who has known the mind of the LORD?
Or who has become His counselor?"
35 "Or who has first given to Him
And it shall be repaid to him?"
36 For of Him and through Him and to Him are all things,
to whom be glory forever. Amen.

(Rom. 11:33-36)

If Reformed theology does not humble you and exalt God, reveal the world and the flesh as ugly and Christ as irresistibly beautiful, and give you a heart of fear, love, obedience, and worship toward God, then you neither know God nor yourself. It is merely a lifeless ideology to you; one which exalts your intellect, not your humility. And this love for the praise of men rather than of God (Jn. 12:43) serves to remove the theological regulator mentioned under implication 4 described earlier in this chapter. This is why people become liberals—they are in love with their big heads rather than God. Which is why the Reformed resurgence of 1990-2020 has waned and largely self-destructed —too many professing Calvinists, like the Pharisees, were in love with themselves and the praise of men (Matt. 23:5; Jn. 5:44) rather than in love with God and His praise for what is done in secret (Matt. 6:4, 6, 18). We need to check ourselves, brothers, to make sure that we are not merely Reformed, but truly regenerate (2 Cor. 13:5).

THE FREE WILL OF GOD

1 And Hannah prayed and said:
"My heart rejoices in the LORD;
My horn is exalted in the LORD.
smile at my enemies,
Because I rejoice in Your salvation.
2 "No one is holy like the LORD,
For there is none besides You,
Nor is there any rock like our God.
3 "Talk no more so very proudly;
Let no arrogance come from your mouth,
For the LORD is the God of knowledge;
And by Him actions are weighed.
4 "The bows of the mighty men are broken,
And those who stumbled are girded with strength.
5 Those who were full have hired themselves out for
bread,
And the hungry have ceased to hunger.
Even the barren has borne seven,
And she who has many children has become feeble.
6 "The LORD kills and makes alive;
He brings down to the grave and brings up.
7 The LORD makes poor and makes rich;
He brings low and lifts up.
8 He raises the poor from the dust
And lifts the beggar from the ash heap,
To set them among princes
And make them inherit the throne of glory.
"For the pillars of the earth are the LORD's,
And He has set the world upon them.
9 He will guard the feet of His saints,
But the wicked shall be silent in darkness.
"For by strength no man shall prevail.
10 The adversaries of the LORD shall be broken in
pieces;
From heaven He will thunder against them.
The LORD will judge the ends of the earth.

"He will give strength to His king,
And exalt the horn of His anointed."

(1 Sam. 2:1-10)

APPENDIX A: WHO IS THE WORLD?

When you hear the question, "For whom did Jesus die?" what do you think? The answer may seem obvious—for the world:

· **Jn. 1:29:** "The next day John saw Jesus coming toward him, and said, 'Behold! The Lamb of God who takes away the sin of the world!'"

· **Jn. 3:16-17:** "'[16] For God so loved the world that He gave His only begotten Son, that whoever believes in Him should not perish but have everlasting life. [17] For God did not send His Son into the world to condemn the world, but that the world through Him might be saved.'"

· **Jn. 4:42:** "Then they said to the woman, 'Now we believe, not because of what you said, for we ourselves have heard Him and we know that this is indeed the Christ, the Savior of the world.'"

· **Jn. 12:47:** "'And if anyone hears My words and does not believe, I do not judge him; for I did not come to judge the world but to save the world.'"

· **2 Cor. 5:19:** "that is, that God was in Christ reconciling the world to Himself, not imputing their trespasses to them, and has committed to us the word of reconciliation."

· **1 Jn. 2:2:** "And He Himself is the propitiation for our sins, and not for ours only but also for the whole world."

· **1 Jn. 4:14:** "And we have seen and testify that the Father has sent the Son as Savior of the world."

As a result of these verses, many well-meaning interpreters assert that Jesus died for the entire world, rather than just a predestined number of people.[1] But does the word *world* really mean *world*? Does it actually mean everyone everywhere at all times? Or are there other uses of the term *world* in the Bible?

---

[1] It should be obvious that, without being read not only in context but also in light of all of Scripture, every single one of these

The Greek word translated world is *kosmos*, which has at least ten meanings in the New Testament: [3]

1. **The entirety of creation (i.e., the seen and unseen universe):** "'God, who made the world and everything in it, since He is Lord of heaven and earth, does not dwell in temples made with hands'" (Acts 17:24).

2. **The earth itself:** "[J]ust as He chose us in Him before the foundation of the world, that we should be holy and without blame before Him in love" (Eph. 1:4; see also Lk. 11:50 ("world") compared with Matt. 23:35 ("earth")).

3. **The temporal realm:** This present, passing world as compared to the eternal, spiritual realm—"For we brought nothing into *this* world, and it is certain we can carry nothing out" (1 Tim. 6:7; emphasis added; see also Matt. 16:26; Mk. 8:36; Lk. 9:25; Jn. 12:25, 13:1, 18:36; 1 Cor. 7:31; 1 Jn. 3:17).

4. **The inhabitants of earth:** "'The field is the world, the good seeds are the sons of the kingdom, but the tares are the sons of the wicked one'" (Matt. 13:38; see also Rom. 3:19; 1 Cor. 1:27, 4:9).

5. **The majority of inhabitants of a specific local or region:** "The Pharisees therefore said among themselves, 'You see that you are accomplishing nothing. Look, the world has gone after Him!'" (Jn. 12:19; see also 7:4).

6. **The inhabitants of earth minus the Jews (i.e., Gentiles):** "Now if their [the Jews] fall is riches for the world, and their failure riches for the Gentiles, how much more their fullness!" (Rom. 11:12). Here the Apostle Paul uses the terms *world* and *Gentiles* interchangeably.

---

verses—read superficially and by itself—doesn't merely stand for the proposition of unlimited atonement but of universal salvation as well. It is only the universalist who doesn't have to exegete.

[3] Scholars debate the number of categories and which verses belong in which, but the wide-range of uses for *kosmos* is a linguistic reality that cannot be denied.

7. **The inhabitants of earth minus the elect (i.e., unbelievers):** "'I pray for them. I do not pray for the world but for those whom You have given Me, for they are Yours'" (Jn. 17:9; see also Jn. 15:18-19; Rom. 3:6; 1 Cor. 1:21, 6:2, 11:32, 2 Cor. 7:10; Jas. 1:27; 1 Pet. 5:9; 1 Jn. 3:1, 13, 4:5, 5:19).

8. **The ungodly, carnal, fleshly desires of this world:** "But God forbid that I should boast except in the cross of our Lord Jesus Christ, by whom the world has been crucified to me, and I to the world" (Gal. 6:14; see also Col. 2:20; 1 Jn. 2:16).

9. **Aggregate:** "And the tongue is a fire, a world of iniquity..." (Jas. 3:6a).

10. **Adornment:** "Do not let your adornment be merely outward —arranging the hair, wearing gold, or putting on fine apparel—" (1 Pet. 3:3).   Rather than "fine apparel," a more literal translation would be "adorning garments" or "arranging" or "putting on" clothing. The word for *fine*, *adorning*, *arranging*, or *putting on* is, in fact, *kosmos*. This use of *kosmos* is where we derive the English word cosmetic.

And, ostensibly, the term *kosmos* in John 1:10 may be a play on words conveying at least two, if not three, meanings: "He was in the world, and the world was made through Him, and the world did not know Him." It could easily and properly be rendered: "He was on the earth, which He made when He created the entire universe (vs. 3), and yet incredibly the majority of the inhabitants of the earth did not know Him." There are at least two, and likely three, meanings for *kosmos* in this one verse alone: earth, universe, and (unbelieving) inhabitants.

And so we see that the meaning of kosmos, as with many words in both English and Greek, depends on the context. One cannot just look at the word *world* and assume that it means everyone, everywhere, at all times.   That's sloppy and lazy exegesis.   One must look at how the term *world* is defined, not just in the immediate passage itself, but also in parallel passages.

So in examining the proof-texts employed for universal atonement listed at the beginning of this appendix, we find that there is yet an eleventh category of uses for the word *kosmos*—

as a term for *believers* and believers only. The inhabitants of earth minus the sons of perdition. For instance, let us look at the larger context for John 3:16-17, the **first proof-text**, where we find Jesus telling Nicodemus (and us):

> 14 "And as Moses lifted up the serpent in the wilderness, even so must the Son of Man be lifted up, 15 that whoever believes in Him should not perish but have eternal life. 16 For God so loved the world that He gave His only begotten Son, that whoever believes in Him should not perish but have everlasting life. 17 For God did not send His Son into the world to condemn the world, but that the world through Him might be saved. 18 He who believes in Him is not condemned; but he who does not believe is condemned already, because he has not believed in the name of the only begotten Son of God."
>
> (Jn. 3:14-18)

Why did God give His only begotten Son (vs. 16)? So that—by being lifted up and dying upon the cross as Moses lifted up the bronze serpent in the wilderness (vs. 14)—*some* would be saved from condemnation (vs. 17-18) and thereby enjoy everlasting life (vs. 15-16). Who? Not the entire world, but only "whoever believes" (vs. 15, 16). Not everyone, everywhere, at all times, but only, "He who believes in Him" (vs. 18). They, and they alone, are the object of God's love in this passage.

Often in the Gospel of John the context reveals that seemingly different terms are being used interchangeably. For instance, look at what the Lord Christ tells us about the Holy Spirit:

> **14** 16 And I will pray the Father, and He will give you another Helper, that He may abide with you forever— 17 the Spirit of truth, whom the world cannot receive, because it neither sees Him nor knows Him; but you know Him, for He dwells with you and will be in you. 18 I will not leave you orphans; I will come to you…

²⁰ At that day you will know that I am in My Father, and you in Me, and I in you....²³ ...We will come to him and make Our home with him....²⁶ But the Helper, the Holy Spirit, whom the Father will send in My name, He will teach you all things, and bring to your remembrance all things that I said to you...

16 ⁷ Nevertheless I tell you the truth. It is to your advantage that I go away; for if I do not go away, the Helper will not come to you; but if I depart, I will send Him to you...¹⁴ He will glorify Me, for He will take of what is Mine and declare it to you.

(Jn. 14:16-18, 20, 23, 26, 16:7, 14)

We see two important things in this passage.   First, that the Holy Spirit is a Person distinct from both the Father, who will send Him (14: 16, 26), and the Son, who also will send Him (16:7) and be glorified by Him (16:14).   Secondly, however, we see that the Holy Spirit is the Spirit of both Christ (14:18, 20, 23) and the Father (14:20, 23)—for They "will come to [a believer] and make Our home with him" (vs. 23).   The term *Helper* or *Spirit* is used, in context, interchangeably with *I* (14:18), *the Father* (14:20, 23), *Me* (14:20), *We* (14:23), *Our* (14:23).[4]

It is also important to note that John 3:16 has two nearly identical sister verses in the Apostle John's first epistle.   The first is 1 John 4:9: "In this the love of God was manifested toward us, that God has sent His only begotten Son into the world, that we might live through Him."   Why did God send HIs one and only begotten Son into the kosmos (*universe* or *earth*)?   Not because He loved the kosmos, but because He loved us—the elect—and redeemed us that we might live through Christ.   We see this confirmed by the entire passage:

⁴ You are of God, little children, and have overcome them, because He who is in you is greater than he who is

---

⁴ For a very similar interchangeable use of such terminology for the Spirit, please refer to Romans 8:9-11.

in the world. 5 They are of the world. Therefore they speak as of the world, and the world hears them. 6 We are of God. He who knows God hears us; he who is not of God does not hear us. By this we know the spirit of truth and the spirit of error. 7 Beloved, let us love one another, for love is of God; and everyone who loves is born of God and knows God. 8 He who does not love does not know God, for God is love. 9 In this the love of God was manifested toward us, that God has sent His only begotten Son into the world, that we might live through Him. 10 In this is love, not that we loved God, but that He loved us and sent His Son to be the propitiation for our sins. 11 Beloved, if God so loved us, we also ought to love one another.

(Jn. 4:4-11)

We see therefore, the apostle drawing a contrast between the world (i.e., the inhabitants of the earth minus believers) and the elect. Those who "are of the world," "speak as of the world," and are heard by the world (vs. 5) are not loved by God. Christ did not propitiate the wrath of His Father (vs. 10) for them. Their sins remain. Rather, God loved and sent HIs Son to propitiate His wrath for "you [who] are of God" (vs. 4), "We [who] are of God" (vs. 6), who are "born of God and knows God" (vs. 7).

The second nearly identical sister passage is 1 John 3:16: "By this we know love, because He laid down His life for us. And we also ought to lay down our lives for the brethren." Christ laid down HIs life because He loved who? "[W]e," "us," the brotherhood of Christians. We see this confirmed by the entire passage:

10 In this the children of God and the children of the devil are manifest: Whoever does not practice righteousness is not of God, nor is he who does not love his brother. 11 For this is the message that you heard from the beginning, that we should love one another, 12 not as Cain who was of the wicked one and murdered his brother. And why did

he murder him? Because his works were evil and his brother's righteous.

13 Do not marvel, my brethren, if the world hates you. 14 We know that we have passed from death to life, because we love the brethren. He who does not love his brother abides in death. 15 Whoever hates his brother is a murderer, and you know that no murderer has eternal life abiding in him.

16 By this we know love, because He laid down His life for us. And we also ought to lay down our lives for the brethren. 17 But whoever has this world's goods, and sees his brother in need, and shuts up his heart from him, how does the love of God abide in him? 18 My little children, let us not love in word or in tongue, but in deed and in truth. 19 And by this we know that we are of the truth, and shall assure our hearts before Him.

(1 Jn. 3:10-19)

As in the the fourth chapter of 1 John, so here we see that Christ did not love and die for "the children of the devil" (vs. 10), who are of the world (13), who abide in death (vs. 14), who are murderers (vs. 15). Rather, He loved and died for "the children of God" (vs. 10), who practice righteousness (vs. 10), who are hated by the world (vs. 13), who are "of the truth" (vs. 19).

With this necessary background in mind, therefore, we see from the context of the entire passage that the term *world* in the third chapter of John is used interchangeably for those, and only those, believing in the Lord Christ:

14 "And as Moses lifted up the serpent in the wilderness, even so must the Son of Man be lifted up, 15 that everyone believing in Him should not perish but have eternal life. 16 For God so loved the world of believers— the elect in all times and places without regard to ethnicity—that He gave His only begotten Son, that everyone believing in Him should not perish but have everlasting life. 17 For God did not send His Son to the

223

elect to condemn the elect, but that the elect through Him might be saved. [18] He who is believing in Him is not condemned; but he who is not believing is condemned already, because he has not believed in the name of the only begotten Son of God."

(Jn. 3:14-18; author's paraphrase)

If, instead, it read, "'For God so loved everyone who has ever walked the face of the earth that He gave His only begotten Son so that only those who believe in Him should have everlasting life,'" we might rightly wonder where the Good News is in this "gospel." O, what a God who loves so much that He leaves it to men to decisively save themselves! O, what a God who loves so much that He leaves it to men to figure this whole salvation thing out! O what impotent love! O, what an amazing God that loves those in hell just as much as He loves those in heaven!

Of course, this is ludicrous, which is why Scripture no where says that God loves the entire world. No where. Not one single verse in context. Rather, He only loves:

- **"Us"** believers (Rom. 5:8, 8:37; 1 Jn. 3:1, 4:10, 16, 19; see also Rom. 5:5 ("our"))
- **"You"** believers (Jn. 15:9).
- **"Me"** believer (Gal. 2:20).
- **"Friends"** believers (Jn. 15:13).

God only hates the damned; He abhors both the sin and the sinner (Ps. 5:4-6, 7:11-13, 11:5-6). He may show kindness to them (Lk. 6:35) and endure them with much long-suffering (Rom. 9:22). But He never—not even for one trilisecond—loves them, for "As it is written, 'Jacob I have loved, but Esau I have hated'" (9:13). Before they have been born or done anything good or evil (vs. 11), God loves the elect and hates the damned from eternity past (vs. 13). Consequently, God loves everyone who believes throughout the entire world without distinction. Not without exception; His love is not universal and His atonement is not indefinite. But without distinction—loving and atoning all kinds and manner of sinners from a myriad of tongues, tribes, peoples, and nations.

We see this clearly demonstrated in the **second proof-text** that comes from the mouth of John the Baptist, "The next day John saw Jesus coming toward him, and said, 'Behold! The Lamb of God who takes away the sin of the world!'" (Jn. 1:29). The context in the first chapter of John is admittedly limited. However, the Apostle John told us just a few verses earlier that Christ came unto His own people but they rejected Him (vs. 11). Rather, He was received by those "who were born, not of blood, nor of the will of the flesh, nor of the will of man, but of God" (vs. 13).

In other words, ethnicity does not determine election. And a few verses after John the Baptist proclaims that Jesus is the "Lamb of God who takes away the sins of the world!" (vs. 29), he testifies that he did not know Jesus before that date but only that "He should be revealed *to Israel*" (vs. 31; emphasis added). And we know that John the Baptist—as did Christ Himself (Jn. 8:33, 39, 53)—regularly faced opposition from those who believed they were automatically, eternally saved because they were children of Abraham (Matt. 3:9-10, Lk. 3:8). It is against this backdrop, therefore, that verse 29 should be understood to read, "Behold! The Lamb of God who takes away the sins, not only of Jewish believers, but of believers from every ethnicity!"

The **third proof-text** is found in the fourth chapter of John: "Then they said to the woman, 'Now we believe, not because of what you said, for we ourselves have heard Him and we know that this is indeed the Christ, the Savior of the world'" (Jn. 4:42). Jesus, a Jewish rabbi, stopped to rest in Samaria—an unclean, sub-par ethnic region made up of half-breed Jews who had their own religious customs—and talked alone with a woman—which was considered scandalous in those days—who was a serial fornicator—yet a third taboo He scorned.

And on top of these indiscretions of Jewish religious practice, He freely offered salvation to her (vs. 13-14) and to her city (vs. 39-41). And she and many others believed. So the testimony in verse 42 by the believing Samaritans appears to be best understood as: "We believe that He is the Jewish Messiah, who

225

is the Savior not only of Israel but of believers from all ethnic groups, including us Samaritans!"

The **fourth proof-text**—verse 47—comes from the following passage in the twelfth chapter of John:

> 44 Then Jesus cried out and said, "He who believes in Me, believes not in Me but in Him who sent Me. 45 And he who sees Me sees Him who sent Me. 46 I have come as a light into the world, that whoever believes in Me should not abide in darkness. 47 And if anyone hears My words and does not believe, I do not judge him; for I did not come to judge the world but to save the world. 48 He who rejects Me, and does not receive My words, has that which judges him—the word that I have spoken will judge him in the last day. 49 For I have not spoken on My own authority; but the Father who sent Me gave Me a command, what I should say and what I should speak. 50 And I know that His command is everlasting life. Therefore, whatever I speak, just as the Father has told Me, so I speak."
>
> (Jn. 12:44-50)

The first thing to note in this passage is that it presents a contrast—it is the Lord Christ's words that brings life (vs. 50; see also Jn. 5:24, 6:63, 68), and it is Christ's words that will bring condemnation (vs. 48). Secondly, Christ is not saying that unbelievers will not be condemned, for they are *already* under condemnation (Jn. 3:18) and that condemnation will be consummated in the future (vs. 48; see also 5:45; Rev. 20:11-15).

Third, Christ is clarifying that the purpose of His first Advent is not wrath and judgment, but to serve as a light (vs. 46) and Savior (vs. 48) (see also Matt. 18:22; Lk. 19:10; Jn. 1:17, 10:10; 1 Tim. 1:15). But light and Savior of whom? "[W]hoever believes in Me" (vs. 46). "He who believes in Me" (vs. 44). "[H]e who sees Me" (vs. 45; see also 2 Cor. 3:18, 4:4, 6). Therefore, like we saw earlier in this appendix in looking at John 1:10, the use of the word *kosmos* appears to have different meanings in a single verse: "My present mission is not to try and condemn unbelievers before the Judgment Seat of Christ (that is coming later) *because* I still have believers throughout the earth to save." This understanding is reinforced by Christ's parable of the tares and wheat:

> [24] Another parable He put forth to them, saying: "The kingdom of heaven is like a man who sowed good seed in his field; [25] but while men slept, his enemy came and sowed tares among the wheat and went his way. [26] But when the grain had sprouted and produced a crop, then the tares also appeared. [27] So the servants of the owner came and said to him, 'Sir, did you not sow good seed in your field? How then does it have tares?' [28] He said to them, 'An enemy has done this.' The servants said to him, 'Do you want us then to go and gather them up?' [29] But he said, 'No, lest while you gather up the tares you also uproot the wheat with them. [30] Let both grow together until the harvest, and at the time of harvest I will say to the reapers, "First gather together the tares and bind them in bundles to burn them, but gather the wheat into my barn."'"

(Matt. 13:24-30)

The **fifth proof-text** is verse 19 of the fifth chapter of 2 Corinthians:

> [17] Therefore, if anyone is in Christ, he is a new creation; old things have passed away; behold, all things have become new. [18] Now all things are of God, who has reconciled us to Himself through Jesus Christ, and has given us the ministry of reconciliation, [19] that is, that God was in Christ reconciling the world to Himself, not imputing their trespasses to them, and has committed to us the word of reconciliation. [20] Now then, we are ambassadors for Christ, as though God were pleading through us: we implore you on Christ's behalf, be

reconciled to God. 21 For He made Him who knew no sin to be sin for us, that we might become the righteousness of God in Him.

(2 Cor. 5:17-21)

Who is 'the world" that God in Christ is reconciling to Himself (vs. 19)? Not everyone, everywhere, at all times. But rather "us" (vs. 18). "[A]nyone…in Christ" who "is a new creation" (vs. 17). "[Us]" and "we" (vs. 21). It is every member of the elect everywhere at all times without distinction to ethnicity. It is the world of the elect. The world of God's foreloved. The world of the predestined. These and only these are being reconciled to God (ongoing, continuous action throughout the centuries) through double-imputation—Christ bearing an alien (the elect's) sin and dying for it so that the elect might bear an alien (His) righteousness and live through it (vs. 21). The words "that is" at the beginning of verse 19 indicates that it is but a restatement of verse 18, merely changing the scope from the "us" who have already been saved (has *been* reconciled) to the "us" throughout the world in every age that have yet to be saved (are *being* reconciled) and therefore are in need of imploring ambassadors for Christ.

The **sixth proof-text** comes from 1 John 2:2: "And He Himself is the propitiation for our sins, and not for ours only but also for the whole world." The Apostle John uses the term *propitiation* only one other time, which is found in 1 John 4:10 which we looked at earlier in our examination of John 3:16-17. I would encourage the reader to refer back to that discussion for the context of 1 John 4:10, which revealed that the term *propitiation* was clearly reserved for believers and believers only. This is reinforced by a passage we looked at in Chapter 5:

49 And one of them, Caiaphas, being high priest that year, said to them, "You know nothing at all, 50 nor do you consider that it is expedient for us that one man should die for the people, and not that the whole nation should perish." 51 Now this he did not say on his own authority;

but being high priest that year he prophesied that Jesus would die for the nation, 52 and not for that nation only, but also that He would gather together in one the children of God who were scattered abroad.

(Jn. 11:49-52)

Notice the striking similarity between the "not only but for" language of both 1 John 2:2 and John 11:52. In the later the Apostle is clarifying that Jesus' death was not only for the elect ("the children of God") of ethnic Israel, but also for all the elect scattered around the kosmos. Therefore, in light of 1 John 4:10 and its surrounding context, and of John 11:52 and its surrounding context, it is best to interpret 1 John 2:2 as saying, "And He Himself is the propitiation for the sins of those of us who currently believe in this time and place and ethnic group(s), but for all those who will come to believe in all times and place and ethnic groups."

The **seventh and final proof-text** is found in the 14th verse of the fourth chapter of 1 John:

4 You are of God, little children, and have overcome them, because He who is in you is greater than he who is in the world. 5 They are of the world. Therefore they speak as of the world, and the world hears them. 6 We are of God. He who knows God hears us; he who is not of God does not hear us. By this we know the spirit of truth and the spirit of error. 7 Beloved, let us love one another, for love is of God; and everyone who loves is born of God and knows God. 8 He who does not love does not know God, for God is love. 9 In this the love of God was manifested toward us, that God has sent His only begotten Son into the world, that we might live through Him. 10 In this is love, not that we loved God, but that He loved us and sent His Son to be the propitiation for our sins. 11 Beloved, if God so loved us, we also ought to love one another. 12 No one has seen God at any time. If we love one another, God abides in us, and His love

has been perfected in us. [13] By this we know that we abide in Him, and He in us, because He has given us of His Spirit. [14] And we have seen and testify that the Father has sent the Son as Savior of the world. [15] Whoever confesses that Jesus is the Son of God, God abides in him, and he in God. [16] And we have known and believed the love that God has for us. God is love, and he who abides in love abides in God, and God in him.

(1 Jn. 4:4-11)

In light of our examination of verse 10 earlier in this Appendix, as will as verses with similar language (Jn. 1:29, 4:42, 12:42), let it suffice to say that kosmos in verse 14 should be understood as referring to elect believers everywhere at all times without regard for ethnic distinctions.

In conclusion, therefore, we have seen that the Greek word for *world—kosmos—*has a number of different meanings, depending on the context. We gave examples of ten of them, and then demonstrated that there is an eleventh meaning—the world of believers only—which neuters these seven proof-texts of any universal exegesis. For God so loved all kinds and manner of people from a myriad of tongues, tribes, peoples, and nations that He gave His only begotten Son to propitiate His wrath and atone for their sins so that they might pass from death to life, condemnation to reconciliation. The non-elect God has, is, and will always hate.

APPENDIX B: WHO IS "ALL"?

*T*hose objecting to definite atonement, however, may point to the following verses to persist in arguing that, though God may not have died for the entire *world*, He certainly died for *all*:[1]

· **Is. 53:6:** "All we like sheep have gone astray; We have turned, every one, to his own way; And the LORD has laid on Him the iniquity of us all."

· **Rom. 5:18:** "Therefore, as through one man's offense judgment came to all men, resulting in condemnation, even so through one Man's righteous act the free gift came to all men, resulting in justification of life."

· **Rom. 8:32:** "He who did not spare His own Son, but delivered Him up for us all, how shall He not with Him also freely give us all things?"

· **2 Cor. 5:14-15:** "[14] For the love of Christ compels us, because we judge thus: that if One died for all, then all died; [15] and He died for all, that those who live should live no longer for themselves, but for Him who died for them and rose again."

· **Tit. 2:11:** "For the grace of God that brings salvation has appeared to all men,"

· **Heb. 2:9:** "But we see Jesus, who was made a little lower than the angels, for the suffering of death crowned with glory and honor, that He, by the grace of God, might taste death for everyone."

Before we exegete each individual text, we must note that the term *all*—both in English and in Greek—doesn't necessarily mean an unlimited, universal *all*. Context is everything. For

---

[1] Again, it should be obvious that, without being read not only in context but also in light of all of Scripture, every single one of these verses—read superficially and by itself—doesn't merely stand for the proposition of unlimited atonement but of universal salvation as well. It is only the universalist who doesn't have to exegete.

instance, if I were describing a plane crash and reported that all survived, I do not mean that everyone, everywhere, at all times survived that plane crash, but only those on board. Or if I told my wife that a weasel killed all the chickens, I do not mean every chicken, everywhere, at all times was killed by that weasel, but only our flock. Or if I were announcing an upcoming church potluck and said that all were invited, I do not mean everyone, everywhere, at all times are invited, but only those connected with our church.

We see this need for context in understanding the word *all* throughout the New Testament:

- **Matthew 4:23:** Jesus likely didn't heal *all* (i.e., every single known) diseases and sicknesses, but rather every type and manner of disease and sickness.
- **Matthew 23:27:** The teachers of the law and Pharisees were probably not literally full of every single known uncleanness, but merely all kinds of unclearness.
- **Acts 2:5:** Jews from every single nation under heaven were not in Jerusalem for Pentecost, in part because there were no Jews living in every single nation on earth at that time. Rather, every Jew from all kinds of nations were present.
- **Acts 7:22:** Moses doubtless was learned in all kinds of Egyptian wisdom, but it is highly doubtful that he had mastered *all* of their wisdom—law, medicine, engineering, war, literature, etc.
- **Acts 10:11-14:** The large sheet which Peter saw being lowered from heaven did not literally contain *all* four-footed animals that have every walked the face of the earth, but rather *all kinds* of such quadrupeds. Most modern English translations have written that explanation into their versions for you, but it is not in the original Greek.
- **Romans 7:8:** It seems dubious to believe that sin, seizing an opportunity afforded by the commandment, produced in Paul *all* coveting, but rather *every kind* or *all manner* of covetousness.
- **Romans 11:26:** While it is certainly possible that every single Jew alive at the time of Christ's second (and final) coming will

be saved, it is equally if not more plausible that Paul merely means every kind or manner of Jew will be saved without distinction. Mass conversions among the Jewish people will certainly take place, but perhaps not universal conversions.

• **1 Tim. 6:10:** The love of money produces *all kinds* of evil, rather than *all* evil. Again, most modern translations have already paraphrased this for the reader, though it is not in the original Greek.

With that in mind, we turn to our **first proof-text:** "All we like sheep have gone astray; We have turned, every one, to his own way; And the LORD has laid on Him the iniquity of us all" (Is. 53:6). Who is the "us all"? While there are ample clues throughout the passage, verses ten and eleven make the answer explicit—"He shall bear their iniquities" and thereby "justify many" —not *all*, but *many*—so that "He shall see the labor of His soul"— "His seed"—and be satisfied. In light of the context of the entire chapter, therefore, "us all" in verse 6 actually means "all of us believers." The elect. His seed.

The **second proof-text** comes from the 18th verse of the fifth chapter of Romans:

> [12] Therefore, just as through one man sin entered the world, and death through sin, and thus death spread to all men, because all sinned— [13] (For until the law sin was in the world, but sin is not imputed when there is no law. [14] Nevertheless death reigned from Adam to Moses, even over those who had not sinned according to the likeness of the transgression of Adam, who is a type of Him who was to come. [15] But the free gift is not like the offense. For if by the one man's offense many died, much more the grace of God and the gift by the grace of the one Man, Jesus Christ, abounded to many. [16] And the gift is not like that which came through the one who sinned. For the judgment which came from one offense resulted in condemnation, but the free gift which came from many offenses resulted in justification. [17] For if by the one

man's offense death reigned through the one, much more those who receive abundance of grace and of the gift of righteousness will reign in life through the One, Jesus Christ.)

18 Therefore, as through one man's offense judgment came to all men, resulting in condemnation, even so through one Man's righteous act the free gift came to all men, resulting in justification of life. 19 For as by one man's disobedience many were made sinners, so also by one Man's obedience many will be made righteous.

20 Moreover the law entered that the offense might abound. But where sin abounded, grace abounded much more, 21 so that as sin reigned in death, even so grace might reign through righteousness to eternal life through Jesus Christ our Lord.

(Rom. 5:12-21)

Who is the "all men" mentioned in verse 18—all men who have ever walked the face of the earth, or a more definite category of all men? The answer is yes. Both. The phrase *all men* here in verse 18 has the same meaning, but in reference to two different categories. This entire passage is one of the most important in Christian theology for its significance in explaining original sin and federal headship. Here the Apostle Paul is juxtaposing two Adams—two federal heads—the First Man Adam and his biological progeny who share in his defeat, and the Second Adam Jesus Christ and His spiritual progeny (Is. 53:10) who share in His victory. The *all men* condemned by the First Man Adam's Fall refers to all those in Adam—i.e., everyone, everywhere, at all times (see also vs. 12). And the *all men* justified by the Second Adam Jesus Christ's righteousness refers to all those in Christ—i.e., all believers everywhere at all times (see also vs. 17). We see this confirmed in the fifteenth chapter of 1 Corinthians: "21 For since by man came death, by Man also came the resurrection of the dead. 22 For as in Adam all die, even so in Christ all shall be made alive."

The **third proof-text** is verse 32 from chapter 8 of Romans:

28 And we know that all things work together for good to those who love God, to those who are the called according to His purpose. 29 For whom He foreknew, He also predestined to be conformed to the image of His Son, that He might be the firstborn among many brethren. 30 Moreover whom He predestined, these He also called; whom He called, these He also justified; and whom He justified, these He also glorified.

31 What then shall we say to these things? If God is for us, who can be against us? 32 He who did not spare His own Son, but delivered Him up for us all, how shall He not with Him also freely give us all things? 33 Who shall bring a charge against God's elect? It is God who justifies. 34 Who is he who condemns? It is Christ who died, and furthermore is also risen, who is even at the right hand of God, who also makes intercession for us. 35 Who shall separate us from the love of Christ? Shall tribulation, or distress, or persecution, or famine, or nakedness, or peril, or sword? 36 As it is written:

"For Your sake we are killed all day long;

We are accounted as sheep for the slaughter."

37 Yet in all these things we are more than conquerors through Him who loved us. 38 For I am persuaded that neither death nor life, nor angels nor principalities nor powers, nor things present nor things to come, 39 nor height nor depth, nor any other created thing, shall be able to separate us from the love of God which is in Christ Jesus our Lord.

(Rom. 8:28-39)

Who is the "all" of verse 32? Not the world. Not everyone, everywhere, at all times. But only those whom God foreloved (vs. 29), predestined, called, justified, and glorified (vs. 30), the elect (vs. 33), who are without condemnation because of Christ's High Priestly intercession (vs. 34), who are conquerors through Him who loved us (vs. 37), and who are unable to be separated from

His love (vs. 38-39). "All," therefore, refers only to the entire class of believers the world over in every time period, and it is grossly irresponsible to pretend otherwise with this passage.

The **fourth proof-text** comes from verses 14-15 of the fifth chapter of 2 Corinthians:

> 1 For we know that if our earthly house, this tent, is destroyed, we have a building from God, a house not made with hands, eternal in the heavens. 2 For in this we groan, earnestly desiring to be clothed with our habitation which is from heaven, 3 if indeed, having been clothed, we shall not be found naked. 4 For we who are in this tent groan, being burdened, not because we want to be unclothed, but further clothed, that mortality may be swallowed up by life. 5 Now He who has prepared us for this very thing is God, who also has given us the Spirit as a guarantee.
>
> 6 So we are always confident, knowing that while we are at home in the body we are absent from the Lord. 7 For we walk by faith, not by sight. 8 We are confident, yes, well pleased rather to be absent from the body and to be present with the Lord.
>
> 9 Therefore we make it our aim, whether present or absent, to be well pleasing to Him. 10 For we must all appear before the judgment seat of Christ, that each one may receive the things done in the body, according to what he has done, whether good or bad. 11 Knowing, therefore, the terror of the Lord, we persuade men; but we are well known to God, and I also trust are well known in your consciences.
>
> 12 For we do not commend ourselves again to you, but give you opportunity to boast on our behalf, that you may have an answer for those who boast in appearance and not in heart. 13 For if we are beside ourselves, it is for God; or if we are of sound mind, it is for you. 14 For the love of Christ compels us, because we judge thus: that if One died for all, then all died; 15 and He died for all, that

those who live should live no longer for themselves, but
for Him who died for them and rose again.

(2 Cor. 5:1-15)

Who is the "all" of verses 14-15? All those who groan with
earnest desire to be further clothed as mortality is swallowed up
by life (vs. 1-4), who have the Spirit as a guarantee (vs. 5), who
walk by faith and not by sight (vs. 7), who would rather be absent
from the body to be present with Christ (vs. 8), who aim to be
well-pleasing to God (vs. 9), who know the terror of the Lord (vs.
11), and are well known to God (vs. 11), who are compelled by
the love of Christ (vs. 14) to "persuade men" (vs. 11).

Consequently, these verses should be understood as follows:
"14 For the love of Christ compels us, because we judge thus:
that if One died for the entire, universal body of believers in all
times and places, then they all died in Him, 15 and because He
died for them, they should no longer live for themselves but for
Him who died and rose again for them." We see this confirmed in
the previous chapter, where Paul writes: "13 And since we have
the same spirit of faith, according to what is written, "I believed
and therefore I spoke," we also believe and therefore speak,
14 knowing that He who raised up the Lord Jesus will also raise us
up with Jesus, and will present us with you" (2 Cor. 3:13-14). The
"all" of 5:14-15 is the same as the "we," "us," and "you" of 4:13-14
—the entire world of believers.

The **fifth proof-text** reads, "For the grace of God that brings
salvation has appeared to all men" (Tit. 2:11). The verse does not
say that the grace of God *has brought* salvation to all men, but
only that it *has appeared* to all men. This verse is saying nothing
more than what we read in the first chapter of the Gospel of John
—that Christ, the true Light, has come into the world to enlighten
every man (Jn. 1:9; see also Jn. 3:19, 6:14, 12:46). This light is a
light of common grace—ineffectually appearing to all men leaving
them without excuse (Ps. 19:1-4; Rom. 1:18-20, 2:13-16).

But some translators render verse 11 to read that "the grace of
God has been revealed, bringing salvation to all men." That
certainly *seems* to change the focus of the verse from common

enlightenment to effectual salvific sight. Even assuming, arguendo, that such a rendering is more accurate than the NKJV, the rest of the passage explains who the *all men* are:

> 11 For the grace of God that brings salvation has appeared to all men, 12 teaching us that, denying ungodliness and worldly lusts, we should live soberly, righteously, and godly in the present age, 13 looking for the blessed hope and glorious appearing of our great God and Savior Jesus Christ, 14 who gave Himself for us, that He might redeem us from every lawless deed and purify for Himself His own special people, zealous for good works.
>
> (Tit. 2:11-14)

Who are the "all men" of verse 11? Those who are taught (vs. 12) by "the grace of God that brings salvation" (vs. 11) and only them. The "for" (or *because*) at the beginning of verse 11 is vital, for it shows that the subject of salvation is the "us" and "we" (vs. 12), and "our" (vs. 13), and "us" and "own special people" and "redeem[ed]" and "purif[ied]" (vs. 14). "All men," therefore, means "all of us believers in all times and places."

The **sixth and final proof-text** comes for the 9th verse of the second chapter of Hebrews:

> 9 But we see Jesus, who was made a little lower than the angels, for the suffering of death crowned with glory and honor, that He, by the grace of God, might taste death for everyone. 10 For it was fitting for Him, for whom are all things and by whom are all things, in bringing many sons to glory, to make the captain of their salvation perfect through sufferings. 11 For both He who sanctifies and those who are being sanctified are all of one, for which reason He is not ashamed to call them brethren, 12 saying:
>
> "I will declare Your name to My brethren;
> In the midst of the assembly I will sing praise to You."

[13] And again:

> "I will put My trust in Him."

And again:

> "Here am I and the children whom God has given Me."
>
> (Heb. 2:9-13)

Who is the "everyone" for whom Christ tasted death in verse 9? Not all men everywhere in every age, but rather all "the children whom God has given Me" (vs. 13). All of "My brethren" (vs. 12). All of the "many sons [brought] to glory" (vs. 10). "[A]ll those who are being sanctified" and therefore "are all of one" with "He who sanctifies" (vs. 11). Once again, "everyone" means "all of us believers in all times and places."

In conclusion, therefore, the term *all* does not necessarily mean everyone, everywhere, at all times. Rather, it may merely mean all of a particular, defined class of individuals. Only the context can determine its meaning. And as we have seen, the context of these verse do not mean that Christ died for all *men*, but rather all *believers* and them only.

APPENDIX C: DOES GOD DESIRE ALL TO BE SAVED?

Some may object to the doctrine of particular propitiation, or definite atonement, by pointing primarily to the following verses which seem to indicate that God desires all men to be saved:

> • **1 Tim. 2:4:** "who [God] desires all men to be saved and to come to the knowledge of the truth."
>
> • **2 Pet. 3:9:** "The Lord is not slack concerning His promise, as some count slackness, but is longsuffering toward us, not willing that any should perish but that all should come to repentance."
>
> • **Ezek. 18:23:** "'Do I have any pleasure at all that the wicked should die?' says the LORD God, 'and not that he should turn from his ways and live?'" (see also vs. 32).
>
> • **Matt. 23:37:** "'O Jerusalem, Jerusalem, the one who kills the prophets and stones those who are sent to her! How often I wanted to gather your children together, as a hen gathers her chicks under her wings, but you were not willing!'"

Before exegeting these particular texts, let us take a step back and look at the big picture and see what, exactly, the objector is (unknowingly) arguing for. For Scripture and reality clearly deny universalism—the belief that all men will be saved, whether in this life or the next (Matt. 7:13-14, 22:14). Consequently, the objector wishes us to believe that Scripture teaches that what God decisively desires—the salvation of all—will not, in fact, come to pass.

Now there are only three possible solutions to this quandary. The first is that God is lying in these proof-texts presented by the objector, a notion which Scripture repeatedly and emphatically denies (Num. 23:19; 1 Sam. 15:29; Tit. 1:2; Heb. 6:18). The second is that God means well but is just impotent or incompetent or both. He wants all men to be saved, but He is powerless to save anyone. He desires all men to be with Him in heaven, but His Plan A of Calvary isn't quite working the way He thought it would and He's struggling to come up with a Plan B. And that's blasphemy.

The third and final solution is that the Trinity is divided. That God the Father really wants all men to be saved, but that God the Son only wants to atone for but a few and thereby thwarts His Father's will. Or God the Father does desire all men to be saved and God the Son is in agreement with He plan, but God the Holy Spirit vetos the majority of the Godhead and instead only effectuates salvation for a definite minority of mankind. And that's heresy.

There is no other viable solution if these proof-texts do, in fact, teach that God's primary and decisive will is for all men to be saved. But is that, in fact, what they teach? Again, before exegeting these specific texts, let us look at two considerations. The first is that God often simultaneously commands what He does not effectually will. We saw this earlier in Chapter 4 when we examined God's free will over sin. To briefly reiterate, God wills men not to murder (Ex. 20:13), yet He Himself wills murder to happen (Acts 4:27-28). He wills men not to lie (Ex. 20:16), yet He Himself wills lies to happen (1 Kings 22:22-23; Ezek. 14:9; 2 These. 2:10-12). Theologians distinguish between these two wills by calling the former the "will of command" and the later the "will of decree." Or God's revealed will and His secret will. Or His moral will and His sovereign will.

Therefore, in considering these proof-texts, the divine desire spoken of may simply be God's revealed will—His will of command or His moral will—that all men everywhere repent and believe the Gospel (Mk. 1:15). We often view the Gospel call as an offer rather than a command, but it is clearly depicted as both in Scripture. God "now commands all men everywhere to repent!" (Acts 17:30). Therefore, just as God wills—on one level —that all men everywhere should not murder or lie, so He also wills—on one level—that all men everywhere should repent and believe the Gospel. But this willing isn't necessarily His will of decree (or secret will, sovereign will, or effectual will).

The second consideration is that it is not at all unusual to experience conflicting emotions. This does not mean that one is schizophrenic, but merely that one is not a robot. That one is a complex individual who takes multiple considerations into account, including emotions, before reaching a final, decisive course of action. For instance, I desire to lose weight. But I do not effectuate that desire because it is outweighed (pun unintended...) by a plethora of other factors. We may experience these conflicting emotions simultaneously, sincerely, and effectually. Believers, for instance, are exhorted in the midst of their sorrow to also, simultaneously, be always rejoicing (2 Cor. 6:10).

And this divided will, this mix of emotions, these conflicting emotions is not absent from our Triune God. We see this clearly illustrated in the example of Christ the night before His death. Three times (Matt. 22:44) He "offered up prayers and supplications, with vehement cries and tears to Him who was able to save Him from death" (Heb. 5:7) as He sweated great drops of blood (Lk. 22:44). And yet, despite not wanting—on one level—to experience the hell of His Father's wrath, He submitted —on another, much more decisive level—His emotions, His will, His desire, to that of HIs Father's in humble obedience (Matt. 26:39; Mk. 14:36; Lk. 22:42; Jn. 6:38; Phil. 2:8).[1]

Therefore, while God may—on one level—sincerely desire many things (1 Sam. 15:22; Ps. 51:16-17; Hosea 6:6; Mal. 6:8), on another, much more decisive level He does not effectuate those desires. This distinction may be called His subordinate will(s) and His dominate will. His subordinate will may be for all men to be saved, but He does not effectually will that all men be saved. His subordinate will is not to punish HIs children from HIs heart (Lam. 3:33), and yet as a loving Father He effectually wills their discipline. His subordinate will is not to harm His beloved

---

[1] These two wills or desires do not mean that God has unfulfilled desires and is therefore thwarted in His joy. To the contrary, all of His desires are perfectly and infinitely satisfied in His dominate or controlling will. We again see this clearly in the example of the Lord Christ in Gethsemane, where His desires were infinitely and perfectly satisfied in doing the will of His Father *for* the joy that was set before Him (Heb. 12:2).

Son, and yet He effectually wills to smite and crush (Is. 53:4, 10) and slaughter Him (Rev. 5: 6, 9, 12).

With these considerations in mind, now let us turn to examine the various proof-texts offered by our objector. The **first** comes from 1 Timothy 2:4, which reads, "who [God] desires all men to be saved and to come to the knowledge of the truth." The words *all men* (*pantas anthropous*) are clearly in the original Greek. Case closed, right? God wants all men to be saved, end of story. Perhaps on a subordinate level He does, but let us look at the big picture without chapter or verse divisions which are not original to the text and often cloud the meaning of a passage.

The Apostle Paul had just issued a doxology (1:17) because "Christ Jesus came into the world to save sinners, of whom I am chief" (1:15). He then exhorted his "son Timothy" to "wage the good warfare" (1:18) in faith and a good conscience (1:19), not as those who have suffered shipwreck (1:19) such as Hymenaeus and Alexander whom Paul "delivered to Satan that they may learn not to blaspheme" (vs. 20). And immediately thereafter we read:

> 1 Therefore I exhort first of all that supplications, prayers, intercessions, and giving of thanks be made for all men, 2 for kings and all who are in authority, that we may lead a quiet and peaceable life in all godliness and reverence. 3 For this is good and acceptable in the sight of God our Savior, 4 who desires all men to be saved and to come to the knowledge of the truth. 5 For there is one God and one Mediator between God and men, the Man Christ Jesus, 6 who gave Himself a ransom for all, to be testified in due time, 7 for which I was appointed a preacher and an apostle—I am speaking the truth in Christ and not lying—a teacher of the Gentiles in faith and truth.
>
> (1 Tim. 2:1-7)

We see three *alls* in this passage:

• **Verse 1:** "I exhort first of all that supplications, prayers, intercessions, and giving of thanks be made for *all men*" (emphasis added).

• **Verse 4:** God "desires *all men* to be saved" (emphasis added).

• **Verse 6:** Jesus—the "one Mediator between God and men" (vs. 5)—"gave Himself a ransom for *all*" (vs. 6; emphasis added).

Who are the *all men* of verse 1? They are found in verse 2—kings and all who are in authority. So we see that the first *all* we come to in this passage is not unlimited. It is not universal. It does not mean all men everywhere at all times. And why are we to pray for these *definite all*? So "that we may lead a quiet and peaceable life in all godliness and reverence" (vs. 2). Why? So the Gospel can spread unhindered because God "desires all men to be saved and to come to the knowledge of the truth" (vs. 4). Who are these *all men* of verse 4? Those whom Jesus—the "one Mediator between God and men" (vs. 5)—gave Himself as a ransom for (vs. 6).

If *all men* in verse 1 is not universal but rather defined and limited by the Apostle in verse 2, then it stands to reason that the *all men* of verse 4 may well not be universal but rather defined and limited by the Apostle in the subsequent two verses. This view is buttressed by passage after passage in which the Apostle clearly teaches that Christ only atoned, or ransomed, a definite few—His Bride (Eph. 5:25), His sheep (Acts 20:28), His elect (Eph. 1:4-7), His people (Rom. 4:25; 1 Cor. 15:3; Gal. 2:20; Eph. 5:2).

Therefore, using Scripture to interpret Scripture as well remembering our discussion of the possible meanings of the word *all* in Appendix B, it seems best to interpret the *all men* of 1 Timothy 2:4 as, *all kinds of men*. All the elect everywhere in every place at all times without distinction as to rank, class, standing, ethnicity, etc.

The **second proof-text** raised by our objector reads, "The Lord is not slack concerning His promise, as some count slackness, but is longsuffering toward us, not willing that any should perish but that all should come to repentance" (2 Pet. 3:9). Who are the *any* and *all* in this verse? The first part of the verse provides the answer—*us*. Or as some of the underlying Greek texts states, *you*. In either case, Peter is exhorting believers (the "beloved" of verse 1) to patiently endure despite the fact that Christ has not yet returned a second (and final) time because He is waiting for the full number of elect to repent and not to perish (Matt. 13:24-30; Jn. 12:47).

The **third proof-text** enlisted by our objector are several statements made by God through the prophet Ezekiel:

• **Ezek. 18:23:** "'Do I have any pleasure at all that the wicked should die?' says the LORD God, 'and not that he should turn from his ways and live?'"

• **Ezek. 18:32:** "'For I have no pleasure in the death of one who dies," says the LORD God. "Therefore turn and live!'"

• **Ezek. 33:11:** "'Say to them: "As I live," says the LORD God, "I have no pleasure in the death of the wicked, but that the wicked turn from his way and live. Turn, turn from your evil ways! For why should you die, O house of Israel?"'"

We should first note that whatever God does, He takes pleasure in (Ps. 115:3). This is part and parcel of being God. Everything that God does must, of necessity, be infinitely perfect. And if God would cease to take pleasure in the infinitely perfect work of His hands, He would be committing idolatry by taking pleasure in the works of the hands of a creature rather than Himself. He does everything for His own glory, and should He stop taking pleasure in the pursuit of His own glory He would no longer be the most infinitely valuable Being imaginable.

God, therefore, even takes delight in executing judgment upon the wicked, for He tells us that because simple ones, scorners, and fools disdain and refuse Him, "'I also will laugh at your calamity; I will mock when your terror comes'" (Prov. 1:26; see also Ps. 37:13, 59:8). "He who sits in the heavens shall laugh; The Lord shall hold them in derision" (Ps. 2:4). In destroying

Judah, Yahweh pronounces that, "'Thus shall my anger spend itself, and I will vent my fury upon them and satisfy myself. And they shall know that I am the LORD—that I have spoken in my jealousy—when I spend my fury upon them'" (Ezek. 5:13 ESV). God was satisfied in executing His vengeance upon Jerusalem. Elsewhere we are told that He took pleasure in bringing judgment upon Babylon (Is. 48:14).

Therefore, these proof-texts from Ezekiel should not be interpreted in an absolute sense, but rather that God does not— on one level—take pleasure in disobedience. Again, this is an example of the distinction between God's moral will and His sovereign will. The point of the eighteenth chapter of Ezekiel, for instance, is God rebuking a Jewish proverb that a child should pay for the sins of his father and vice versa. Rather, Yahweh proclaims:

4 "Behold, all souls are Mine;
The soul of the father
As well as the soul of the son is Mine;
The soul who sins shall die.
5 But if a man is just
And does what is lawful and right...
9 If he has walked in My statutes
And kept My judgments faithfully—
He is just;
He shall surely live!"
Says the LORD God...
20 The soul who sins shall die. The son shall not bear the guilt of the father, nor the father bear the guilt of the son. The righteousness of the righteous shall be upon himself, and the wickedness of the wicked shall be upon himself...
25 "Yet you say, 'The way of the Lord is not fair.' Hear now, O house of Israel, is it not My way which is fair, and your ways which are not fair? 26 When a righteous man turns away from his righteousness, commits iniquity, and dies in it, it is because of the iniquity which he has done

that he dies. 27 Again, when a wicked man turns away from the wickedness which he committed, and does what is lawful and right, he preserves himself alive. 28 Because he considers and turns away from all the transgressions which he committed, he shall surely live; he shall not die. 29 Yet the house of Israel says, 'The way of the LORD is not fair.' O house of Israel, is it not My ways which are fair, and your ways which are not fair?

30 "Therefore I will judge you, O house of Israel, every one according to his ways," says the LORD God. "Repent, and turn from all your transgressions, so that iniquity will not be your ruin. 31 Cast away from you all the transgressions which you have committed, and get yourselves a new heart and a new spirit. For why should you die, O house of Israel? 32 For I have no pleasure in the death of one who dies," says the LORD God. "Therefore turn and live!"

(Ezek. 18:4-5, 9, 20, 25-32)

God, therefore, takes no delight, no pleasure, in disobedience. In rebellion. In sin. In having His moral law trampled and mocked and ignored. And it must not be overlooked that Yahweh is rebuking a people who—save for a small remnant according to election (Rom. 11:5)—He has "has not given you a heart to perceive and eyes to see and ears to hear, to this very day" (Deut. 29:4). The promise of the New Covenant (Jer. 31:31-34, 32:39-40; Ezek. 11:19-20, 36:26-27) was not fulfilled until centuries after Ezekiel's ministry. And yet man is absolutely responsible to do what man is absolutely morally unable to do.

The **fourth and final verse** raised by our objector comes from the Lord Christ Himself, "'O Jerusalem, Jerusalem, the one who kills the prophets and stones those who are sent to her! How often I wanted to gather your children together, as a hen gathers her chicks under her wings, but you were not willing!'" (Matt. 23:37). This, like the passages we just looked at from Ezekiel, further illustrates the difference between God's commands and His decrees. On one level God commands and delights in obedience, and yet on the other hand God decrees disobedience for good purposes (namely, the fuller display of His glory).

APPENDIX D: BUT CAN'T YOU LOSE YOUR SALVATION?

Salvation is absolutely and unequivocally conditional upon persevering faith—evidenced by fruit-bearing obedience—until one's final breath. Let me repeat that to avoid any confusion whatsoever—salvation is conditional. If anyone tells you otherwise, they are negligently mishandling the Word of God by misinterpreting Scripture with their preconceived theological blinders on, thereby doing a gross disservice to the faith of believers. If one does not continue fighting the fight of faith, one will go to hell. That is an undeniable Scriptural reality.

However, Scripture is also absolutely and unequivocally clear that genuine, Born Again, regenerated believers will always satisfy the conditionality of salvation. Let me repeat that to make sure we are absolutely clear—salvation is conditional, and the elect of God will always meet that condition by heeding both the warnings and promises, admonitions and assurances, of Scripture. If anyone tells you otherwise, they, too, are negligently mishandling the Word of God by exegeting Scripture through an already established theological system rather than letting the Word of God speak for itself. And by doing so, they do a gross disservice to the faith of believers, for authentic children of God will always continue to abide in Christ and therefore enter into His heavenly rest. That is an undeniable Scriptural reality.

The warnings and promises, admonitions and assurances, of Scripture are not in opposition to one another but rather support one another. They are not incompatible, but helpmates joined at the hip. For the goal of both is not to cause a believer to question their faith, but rather to spur them on with confidence towards the finish line. Their purpose is not to create doubt, but assurance; not to produce despondent introspection that results in self-condemnation and self-loathing, but bold looking unto Jesus (Heb. 12:2); not limping between two minds (1 Kings 18:21 ESV), but courageous laying hold on Him who first laid hold of us (Phil. 3:12).

Nor is it at all insincere to simultaneously believe both the warnings and the promises, the admonitions and the assurances. Faith in one does not make faith in the other hypocritical, double-minded, or duplicitous. For both are simply extensions of the Gospel call—repent and believe or remain under eternal condemnation. Penitent faith—the faith that saves, sanctifies, and perseveres—is but humbly and fearfully recognizing that one is unable to save himself, much less stay saved, by one's own power, but rather that one but must turn to God in faith that He, and He alone, can save and keep you. It is an absolute helplessness, a desperate despairing, of one's own ability but a resolute hope, a confident assurance, of God's ability to save and to preserve. It is a fear of self, not of God's faithfulness. A distrust of self, not of God's promises. And these warnings and admonitions, just as much as the promises and assurances, are the *means* decreed by God to keep the Born Again in the faith.

Salvation is a process, not merely a once-for-all completed event in time. The race isn't won at the starting line but at the finish line. There is the Exodus, but then there still remains entering the Promised Land. There is Passover, but then there is still the Day of Atonement (Yom Kippur). Believers are saved, they are being saved, and they will be saved. The later two are predicated upon the first and are no less infallibly certain than the first.

Born Again believers are saved—past-tense:

• **Rom. 5:1:** "Therefore, *having been* justified by faith, we have peace with God through our Lord Jesus Christ" (emphasis added). We have been justified—past-tense—at the moment of conversion, and therefore are currently enjoying peace with God.

• **Rom. 8:14-16:** "14 For as many as are led by the Spirit of God, these are sons of God. 15 For you did not receive the spirit of bondage again to fear, but you *received* the Spirit of adoption by whom we cry out, "Abba, Father." 16 The Spirit Himself bears witness with our spirit that we are children of God" (emphasis added).

• **Rom. 8:30:** "Moreover whom He predestined, these He also called; whom He called, these He also *justified*; and whom He justified, these He also *glorified*" (emphasis added). Not only have we been justified in the past at a point in time, but we have also been already glorified!

• **1 Cor. 1:2:** "To the church of God which is at Corinth, to those who *are sanctified* in Christ Jesus, called to be saints…" (emphasis added).

• **Eph. 1:7:** "In Him we *have redemption* through His blood, the forgiveness of sins, according to the riches of His grace" (emphasis added).

• **Eph. 2:4-6:** "⁴ But God, who is rich in mercy, because of His great love with which He loved us, ⁵ even when we were dead in trespasses, *made* us alive together with Christ (by grace you *have been saved*), ⁶ and *raised us* up together, and *made us* sit together in the heavenly places in Christ Jesus" (emphasis added).

• **Eph. 2:8:** "For by grace you *have been saved* through faith, and that not of yourselves; it is the gift of God" (emphasis added).

• **Col. 1:13-14:** "¹³ He has deliver*ed* us from the power of darkness and convey*ed* us into the kingdom of the Son of His love, ¹⁴ in whom we *have redemption* through His blood, the forgiveness of sins" (emphasis added).

But Born Again believers are currently, progressively saved—present-tense:

• **Acts 2:47:** "…And the Lord added to the church daily those who *were being saved*" (emphasis added).

• **1 Cor. 1:18:** "For the message of the cross is foolishness to those who are perishing, but to us who *are being saved* it is the power of God" (emphasis added).

• **2 Cor. 2:15:** "For we are to God the fragrance of Christ among those who *are being saved* and among those who are perishing" (emphasis added).

• **2 These. 2:13:** "But we are bound to give thanks to God always for you, brethren beloved by the Lord, because God from the beginning chose you *for salvation through sanctification* by the Spirit and belief in the truth" (emphasis added).

And Born Again believers will be saved from the Day of God's Wrath yet to come—future-tense:

• **Rom. 5:9-10:** "9 Much more then, having now been justified by His blood, we shall be saved from wrath through Him. 10 For if when we were enemies we were reconciled to God through the death of His Son, much more, having been reconciled, we shall be saved by His life" (emphasis added).
• **Rom. 8:17, 23:** "17 and if children, then heirs—heirs of God and joint heirs with Christ, *if* indeed we suffer with Him, that we *may also* be glorified together...23 Not only that, but we also who have the firstfruits of the Spirit, even we ourselves groan within ourselves, *eagerly waiting* for the adoption, the redemption of our body" (emphasis added).
• **Rom. 13:11:** "And do this, knowing the time, that now it is high time to awake out of sleep; for now *our salvation is nearer* than when we first believed" (emphasis added).
• **Gal. 5:5:** "For we through the Spirit *eagerly wait* for the hope of righteousness by faith" (emphasis added).
• **Eph. 4:30:** "And do not grieve the Holy Spirit of God, by whom you were sealed *for the day of redemption*" (emphasis added).
• **1 Thess. 1:10:** "and to wait for His Son from heaven, whom He raised from the dead, even Jesus who delivers us *from the wrath to come*" (emphasis added).
• **1 Thess. 5:9-10:** "9 For God did not appoint us to wrath, but *to obtain* salvation through our Lord Jesus Christ, 10 who died for us, that whether we wake or sleep, we *should* live together with Him" (emphasis added).
• **1 Thess. 5:23:** "Now may the God of peace Himself sanctify you *completely*; and *may* your whole spirit, soul, and body *be*

preserved blameless at the coming of our Lord Jesus Christ" (emphasis added).

• **2 Tim. 4:18:** "And the Lord *will deliver* me from every evil work and *preserve* me for His heavenly kingdom. To Him be glory forever and ever. Amen!" (emphasis added).

• **Heb. 9:28:** "so Christ was offered once to bear the sins of many. To those who eagerly wait for Him He will appear a second time, apart from sin, *for salvation*" (emphasis added).

• **1 Pet. 1:5:** "who are kept by the power of God through faith *for salvation ready to be revealed in the last time*" (emphasis added).

Scripture, therefore, is emphatically clear that Born Again believers have already been saved and yet will be saved in the future. We are justified, past-tense, in a legal, forensic sense. All of our sins—past, present, and future—are already forgiven and we bear them no more. The banner of not guilty flies over our heads as we are clothed with the righteousness of Christ. This salvation is applied to us in the here-and-now, and It will decisively determine our immediate state in the afterlife.

But our salvation will not be fully realized until we appear before the Judgment Seat of Christ where we will be saved from the wrath and fury of Almighty God. For everyone—believer and nonbeliever—must stand before the Great White Throne and be held accountable for every word, thought, and deed done in this life (Rom. 14:10; see also Matt. 12:36; Jn. 5:22; Acts 10:42; 2 Cor. 5:10; Heb. 4:13, 9:27; 1 Pet. 4;5; Rev. 20:12).

And between having already been saved and our future salvation we are currently being saved through persevering sanctification (2 Thess. 2:13; see also 2 Cor. 3:18). Salvation, therefore, is a race that is conditional upon finishing it. This is seen most clearly in the "word exhortation" of the book of Hebrews (Heb. 13:22), which constantly refers to salvation in the ongoing, not-yet-fully-realized tense. For instance:

• **1:14:** "Are they not all ministering spirits sent forth to minister for those who *will inherit* salvation?" (emphasis added).

- **2:3:** "how *shall we escape if* we neglect so great a salvation, which at the first began to be spoken by the Lord, and was confirmed to us by those who heard Him" (emphasis added).
- **2:10:** "For it was fitting for Him, for whom are all things and by whom are all things, *in bringing* many sons to glory, to make the captain of their salvation perfect through sufferings" (emphasis added).
- **9:15:** "And for this reason He is the Mediator of the new covenant, by means of death, for the redemption of the transgressions under the first covenant, that those who are called *may receive* the promise of the eternal inheritance" (emphasis added).

Genuine, Born Again believers are being brought to glory (2:10) where, in the future, they will inherit salvation (1:14)—escape from the coming wrath of God (2:3). We see this most clearly in the analogy of a Sabbath rest (eternal salvation) awaiting persevering believers:

> [1] Therefore, since a promise remains of entering His rest, let us fear lest any of you seem to have come short of it. [2] For indeed the gospel was preached to us as well as to them; but the word which they heard did not profit them, not being mixed with faith in those who heard it. [3] For we who have believed do enter that rest, as He has said:
>
> > "So I swore in My wrath,
> > 'They shall not enter My rest,' "
>
> although the works were finished from the foundation of the world. [4] For He has spoken in a certain place of the seventh day in this way: "And God rested on the seventh day from all His works"; [5] and again in this place: "They shall not enter My rest."
>
> [6] Since therefore it remains that some must enter it, and those to whom it was first preached did not enter because of disobedience, [7] again He designates a certain day, saying in David, "Today," after such a long time, as it has been said:

"Today, if you will hear His voice,
Do not harden your hearts."

[8] For if Joshua had given them rest, then He would not afterward have spoken of another day. [9] There remains therefore a rest for the people of God. [10] For he who has entered His rest has himself also ceased from his works as God did from His.

[11] Let us therefore be diligent to enter that rest, lest anyone fall according to the same example of disobedience.

(Heb. 4:1-11)

The ancient Hebrews had been delivered from the bondage of slavery in Egypt, but the rest was not life in the wilderness but of inheriting the Promised Land. They were absolutely free, redeemed, and delivered, but not yet. Similarly, our eternal rest is in the future—it remains to be obtained—and, while assuring that "we who have believed *do enter* that rest" (vs. 3; emphasis added), at the same time the author exhorts believers to:

- **Vs. 1:** Fear lest we come short.
- **Vs. 11:** "Be diligent to enter that rest."

We also see this already-not-yet salvation depicted in the Jewish calendar where all the Jewish feasts point to Jesus. It is so easy to glance over these God-appointed feasts in the Old Testament as simply part of the ritual and ceremony of His covenant with Israel that has no real bearing on us today. But a moment's reflection will show the deep symbolism of the Jewish Calendar. According to Exodus 12:2, God mandated the first day of the spring month of Nissan is to be their "beginning of months; it shall be the first month of the year to you."[1] The holiday called Rosh Hashanah, which literally means "head of the year."

---

[1] For reasons unbeknownst to history, the Jewish new year was inexplicably (and unscripturally) changed to the first day of the seventh month.

Then fourteen days later is Passover when, nearly 2,000 years ago, God offered His one and only Son as the final and perfect Passover Lamb for sins. We spent some time in chapter 5 examining how Jesus serves as both the atoning sacrificial goat and scapegoat of the Day of Atonement. But He also serves as the our Passover Lamb (Is. 53:7; Jn. 1:29; 1 Cor. 5:7)—"a lamb without blemish and without spot" (1 Pet. 1:19; see also Ex. 12:5) whose body did not remain until morning (Ex. 12:10). And when God sees the blood of the Lamb, He "will pass over the door and not allow the destroyer to come into your houses to strike you" (Ex. 12:23). Our Passover Lamb has—for those who believe— propitiated God's wrath upon the world.

Then the first day after the Saturday Sabbath immediately following Passover is the Jewish Feast of First Fruits, on which the Messiah was raised from the dead and become the first fruits of the resurrection promise (1 Cor. 15:23). Finally, fifty days after the Feast of First Fruits is the Jewish festival of Pentecost, in which in Acts 2 God poured out the Holy Spirit upon the early Church to empower Her for ministry.

Then there is a long pause—foreshadowing the current Church Age—between the spring Jewish feasts and the cluster of fall feasts.[2] This intermission comes to an end on the first day of the seventh month with the Feast of Trumpets—foreshadowing when Messiah Jesus will return with "the trumpet of God" (1 Thess. 4:16). Next comes Yom Kippur ten days later—the Day of Atonement—foreshadowing the consummated salvation of the corporate elect before the Great White Throne on the Final Judgment Day.[3] Finally, five days later, comes the Jewish Feast

---

[2] No advocate of pre-millenialism, to the author's knowledge, has been able to explain away how, just as there is not measurable gap between the fall feasts, there isn't one between the end-time events they foreshadow. Just as the events foreshadowed by the fist cluster of spring feasts happened back-to-back, so to will the second cluster of events.

[3] The sacrificial goat and scapegoat on the Day of Atonement were primarily corporal (for the entire nation) rather than

of Tabernacles, foreshadowing when the elect will tabernacle with God and God Himself will tabernacle with us (Rev. 21:3) at the marriage supper of the Lamb (Rev. 19:9).

In conclusion, therefore, we have seen—from the testimony of Scripture, the Exodus of Israel, and the long delay between Passover and Yom Kippur on the Jewish calendar—that full and final salvation is conditional upon enduring the race of life with persevering faith. This is why we see exhortation after exhortation in Scripture commanding us to work out our salvation with fear and trembling (Phil. 2:12).[5] Unlike many of my Calvinist friends, I am not going to engage in linguistic contortions and contradictory flights of (il)logic to rewrite these passages in the image of Reformed theology.

But by the same token, we must be careful not to read into these verses more than what they actually say. Just as it is exegetically dishonest to read these passages out of Scripture by imposing the perseverance of the saints upon them, so it is exegetically dishonest to interpret these passages by imposing the possibility that believers could lose their salvation upon them. Rather, all these passages merely say is that salvation is conditional upon persevering. That's it. No more and no less. We know from our discussion in Chapter 6 that believers will always persevere and, therefore, satisfy the conditional requirement of salvation. But that is no reason to dull these warnings and admonitions by making them retrospective (i.e.,

---

individual, whereas at Passover each family unit had to slaughter a lamb and, at the original Passover, apply its blood to their house. At the final Day of Atonement before the Judgment Seat of Christ, our combined Sacrificial Goat/Scapegoat will publicly acknowledge to His Father that, "This one is Mine, for I foreloved him and purchased him with My blood" (Matt. 7:21-23, 10:32).

[5] For a much more detailed explanation of this view, please see *The Race Set Before Us: A Biblical Theology of Perseverance and Assurance* by Thomas Schreiner and Ardel Caneday and Schreiner's followup book, *Run to Win the Prize: Perseverance in the New Testament*.

"Test your past faith and its fruit to see if you are really a believer!") rather than prospective (i.e., "Run with endurance!").

The exhortations to persevere are myriad in Scripture, but let us just look at those in the book of Hebrews.

- **2:1:** "Therefore we must give the more earnest heed to the things we have heard, *lest* we drift away" (emphasis added).
- **3:6:** "but Christ as a Son over His own house, whose house we are *if* we hold fast the confidence and the rejoicing of the hope firm to the end" (emphasis added).
- **3:12:** "*Beware*, brethren, *lest* there be in any of you an evil heart of unbelief in departing from the living God" (emphasis added).
- **3:14:** "For we have become partakers of Christ *if* we hold the beginning of our confidence steadfast to the end" (emphasis added).
- **4:1:** "Therefore, since a promise remains of entering His rest, *let us fear lest* any of you seem to have come short of it" (emphasis added).
- **4:11:** *"Be diligent* to enter that rest" (emphasis added).
- **5:9:** "And having been perfected, He became the author of eternal salvation to *all who obey Him*" (emphasis added).
- **6:4-8:** "⁴ For it is impossible for those who were once enlightened, and have tasted the heavenly gift, and have become partakers of the Holy Spirit, ⁵ and have tasted the good word of God and the powers of the age to come, ⁶ if they fall away, to renew them again to repentance, since they crucify again for themselves the Son of God, and put Him to an open shame. ⁷ For the earth which drinks in the rain that often comes upon it, and bears herbs useful for those by whom it is cultivated, receives blessing from God; ⁸ but if it bears thorns and briers, it is rejected and near to being cursed, whose end is to be burned."⁶

---

⁶ Most Reformed theologians argue that this passage describes the almost Christian. There are many exegetical reasons why that view is seriously flawed, but among the most glaring is why

• **9:28:** "so Christ was offered once to bear the sins of many. *To those who* eagerly wait for Him He will appear a second time, apart from sin, for salvation" (emphasis added).

• **10:26-31:** "26 For if we sin willfully after we have received the knowledge of the truth, there no longer remains a sacrifice for sins, 27 but a certain fearful expectation of judgment, and fiery indignation which will devour the adversaries. 28 Anyone who has rejected Moses' law dies without mercy on the testimony of two or three witnesses. 29 Of how much worse punishment, do you suppose, will he be thought worthy who has trampled the Son of God underfoot, counted the blood of the covenant by which he was sanctified a common thing, and insulted the Spirit of grace? 30 For we know Him who said, "Vengeance is Mine, I will repay," says the Lord. And again, "The LORD will judge His people." 31 It is a fearful thing to fall into the hands of the living God."

• **10:35-38:** "35 Therefore do not cast away your confidence, which has great reward. 36 For you have need of endurance, so that after you have done the will of God, you may receive the promise: 37 'For yet a little while, and He who is coming will come and will not tarry. 38 Now the just shall live by faith; but *if anyone draws back*, My soul has no pleasure in him'" (emphasis added).

• **12.25:** "*See that you do not refuse Him* who speaks. For if they did not escape who refused Him who spoke on earth, much more shall we not escape *if* we turn away from Him who speaks from heaven" (emphasis added).

---

we should desire at all to renew such almost Christians to almost repentance (which Calvinists claim is described in verse 6) rather than genuine repentance?   And why do we want to warn these almost Christians against apostasy (falling away) when, in fact, they are already apostates who have nothing to fall from?   And why should they be in more danger of hellfire for being apostate almost Christians than they are for being almost Christians in the first place?   How are they crucifying again the Son of God when they haven't stopped crucifying Him?

Every single one of these warnings and admonitions is addressed to believers with the exhortation that they must persevere or perish. They aren't telling them that they can lose their salvation, though such a proposition is denied by the entire testimony of Scripture (1 Sam. 12:22). They aren't telling them that if they perish they were not true believers in the first place, though that is the testimony of the entirety of Scripture (1 Jn. 2:19). These subjects, however, are not their purview. We must not read conditional warnings ("if you") as if they are imperative declarations ("you are"). Rather, they are simply pleading with believers to finish the race called salvation. Their focus is entirely prospective ("you will not be finally saved") rather than retrospective ("you were not saved at all").

It is imperative to note that the promises and assurances of the book of Hebrews are nearly as many as the warnings and admonitions (1:14, 2:10-11, 4:3, 14, 16, 6:9-12, 10:39, 12:1-2) and often interspersed with them. They are two sides of the same coin, both serving to exhort believers—while it is still called "Today" (Heb. 3:13)—to hold fast without wavering (10:23) to the full assurance of faith (10:22) because He who promised is faithful (10:23) (see also 12:12-13). They both serve the same purpose—as the God-ordained means of endurance. And when we eradicate one in favor of the other, we cripple the runners, and hamstrung believers is not the Scriptural way of salvation.

For the believer, these warnings and admonitions are not an intellectual hypothetical, like a virus to the vaccinated. These exhortations are real. Repent, and keep on repenting, or you will perish! Believe, and keep on believing, or you will be condemned! Run, and keep on running, or you will not finish! Hold fast, and keep holding fast, or you will fall! These precious warnings and admonitions are just as real as the promises and assurances of Scripture. Romans 8:32, for instance, is just as true and valid for the believer as Hebrews 6:4-8; you cannot have one without the other.

The promises (Mk. 13:22) are *only* guaranteed through the warnings (vs. 23, 33); the admonitions (Acts 27:31) make the assurance (vs. 22-25) certain. In fact, greater confidence in the promises produces greater confidence in the warnings and vice versa. The greater the assurance a believer has, the greater vigilance to heed the warnings he will also have. The greater love for the Promisor, the more fearful His warnings become. The greater desire for the Prize of our high calling will make the risk of losing Him appear that much more alarming—inducing the runner to, with even more blood-earnestness, cast off everything that hinders and the sin that so easily entangles in order to run with persevering endurance to win his Prize. And just as their counterparts, these warnings and admonitions are always effectual; they have a 100%, no-fail success rate.

Therefore, let us exhort, encourage, and persuade one another to continue walking with the Lord (Acts 11:23b) with grace-wrought (Acts 13:43b) faith (Acts 14:22a) in fear and trembling (2 Cor. 5:11; Phil. 2:12) accompanied by the full assurance of hope until the end (Heb. 6:11).

NATHAN W. TUCKER

COMING 2026!

CATECHIZING AS DOXOLOGY:

THE CHRISTIAN FAITH IN FULL BLOOM

A 365 QUESTION CATECHISM AS A DAILY FAMILY
DEVOTIONAL BASED ON THE 1689 2ND LONDON
BAPTIST CONFESSION OF FAITH

OTHER BOOKS BY NATHAN TUCKER:

Are My Babies in Heaven?   A Grieving Pastor Finds Comfort in the God of Scripture

You Must Be Born Again! An Evangelistic Exposition of John 3:1-8

Agape: The Essence of Saving Faith

The Five Solas: An Expository Exhortation

Julia's Christmas Carol

Letters From Cell No. 73

Constitutional Musings: An Anthology of Legal Columns

We the People: The Only Cure to Judicial Activism

Made in the USA
Middletown, DE
31 May 2025

76231260R00156